Mark Tedeschi AM QC

MURDER AT MYALL CREEK

The trial that defined a nation

SIMON & SCHUSTER

London · New York · Sydney · Toronto · New Delhi

MURDER AT MYALL CREEK – THE TRIAL THAT DEFINED A NATION
First published in Australia in 2016 by
Simon & Schuster,
Level 4, 32 York St. Sydney NSW 2000
This edition published in 2017

10 9 8 7 6 5

New York Amsterdam/Antwerp London Toronto Sydney New Delhi
Visit our website at www.simonandschuster.com.au

National Library of Australia Cataloguing-in-Publication entry
Creator: Tedeschi, Mark, 1952- author.
Title: Murder at Myall Creek/Mark Tedeschi.
ISBN: 9781925533484 (paperback)
9781925456271 (ebook)
Subjects: Plunkett, John Hubert, 1802–1869
Fleming, John Henry
Myall Creek Massacre, 1838.
Trials – New South Wales – Myall Creek.
Aboriginal Australians – Crimes against – New South Wales – Myall Creek.
Massacres – New South Wales – Myall Creek.
Aboriginal Australians – New South Wales – Myall Creek – History – 19th century.
Australia – Law and legislation – History – 19th century
Myall Creek (N.S.W.) – History – 19th century.
Australia – History – 19th century
Dewey Number: 305.89915

Cover design: Christabella Designs
Cover image: K Means/Shutterstock
Typeset by Midland Typesetters, Australia
Printed and bound in Australia by Griffin Press

The paper this book is printed on is certified against the Forest Stewardship Council® Standards. Griffin Press – a member of the Opus Group holds chain of custody certification SCS-COC-001185. FSC® promotes environmentally responsible, socially beneficial and economically viable management of the world's forests.

Praise for *Murder at Myall Creek*

'The Myall Creek massacre is a stain on our nation's soul, with the only positive note being that the law brought the evil perpetrators to justice in a key trial that was a foundation stone for the integrity of our legal system. This wonderful book brings that trial, and the marvellous prosecutor, John Hubert Plunkett, back to life.'

Peter FitzSimons

'A much needed and appreciated historical insight into the profession of a man who gained respect through the colonial era of Australia and his fight for justice through the law for my people, the Kamilaroi.'

Aunty Noeline Briggs-Smith OAM, Aboriginal researcher

'Tedeschi's narrative and portrayal of John Plunkett is evocative and intense . . . [Plunkett was] a very remarkable man.'

Kelvin Brown, Anaiwan Peoples of the Gamilaroi Nation

'a considered and elegant work'

Bookseller and Publisher

Praise for *Kidnapped*

'Masterfully pieced together by the New South Wales Senior Crown Prosecutor'

Daily Telegraph

'A broad-brush morality tale about the consuming power of greed'

Sydney Morning Herald

Praise for *Eugenia*

'Crown Prosecutor and barrister Mark Tedeschi QC has drawn on a wealth of legal knowledge and insight'

Courier-Mail

'an outstanding new true-crime story . . .'

Sunday Age

Also by Mark Tedeschi

Eugenia – A True Story of Adversity, Tragedy, Crime and Courage

Kidnapped – The Crime that Shocked the Nation

I dedicate this book to my immigrant grandparents,
Ernest and Margaret Curtis (Cohn), and Guido and Rosina Tedeschi,
who took the bold and enlightened decision in 1939
to come to Australia, fleeing Nazism, fascism,
discrimination and persecution.

CONTENTS

'To cheapen the lives of any group of men, cheapens the lives of all men, even our own. This is a law of human psychology, or human nature. And it will not be repealed by our wishes, nor will it be merciful to our blindness.'

William Pickens
African-American orator, educator, journalist, essayist
and son of liberated slaves

ACKNOWLEDGEMENTS

For a third time I must acknowledge the inspiration and encouragement of my friend and literary mentor, Alan Gold, who encouraged me to continue writing this book at a time when I was doubtful about its viability. His generosity with his time and his honesty with his comments are much appreciated, as is his and his wife, Eva's, friendship and hospitality.

I thank Judge Greg Woods QC of the District Court of New South Wales, who many years ago was my inspirational legal history lecturer at Sydney University Law School, and who in recent times discussed with me some of the more complex issues of legal history associated with this book.

I pay tribute to Emeritus Professor Bruce Kercher of Macquarie University, who was responsible (with a team) for publishing online the records of decisions made by the superior courts of New South Wales during the colonial period.

I thank Reverend Donald Richardson, the Dean of St Mary's Cathedral in Sydney, for help in locating the Chalice of Saint Oliver Plunkett and giving me the opportunity to photograph it.

I wish to acknowledge Peter Hodges of Tea Gardens and his sister, the late Christine Jones, a former police officer, who brought John Henry Fleming to my attention.

I thank Cassie Mercer and Ben Mercer, respectively past and present editor and proprietor of the dynamic Australian magazine *Inside History* – for their enthusiasm for my historical writings over many years.

I pay tribute to Cindy Jones, for her research assistance, her suggestions on my first draft, and her help in locating Archbishop Plunkett's chalice. Her passion for the project gave me the confidence to believe that others would want to share our knowledge of the remarkable John Hubert Plunkett.

I also wish to thank Peter FitzSimons for his generous comments about the book.

I sincerely thank Aunty Noelene Briggs-Smith OAM and Kelvin Brown, both elders of the Gamilaroi nation, for reading my first draft and making some helpful suggestions.

I thank Wayne Gleeson of the Legal Studies Association of New South Wales for his helpful comments on my first draft and I express my gratitude to him and his wife, Julie, for their continuing support of my three true-crime books.

I thank my publishers, Simon & Schuster Australia, and in particular Larissa Edwards, Roberta Ivers, Anabel Pandiella and Anna O'Grady, for their encouragement and support.

Finally, I thank my wife, Sharon, for her patience during the lengthy periods of our holidays and weekends when I was preoccupied with the story of John Hubert Plunkett and the Myall Creek murder trials.

Mark Tedeschi AM QC

PREFACE

I cannot remember when I first became aware of John Hubert Plunkett, the Solicitor General and Attorney General of New South Wales from 1832 to 1856, but I do still recall my initial surprise that a man who had such a profound influence on the colony and was responsible for so many reforms and innovations is so unknown to society at large. That surprise did not dissipate over the years and at some stage I resolved that I would write an easily accessible version of his life story in an attempt to disseminate to the public his well-deserved reputation as one of Australia's unsung heroes and possibly our most important advocate of human rights of all time.

John Plunkett's greatest challenge was to prosecute those responsible for the murders of twenty-eight Aboriginal men, women and children at Myall Creek in the New England district of northern New South Wales. Unusually for the times, there were two trials that arose from the massacre, and both provoked enormous controversy and hostility throughout the colony towards the prosecutor. The powerful forces of the landowning settlers were pitted against him, causing endless difficulties. While a considerable number of books and articles have referred to this massacre, to my knowledge there has not been any analysis of the difficult tactical and legal decisions that John Plunkett took in pursuing justice for those who had been murdered. As I explain in this book, the trials were more akin to modern-day war-crimes trials than to domestic murder trials, even though the concept of war crimes lay more than a hundred years in the future. Plunkett's approach to these prosecutions was innovative and bold in equal measure. He faced massive difficulties in overcoming bigotry and vested interests and, in many respects he had both hands tied behind his back. The biggest hurdle was that despite the fact that there had been an eyewitness to the massacre, the law prevented that person from being called to give evidence in court. Plunkett spent the next twenty-five years trying to remedy this deficiency in the law.

It is not possible to understand John Plunkett's achievements in New South Wales or his conduct of the Myall Creek murder trials without knowing about his background in Ireland. His early years there came at a time of gradual emancipation for Catholics, however, as an Irish Catholic lawyer he still faced considerable discrimination and impediments under the law that he had sworn to uphold. This was a major reason he accepted a prominent government posting in New South Wales. By the time of his arrival, he was adamant that the colony should not experience the same issues of religious discrimination under the law that he and his Catholic colleagues had experienced in Ireland. His whole life can be seen as an attempt to create a society in which the law and all public institutions treated everyone equally.

PREFACE

In attempting to bring to greater prominence the remarkable achievements of John Hubert Plunkett, I have referred to the writings of many other people whom I have listed in the bibliography, but none more so than the two authors of specialist books on Plunkett: John Molony and Tony Earls. Where I have inferred Plunkett's thoughts, motives and emotions, they are entirely my own supposition, based upon the known facts and my own analysis of the man and his times.

In the introduction to his book *An Architect of Freedom: John Hubert Plunkett in New South Wales, 1832–1869*, John Molony decried the fact that so few of Plunkett's personal papers have survived, and stated his opinion that the personality of Plunkett did not emerge from the written records of his professional life. I disagree. In my view, John Plunkett is shown to be a man of many contradictions. He was single-minded and irascible; overly dedicated to his professional work; eclectic in his other interests; rooted in the blighted history of repression over the centuries of his native Ireland and his Catholic forebears; deeply spiritual, but with an abhorrence of sectarian bigotry, racial superiority or tribalism of any kind; outspoken in his views but socially shy; uninterested in all except a few personal connections, but loyal and respectful to those who shared his enlightened views; intensely proud of his family history; loving towards his wife, but rather dismissive of her concerns about their acceptance in Sydney's high society; immune to critical public opinion, but empathetic to the sufferings of the community's underdogs; eloquent when he needed to be, but stolid on most social occasions; and above all else, in possession of an immutable belief in the potency of the law as an instrument of justice and social change.

In some instances I have inserted references in my text to my sources, but I have resisted the temptation to litter it with them, because I believe that they are an impediment to many readers. The bibliography is intended to provide additional reading for those who wish to make further enquiry.

My use of the terms 'blacks' and 'Aborigines' instead of 'Indigenous Australians' is not out of ignorance and does not signify any disrespect, but rather is based on the fact that they were in common usage at the time of the murders. I have used the now generally accepted spelling for the 'Gamilaroi' nation throughout this book, even though 'Kamilaroi' has often been used in the past.

Mark Tedeschi AM QC
Sydney, 2016

1

VERDICT

Western Court, Supreme Court, King Street, Sydney[1]
16 November 1838

'Not guilty!'

The foreman of the jury repeated the same verdict eighty-eight times – representing eight murder charges against each of the eleven accused men in the dock. As each defendant heard the last of his acquittals, he whooped with delight and relief, and the defence counsel seated at the Bar table smirked with barely suppressed pride. The mass of people in the public gallery of the courtroom, representing every echelon of this white colonial society, all of whom were clearly partial to the defence camp, cheered and clapped as each defendant received his final verdict.

The judge seemed unwilling to restrain these public expressions of glee. This case was no mere trifle. It was a matter of life and death, because in the event of a conviction the inevitable sentence would have been death by hanging. Only the man seated in the prosecutor's chair remained unmoved by the infectious celebratory atmosphere. As each fresh set of verdicts was announced, it seemed to strike him like a blow, and each time he slumped imperceptibly lower in his chair, his eyes almost closed and his reddening face suffused with suppressed anger.

For the prosecutor, these verdicts were like piercing arrows that struck at his very core. How could there be such manifest injustice in a supposedly civilised society that professed to be guided by Christian values and the principle of equality of all before the law? In his mind, the prosecution case had been irresistibly strong. How could twelve rational jurors unanimously turn their faces against the clear evidence that these eleven accused men – all convicts or former convicts who had been led by a free man who was not on trial – had been responsible for the most atrocious mass murder of at least twenty-eight defenceless men, women and children at Myall Creek, a tributary of the Big (Gwydir) River[2] in the remote north of the colony, about 350 miles from Sydney and 200 miles from the nearest Police Magistrate's office in Invermein (Scone)? Were the lives of the butchered deceased worth nothing, merely because they were Aboriginal? Did the jurors not think that the law should apply in the distant reaches of the colony just because there was frequent open warfare between the pastoralists and the 'blacks' they were attempting to displace? Did the jurors not know that the Scriptures taught that the life of any human being is as valuable as any other – no matter what their skin colour, religion or status in society? Had the jury been bought off by the rich so-called 'squatters' – those graziers whose illegal, self-declared landholdings beyond the established nineteen counties depended upon putting down 'the black menace' to promote their pastoral self-interests? Had he totally misjudged his own performance in court and failed to mount sufficiently cogent arguments during his case, even though he was universally acknowledged throughout the colony as the pre-eminent advocate of his day – reflecting his official position as the Attorney General of New South Wales? Had he misunderstood the values of the society he had served so faithfully for the previous six years since travelling from his native Ireland to take up the position of Solicitor General?

As the final verdict was delivered and the hubbub from the back of the court died down, the Chief Justice, Sir James Dowling, who had presided over the trial, looked down at the prosecutor and calmly asked him in a rhetorical fashion:

> *Mr Plunkett, is there any reason why these eleven men should not be released to return to their previous locations and occupations?*

John Hubert Plunkett slowly rose to his feet, stared into space a few yards ahead, seemingly ignoring the judge on the raised Bench in front of him, as well as his now haughty opponents at the Bar table to his side and the eleven jubilant defendants in the dock. In reality, he was deep in thought, wondering whether what he was contemplating was legally justified, or not. He realised that what he was about to say was probably the most important utterance of his whole career as a lawyer, and that he would be judged by society upon it. He paused for an undue length of time, before raising his face towards the Bench with a look of sudden revelation, as though he had only just become aware of the Chief Justice's presence and question.

> *Yes, your Honour. There is! These men should be remanded in custody. I intend to present a further indictment against them for murder at the next sittings of this honourable Court.*

Upon the prosecutor uttering these words, the court descended into pandemonium as the defendants, their lawyers and supporters railed with astonishment and dismay at the refusal of the prosecutor to accept the unequivocal verdicts that had just been delivered by the jury. The acquittals accorded with the overwhelming views of every stratum of this colonial society – that these eleven men had been engaged in the legitimate defence of white interests. What right did the prosecutor have to place these men on trial again for murder, when a jury of upright, propertied citizens had just absolved them? What principle of law enabled him to ignore an acquittal and seek a retrial on the same evidence? How presumptuous was it for an Irish Catholic lawyer in a predominantly Anglican British colony to preach his own brand of morality and to seek to manipulate the law to his own ends? Did he not care that this prosecution had, for probably the first time in the fifty years since the colony's establishment by Captain Arthur Phillip, united almost everyone in opposition – the free settlers, the pastoralists, the emancipated former convicts, the magistrates, the military, all but one of the newspapers, and even those who were still serving as convicts? Was he unaware of the depth of hostility towards those who were responsible for the prosecution of these eleven convicts for murdering Aboriginal men, women and children in the most remote and dangerous parts of the colony, where lawlessness prevailed, where possession of land by the squatters was tantamount to ownership, and where the threat of attack from the Indigenous 'blacks' was ever present? Did he not realise that the future prosperity and stability of the colony depended upon the expansion of grazing into these distant, fertile lands? It was one thing for the Colonial Office in London to issue edicts for the protection of the Indigenous population. It was something else for a government official in the colony to enforce them, when whites labouring in harsh and remote environments had met their deaths at the hands of the blacks, and when cattle and sheep belonging to the squatters had frequently been 'rushed' or butchered by them. Outside the established regions of the nineteen counties, neither the Governor, nor his minions, nor the military could provide any support, and the whites were reduced to protecting themselves by enforcing their own self-appointed rules and standards, both on the convicts who worked for them and on the blacks who lived in the bush and were always threatening to confront them. The danger of attacks against whites was so prevalent that even convict workers were permitted to carry weapons when venturing into the bush in these remote areas.

***

When John Plunkett announced that the eleven accused men in the dock of the Supreme Court would be put on trial again for the dreadful murders that had occurred earlier that year at

Myall Creek, he realised that he was going against every tenet of the law that an acquittal by a jury was final and could not be re-litigated, as this would place the defendants in double jeopardy of conviction. However, he was so incensed at the unjustness of the verdicts in the face of overwhelming evidence of guilt, that he decided on the spur of the moment to put them on trial again and to work out the exact legal mechanism later. He saw this case as an opportunity to set a precedent: that the murder of Aborigines by whites would not go unpunished. He fully realised that his move to put the eleven men on trial again would be thoroughly unpopular and would be questioned by almost everyone in the colony, from the lowliest convict to the Governor, Sir George Gipps. However, at that precise moment he did not care about anything other than justice for the twenty-eight departed Aboriginal souls.

Plunkett felt deep in his bones that he, and only he, stood between the unjustified release of these men and the truth that they had committed a most egregious crime for which they should be punished. He felt overwhelmingly that he had a duty to follow his conscience, no matter what the obstacles, no matter what the risks to his reputation or standing, no matter how much hatred and vitriol would be directed at him by society at large. Even his junior counsel, Roger Therry, would question the appropriateness and propriety of the decision that he had just taken, and be dismayed that they had not discussed it beforehand, which was the usual practice between co-counsel. The Governor would insist on some considered, written legal opinion, with past decisions of the superior courts in England to justify a second trial. Plunkett's wife, Maria, would no doubt complain endlessly that even more friends and acquaintances would refuse to associate with them and that once again he had made a decision that would impact her without taking her feelings into account. Despite all this, his conscience dominated his actions, and he felt he had no choice.

Plunkett's concerns for the fate of the Aboriginal victims of atrocities by whites and for the course of justice to play its role were deeply felt. Before coming to New South Wales, as an Irish Catholic in a profession dominated by his native country's English overlords, he had experienced prejudice and discrimination since beginning his working life. It was only a few years before his admission as a barrister in Dublin in 1826 that the requirement was removed for those seeking admission to the Bar to take an oath renouncing a belief in 'transubstantiation' – the miraculous transformation of the Eucharistic bread and wine during Holy Communion to become the body and blood of Christ. The Church of England believed in the symbolic role of the Eucharist, whereas the Catholics believed in a physical transformation. The oath had also included a declaration that the adoration of the Virgin Mary or any other saints was 'superstitious and idolatrous'. As transubstantiation and the veneration of Mary were two of the central tenets of Catholic faith, and points of departure for the Church of England, this was an effective mechanism for keeping Catholics out of the legal profession, which even in Ireland was dominated by the English.

The injustice of oppression by English overlords had been implanted in the Plunkett family's DNA ever since the time of their illustrious ancestor, Archbishop Oliver Plunkett, who became the Roman Catholic Archbishop of Armagh and Primate of all Ireland in 1669. From 1670 to 1678, Archbishop Plunkett was active in resurrecting a severely oppressed and diminished Catholic Church in Ireland, including the building of schools and the creation of educational institutions for the clergy. In Drogheda, he established a Jesuit College for 150 students, 40 of whom were Protestant, making it the first integrated school in Ireland. It has been said of Oliver Plunkett:

> *Whenever a principle in which he believed was at stake, he would defend it robustly and courageously and his pen could be quite sharp in this regard. He had a sense of humour, which also surfaces occasionally. Through the evidence of his letters, he kept meticulous records and accounts, all of which prove he was an excellent administrator, so it must be unusual then, that he could be an outstanding worker out in the field as well. A diplomat, he built bridges between the different traditions and he was soon respected in all quarters.*[3]

In 1678, anti-Catholic measures were re-introduced and Archbishop Plunkett was forced to go into hiding. Despite being on the run and having a price on his head, he refused to leave his flock. He was arrested in Dublin in December 1679 and prosecuted for high treason by the English on fabricated evidence. It was alleged that he had conspired to bring 20 000 French soldiers into Ireland to force out the British and had levied a tax on his clergy to raise a force of 70 000 local men for a rebellion.[4] At his first trial, at Dundalk in Ireland, Plunkett faced an all-Protestant jury; however, the prosecution case collapsed, as the witnesses were themselves wanted men and afraid to turn up in court. The trial was then moved to England and Archbishop Plunkett faced a mockery of a second trial at Westminster Hall, where he was denied the basic rights of all accused: he was not represented by counsel; he was given no reasonable opportunity to call witnesses in his defence; he was deprived of the criminal histories of those who gave evidence against him. When Archbishop Plunkett raised complaints about these aspects, the trial judge, Lord Chief Justice of England Sir Francis Pemberton, said to him:

> *Look you, Mr Plunkett, it is in vain for you to talk and make this discourse here now ... Don't misspend your own time; for the more you trifle in these things, the less time you will have for your defence.*[5]

In other remarks during the trial, Sir Francis Pemberton demonstrated ever more his prejudices:

> *The foundation of Oliver Plunkett's treason was setting up a false religion, which was the most dishonourable and derogatory to God of all religions and that a greater crime could not be committed against God than for a man to endeavour to propagate that religion.*

Archbishop Plunkett's unjustified conviction in June 1681 was assured, and his sentence of death was inevitable. In the sixteen days between his trial and execution, he was visited by a large number of Catholics and Protestants seeking his blessing. On the day of his execution, 1 July 1681, he showed great equanimity and strength of mind. From the three-cornered gallows at Tyburn, in a prepared speech, he refuted his accusers point by point and forgave them all, including the judges and witnesses who had given evidence against him. He was executed in the manner reserved for those convicted of treason – being hanged, drawn and quartered. Within days of his death, those who had been involved in the fabrication of evidence were exposed, but it was too late for the Archbishop.

John Plunkett had known of his famous ancestor's fate since he was a young boy, and the tragedy of what had occurred 150 years earlier burned in his heart as though it had happened in his own lifetime. His most treasured possession was a silver chalice used by Archbishop Plunkett during the celebration of Mass, which, after the martyrdom, had been passed down for generations from father to son. John would regularly bring this prized relic out of the cupboard at his home and perform a ritual of holding it in both his hands while recalling the terrible travesty of justice that had befallen his ancestor.

John Plunkett was deeply mindful of the circumstances of his famous ancestor's two trials: the all-Protestant juries; the fabricated evidence; the inability of Archbishop Plunkett to call witnesses in his defence; the tactic of a second trial to overcome the failure of the first. No man was more aware than John Plunkett of how the law could be misused as an instrument of oppression against a downtrodden section of society. No man was more sensitive to the evils of sectarianism and religious bigotry. No man was more determined that the law should be used to punish the transgressions of oppressors. Despite the fact that he was a deeply religious Catholic, he firmly believed that the divisions and differences between men were illusory and that all were equal in the eyes of God, no matter what their race, background or spiritual beliefs might be.

In 1826, at the age of twenty-four, John Plunkett became a member of the Irish and English Bars. Over the next six years, he distinguished himself in legal practice, primarily on the court circuit in the Irish Province of Connaught. However, he was painfully aware that Protestant barristers frequently prevailed in progression and promotion over their Catholic counterparts, and he realised that as an adherent of the latter faith he would always be treated as a second-class lawyer. This was despite the fact that he had already shown himself to be a practitioner of superior ability to many of his peers. Just as he became aware of the full extent of the restrictions that derived from his origins and faith, he was informed that a position was available for a member of the English or Irish Bar to assume the office of Solicitor General in the far-flung convict colony of New South Wales. Without consulting his family, Plunkett accepted an offer to take up the post, which had been made by those in the Colonial Office in London, who were only too pleased to see an able and industrious lawyer take up a senior government position in what was then a most distant, harsh and unpopular destination. Plunkett was, in fact, the first Catholic to be appointed to a major position of authority in the colony.

The society that John Plunkett found on his arrival in Sydney in June 1832 was solidly based on the availability of free labour by convicts working their way to freedom. Without this ready supply of workers to build the basic foundations, the colony would have floundered. Many male convicts were forced to engage in harsh manual labour on public building projects; however, a large number were assigned to private sector landowners as a source of free labour to work on farms, on cattle and sheep stations, or as domestic servants throughout the colony. In reality, this was a form of slavery, because the convict workers were not paid for their efforts, apart from being provided with barely sufficient food to maintain their ability to work.[6] Most female convicts were either sent to one of the thirteen 'female factories'[7] in New South Wales and Van Diemen's Land,[8] or assigned to free-settler masters as domestic servants. The rate of sexual abuse must have been horrendously high.

The treatment of assigned convicts by their masters varied from case to case. Many masters were brutal and cruel, while others treated their workers with humanity and kindness. By 1832, there was already a sizeable number of ex-convicts, many of whom, on completing their sentences or being granted early release by the issue of a ticket-of-leave, had taken up grants of Crown land and commenced to farm. Others had opened small businesses, and quite a few of them had flourished and become prosperous.

While there were still some restrictions on the legal entitlements of ex-convicts, there were none on their ability to own land, engage in farming and open businesses. Their numbers soon swelled to the extent that they became a social class with increasing political influence. Almost without exception, once these freed convicts found a paying job or acquired property or set up a business, they had an investment in the social cohesion and prosperity of their society, and their crime rate was negligible. This enlightened approach proved to be one of the enduring strengths of the developing colony: it encouraged convicts to peacefully serve out their sentences, and it gave emancipated convicts a sense of identification with their society. This is to be contrasted with the situation in the American colonies, where freed slaves and their offspring were denied social acceptance and did not possess any financial or political investment in their society, with the result that their crime rate remained astronomically high and their poverty overwhelming.[9] Those few settlers who had arrived in New South Wales as free men viewed the emancipated ex-convicts as second-class citizens, tainted by their earlier status as prisoners, and there was a deep social and political divide between these groups. Those in the military, or retired from its ranks, considered themselves as a class of their own, but identified with the interests of the free settlers. While some of them returned to England after their period of service had ended, others remained in the colony after discharge and engaged in farming or business.

Sydney had the atmosphere of a military garrison at the outer reaches of the known world – a wild locality surrounded by dense, threatening bush, with a convict and ex-convict majority and the ever-present threat of violence from the Aborigines. Punishment of convicts was frequent and severe, and the death penalty often invoked. Bushrangers – escaped convicts who lived in the bush on the periphery of white settlement and often survived through robbery – were prevalent. Most whites believed that there was a constant threat from the menace of the black inhabitants, who, they believed, could move about the bush without being seen and appear out of nowhere at any time. In this setting, violence was only just below the surface. The colony was perfused with tension and a sense of everyone constantly being on guard, aware that the threat of starvation had only just been averted during the early years of settlement. It was a society that depended for its survival and smooth running on the division of men into categories that defined their limitations, rights and obligations. It was a settlement that could only prosper because of the ruthless oppression and displacement of the Indigenous population and the rigorous exploitation of the labour of convicts, about one-quarter of whom were of Irish origin. It was a society in which the military, the magistrates and the mounted police were viewed by free settlers as fragile bastions against a constant threat of disintegration of this outpost of British civilisation so remote from the mother country.

***

It was into this society that in 1832 John Hubert Plunkett, a man with an abiding hatred of bigotry and injustice and a belief in the equality of all men under the law, arrived to take up the position of Solicitor General of New South Wales – a posting that made him the second most senior law officer of the colony and answerable only to the Attorney General, John Kinchela, and the Governor, Sir Richard Bourke.[10]

In order to fully understand the actions of John Plunkett during the most important case of his career – the 1838 trials of the men charged with the murders of twenty-eight Aboriginal men, women and children at Myall Creek in the north of the colony – it is necessary to know more about his early life in his native Ireland, about what he achieved in the colony in the six years prior to the trials, and the unique circumstances prevailing at that time in the penal settlement of New South Wales.

2

EARLY YEARS

John Hubert Plunkett was born on 4 June 1802 at Mount Plunkett in the county of Roscommon, which is part of the Province of Connaught in central-western Ireland, an area rich in Gaelic history with some of the most beautiful countryside in the land. In Plunkett's time, the Irish language was frequently spoken. John Plunkett had an older twin brother, Christopher, and a younger sister, Kate Amelia. His father, George Plunkett, was a gentleman farmer who owned 400 acres of land on which he had built an impressive, large manor house for his family,[1] making him one of the more prosperous Catholic landholders in Ireland, although far less so that the prominent Protestant English families. The Plunketts were Catholic aristocracy[2] who had managed to keep a small part of their landholdings during centuries of British persecution by using the services of supportive Protestant friends to hold their land on their behalf. The scion of the Plunkett family in John Hubert's lifetime was Arthur Plunkett, the eighth Earl of Fingall. This branch of the family spoke English, had English ways, identified with their Catholic counterparts in England and were intensely loyal to the British Crown. The Plunketts were not revolutionaries or radicals, but they were very aware of the deep injustices and legal restrictions that still persisted to hamper Catholics, and they pressed strongly for reform of the many anti-Catholic laws. The family motto was 'Festina Lente' – hasten slowly. It was fortuitous for John Plunkett that he was born into a period when the restrictions on Catholics were in the process of being slowly dismantled.

From 1819, John Plunkett attended Trinity College in Dublin at a time when it was a bastion of Protestant hegemony in Ireland. He was the only one of his siblings to go to university, no doubt because he was the one who showed the most promise. At that time, Catholics had only been allowed entrance to university for twenty-six years, and only a few attended the prestigious Trinity College. He enrolled for a Bachelor of Arts degree and from 1821 he was concurrently a student of law at King's Inn, Dublin. By 1823, John had completed his degree at Trinity College and served his terms at King's Inn. The next step was to serve a period as a student of law at one of the Inns of Court in London, and so, like many Irishmen wishing to practise law, he joined Gray's Inn in London. It was here that he made two connections that were to influence the direction of his later life, when he befriended two other law students. The first was Maurice O'Connell, the eldest son of

Daniel O'Connell, who became the most significant proponent of Catholic emancipation of his era. During the period that John Plunkett was in London between 1823 and 1826, Daniel O'Connell was also there for much of the time, and Plunkett came to know him well. The second important connection at Trinity was with fellow student Roger Therry, who preceded Plunkett as a lawyer in New South Wales, and whose career for much of the time ran parallel to, though slightly behind, Plunkett's.

On 20 January 1826, at the age of twenty-three, John Plunkett was admitted as an English and Irish barrister. The ceremony, before Lord Manners – the Chief Judge of the King's Bench in Dublin – left an indelible mark on the budding young lawyer because of the judge's bad manners. The admission of Catholics was still a rare event, and there was not a single Catholic on the Bench or among the senior counsel in Dublin. Although John Plunkett was not required to take an oath abhorrent to his faith, he was obliged during the ceremonial hearing to make a formal, oral request to the Court that he 'take the form of oath for the relief of Catholics', and he could not fail to notice the Chief Judge's change of demeanour when this application was made. When he signed the roll as a new barrister, he used his full name – John Hubert Plunkett – to distinguish himself from another, unrelated John Plunkett already at the Irish Bar, and from then on he was always known by his full name.[3]

At the time of Plunkett's admission as a barrister, there were still numerous restrictions on Catholics. They were ineligible to hold office in the most senior government posts. They could not be judges in the superior courts or become senior counsel.[4] They could not be Attorney General or Solicitor General or participate in Parliament in Westminster.[5] Although seven million of the eight million people in Ireland were Catholic, less than five per cent of those Crown offices that Catholics were eligible to hold were in fact held by Catholics.[6]

The main impediment to Catholics taking high office was the requirement to take the Oath of Supremacy, which included a declaration that the Monarch was 'the only supreme governor of this realm … in all spiritual or ecclesiastical things or causes, as [well as] temporal, and that no foreign prince, person, prelate, state or potentate hath or ought to have any jurisdiction, power, superiority, pre-eminence or authority ecclesiastical or spiritual within this realm'. Obviously, a Catholic could not in conscience acknowledge the spiritual and ecclesiastical supremacy of the head of the Church of England.

In 1823, two prominent Irish lawyers, Daniel O'Connell and Richard Lalor Sheil, set up an organisation known as the Catholic Association to press peacefully for Irish emancipation through the medium of public opinion, the electoral process and changes to existing laws. Like Mahatma Gandhi more than a century later, O'Connell and Sheil rejected any violent means and called for mass participation in the call for the civil rights of Catholics, and indeed for adherents of all other religions. They were passionate voices against slavery in America, and they even advocated for better conditions and equality of opportunity for all in the far-flung colony of New South Wales.

O'Connell and Sheil believed that civil rights were universal, irrespective of colour, creed, class or gender, and that violence in the pursuit of political ends was counterproductive. They were of the view that the principles on which they called for

Catholic emancipation had universal application and they condemned all religious intolerance and discrimination. At a meeting of the Catholic Association in Connaught in 1826, a resolution was passed that stated:

> *The State should have no established religion. It should preserve neutrality between them all.*

and:

> *To attempt seizing on public education with a view to converting it into a monopoly for any particular class or sect, is to disturb in a direct manner the order of society.*

These principles were to play a major role in John Hubert Plunkett's later life.

In October 1823, as a friend of O'Connell's son Maurice, twenty-one-year-old John Plunkett was one of the first Irishmen to sign up for membership of the Catholic Association. Within two years the Association had amassed a great number of supporters throughout Ireland and collected substantial funds. The leadership of the Association was well organised and disciplined, avoiding any violence or disturbances at public meetings. Its accounts were meticulously kept and publicly available, avoiding any accusation that the funds were being used for unlawful purposes. The Association's aims were supported by English Catholics and even by progressive Protestants.

In 1825 Daniel O'Connell and a delegation from the Catholic Association went to London and convinced the government to allow Catholics with a certain landholding to hold high office, including membership of Parliament, and to abolish the requirement to take the Oath of Supremacy. The *Catholic Relief Bill* was passed by the House of Commons, but rejected in the House of Lords. That bastion of inherited Protestant ascendancy had prevailed against the wishes of the elected representatives of the people.

As an O'Connell family intimate, John Plunkett was in the midst of this exciting new movement. He was indeed fortunate at the beginning of his legal career to be present at such a momentous time in the history of Catholic emancipation. He was a young man in search of a mission, and intensely aware of the discrimination that his forebears had suffered under English law. At the same time, he was mindful of the power of the law to effect positive social and political change. Even as a young man, he believed that the most important aspect of any civilised society was the equality of all under the law. He was determined that once he qualified as a lawyer he would devote his professional energies to achieving justice and equality for the underdogs of Irish society, including his own suppressed Catholic majority. He had no idea that his main contribution would be on the opposite side of the world.

Upon his admission as a barrister in 1826, John Plunkett became one of the principal liaison men between the Catholic Association's headquarters in Dublin and the Province of Connaught, where he practised law. He lived in Dublin, but his working life as a barrister and as a representative of the Catholic Association was in Connaught. In both these capacities, Plunkett soon won admiration and respect for his ability, diligence and professionalism. His legal work included both civil and criminal cases, although the latter were almost invariably for the defence. The Catholic Association provided counsel to many of its members, and Plunkett would often have to take such a case without a fee. On many occasions he represented defendants accused of crimes for which they were at risk of forfeiting their lives or being transported to the colonies. In such cases, he was only too aware of his enormous responsibility by virtue of the fact that his advocacy might well determine whether or not a man was to be executed or forced to labour for years in one of the distant British colonies.

In 1828, with the repeal of the *Test and Corporation Acts*, dissenting Protestants (non-Anglicans) were permitted to stand for election to Parliament and to hold other offices of government. Daniel O'Connell decided that the time had finally come to mount a serious challenge to the exclusion of Catholics. An opportunity arose with a by-election in the vacant seat of Clare – the neighbouring county to Connaught – and O'Connell decided to stand as a candidate. As a Catholic, he could not take up the seat because he could not in conscience take the Oath of Supremacy, but there was nothing to prevent him standing for election, and, if he won, it would demonstrate the absurdity and injustice of the exclusion of Catholics and put immense pressure on the government to change the law.

Millions of Irish Catholics supported O'Connell's candidacy and in July 1828 he convincingly won the by-election. London feared that if he attempted to take his seat in Westminster and was denied it, a terrible tide of resentment would inevitably follow, threatening civil disturbance and possibly another Irish uprising, which was the last thing anyone wanted. In addition, there were many Englishmen who felt that the time had come to end the restrictions on Catholics and to allow proper representation of the majority of the Irish in Westminster. O'Connell portrayed himself as a bastion of legality and respectability holding back the tide of resentment and the threat of an uprising.

The English recognised that an accommodation had to be reached. O'Connell was quietly requested to delay his arrival in Westminster for several months. On 13 April 1829, the *Catholic Relief Act* was finally passed by both Houses in Westminster, allowing Catholics to become members of Parliament and to hold most other high offices, and replacing the Oath of Supremacy with one acceptable to those who were Christian, but not Anglican.[7] However, the Act was not retrospective, so O'Connell had to seek re-election, and in July that year was elected unopposed. It was said that King George IV used to joke that 'Wellington is the King of England, O'Connell is the King of Ireland, and I am only the dean of Windsor', reflecting admiration for the role that O'Connell had played in Anglo–Irish relations. John Plunkett was on the sidelines watching these important events.

The death of George IV in 1830 precipitated a general election. O'Connell and his supporters were keen to win as many of the 100 Irish seats in Westminster as possible. The district of Roscommon had two seats in Parliament, and the person chosen to stand for one of them was Owen O'Conor – known as the O'Conor Don – who was the scion of the O'Conor family, which had produced the ancient kings and chieftains of Connaught. The O'Conor Don chose young John Plunkett to be his election campaign manager. It was a natural choice, considering John's passion for Catholic emancipation, his knowledge of the people of Connaught, his closeness to Daniel O'Connell, and his personal attributes as a talented barrister and tireless worker for the Catholic Association. At the 1830 elections, the Tories were defeated by the Whigs, who were committed to many progressive causes, including the abolition of slavery, the emancipation of Catholics and serious electoral reform. A significant reason for the Whigs' win was the considerable success of Daniel O'Connell's candidates, who played a significant role in the formation of the new government. The O'Conor Don was elected to one of the Roscommon seats. John Plunkett's contribution to this success was widely acknowledged and Daniel O'Connell caused a dinner to be held in his honour.

The election of the new Whig government in 1830 marked a significant shift of power away from the landed aristocracy to the urban middle classes. Within three years, Acts were passed to modernise the distorted electoral laws in England, Scotland and Ireland, and to abolish slavery throughout the Empire.

John Plunkett was lucky to be associated with some of the principal political players at a time of significant change in British politics and considerable advancements in the emancipation of Catholics. Although he was on the periphery of the movement, he was present at the cusp of an era of sustained reform, and was ready to take a position of leadership if and when it became available. His association with Daniel O'Connell clearly had a profound influence on him, and his views on the rights of all men, regardless of faith or origin, clearly reflected those of his mentor. His time as a 'shop steward' for the Catholic Association developed his administrative skills and politicised him as an advocate for human rights. His law practice gave him the opportunity to see that many of his clients facing serious consequences for petty crimes were decent people who had reacted unwisely in response to political oppression or financial hardship, or both. His work as a defence barrister on the Connaught circuit taught him much about the British legal system and how it could be used as an instrument of either justice or injustice.

***

On 18 January 1830, the *Catholic Relief Act* became law in New South Wales and the stage was set for a Catholic to assume high office in the colony. In many ways, the colony was more ready for an Irish Catholic to assume a position of influence and authority than was Great Britain. There was such a dearth of talent in so many areas of government in New South Wales that religious affiliation was more easily overlooked. In any event, about a quarter of the population were Irish Catholics, most of whom had come as convicts. Over time, however, many of them had served their sentences or been given early release on a ticket-of-leave, and had taken up life as free men and women.

***

By 1831, John Hubert Plunkett was looking for a change in his life. Despite emancipation and the success of his legal career, he recognised that serious hurdles still stood in the way of his professional advancement in Ireland, where very few opportunities for high office would present themselves. He was ambitious and desperate to make a difference. The colonies offered many more opportunities to an energetic and resourceful young man. In addition, he had suffered a broken engagement to a woman he deeply loved and was keen to make a change to overcome the trauma.[8] No doubt with Plunkett's agreement, O'Connell and the Earl of Fingall successfully lobbied the Colonial Office in London to appoint Plunkett as Solicitor General of New South Wales. The appeal of the colony was enhanced by the knowledge that Plunkett's old Trinity friend Roger Therry had preceded him there and was already in legal practice. The fact that Plunkett would be the first Catholic to hold high office in the colony must also have attracted him to making the momentous decision to move to the other side of the earth. Also of importance was the fact that the Governor, Major-General Richard Bourke, had a reputation as a reformer and a man of compassion and tolerance.

Plunkett received his letter of appointment as Solicitor General on 10 October 1831. Over the next four months, before setting sail for Australia, no doubt still on the rebound from his broken engagement, Plunkett married Maria Charlotte McDonough, the attractive and vivacious daughter of his first cousin, who was a Plunkett on her mother's side. He was thirty and Maria was only nineteen, having just returned from a period in a convent in Paris run by English nuns. Apart from their family connection, John and Maria had two fundamental interests in common: they were both committed to their religion and they both loved music. Maria was a first-rate pianist and John was an accomplished violinist with a passion for Irish folk music.[9]

While awaiting their departure at the port of Cobh, near Cork, Plunkett came across thirty-eight-year-old Catholic priest Father John McEncroe, who was ministering to the convicts as they awaited their passage to the colonies. Plunkett and McEncroe had known each other in Dublin. Coincidentally, McEncroe was keen to go to New South Wales, and had already sought permission from the Colonial Secretary but received no reply. Both had heard that there was only one Catholic priest in the colony, Father John Therry, who had quarrelled with the Governor and the Anglican establishment. McEncroe asked Plunkett if he could accompany him on the voyage, and, in an act of bravado, Plunkett readily agreed. Plunkett's clerk, who was to have gone on the voyage, offered to surrender his berth, and McEncroe took his place. Shortly before they departed, Plunkett sought permission from the Colonial Secretary for McEncroe to proceed to New South Wales as a member of the clergy, which was given but only after their ship, the *Southworth*, had departed on 6 February 1832. Also on this journey with John and Maria Plunkett was John's younger sister, Kate Amelia, and a female domestic servant. Fellow passengers included 134 female convicts, aged between thirteen and seventy, transported to partially redress the gender imbalance in the colony. The voyage to Sydney took 129 days, during which time only one of the prisoners died – an unusually low number considering the length of time that many of them had awaited the journey in leaking hulks or dank prisons and the atrocious conditions under which the convicts were kept at sea. On the trip, Plunkett cemented a friendship with McEncroe that was to last for the rest of their lives.

3

JURIES, OATHS AND WITNESSES

When John Plunkett arrived in Sydney on 14 June 1832, he was a thirty-year-old man with enormous drive and ambition that would have been quite unrealistic for a man of his age and faith in his native Ireland. The Australian colonies offered a bright, energetic, young, Irish barrister many more opportunities than he could ever have expected at home. In order to understand the steps taken by John Plunkett during the 1838 trial of the men responsible for the Myall Creek murders, it is important to set out his efforts as Solicitor General and Attorney General of New South Wales to achieve reforms of the most brutal and retrograde aspects of colonial society in the six years prior to the murders. Considering its physical isolation and its penal function, Sydney was a vibrant town. Many landowners had already become quite prosperous from cattle and sheep farming. There were a number of outspoken newspapers, many places of entertainment and flourishing groups of artists, musicians, sportsmen, tradesmen and professional men.

At the time of his arrival, Plunkett was fortunate that the Governor, Major-General Richard Bourke, was a man who, like himself, believed in the equality of all men and had a desire to see reformist changes in the colony. Plunkett's early years in the colony gave him unprecedented opportunities to join with his Governor in introducing progressive reforms, some of which had not yet been achieved in England and Ireland. Some of the measures were readily accepted in the colony, while others were initially rejected as too far-reaching. A few were not able to be realised in his lifetime.

Major-General Richard Bourke was the first Irish-born Governor of the colony. His arrival had been much feted, because his predecessor, General Ralph Darling, had been most unpopular. Bourke came from a well-established, Anglo–Irish family based in Limerick and Tipperary in southern Ireland. He had been educated in England and attended Westminster School and been greatly influenced by the English statesman and author Edmund Burke, who was a distant relative. Richard Bourke held strong liberal and humanitarian beliefs.[1] He was sympathetic to the reformist ideals advocated by the Whigs, and, although he was a devout Anglican, he was liberal in his attitude to people of other religions, particularly the Roman Catholics. He had seen at first hand the suffering of the Irish poor, and had empathy for them. He had been Chairman of the Irish Relief Association and supported the idea of capital works funded by the state to provide employment for the poor.

In Ireland in 1829, Bourke became involved with Thomas Spring-Rice, the Member of Parliament for Limerick and a friend of the Bourke family, in advocating for public education that would be available for the children of poor Catholic and Protestant families. The non-denominational schools were to be built with government subsidies. Representatives of the Anglican, Catholic and Presbyterian Churches agreed to become members of a National Board of Education.[2] The non-Christian religions were expected to provide for their own children's educational needs. These early steps towards public education in Ireland were to have a profound influence in New South Wales in years to come.

Upon John Plunkett taking up his position as Solicitor General of New South Wales, the colonial government's legal services were in considerable disarray. The fifty-eight-year-old Attorney General, John Kinchela, who had arrived in the colony only the year before Plunkett, was quite deaf, which meant that it was difficult for him to appear in Court. The Crown Solicitor, William Henry Moore, was idle and incompetent, preferring to focus his energies on his private practice. These factors rendered two of the three senior legal roles in government virtually moribund. As a result of Kinchela's disability, Plunkett was compelled to take on many of the criminal trials that would normally have been done by the Attorney General. As a consequence of Moore's ineptitude and inattention, Plunkett was forced to do many of the civil cases normally performed by a government solicitor. Because of his sense of duty and work ethic, this situation resulted in John Plunkett performing much of the work of the three most important legal officers in the colony.

In November 1833, he wrote a letter to the Secretary of State for the Colonies in London, Lord Stanley, complaining:

> *Previous to the last Criminal Sessions, which commenced on the first of August last, His Excellency the Governor thought it necessary that I should relieve the Attorney General from that part of his duty which required his presence in court; and, having conveyed to me his desire to that effect, I attended in Court for the Attorney General every day during the entire of the Criminal Sessions, which lasted without intermission from the 1st of August to the 5th of September. I conducted during that time ninety one cases, and of that number there were 64 convictions, of which there were 26 capital convictions; and, notwithstanding their heavy and extraneous duty, not the least assistance was afforded to me in my own peculiar business, Viz., the civil department, by either the Attorney General or the Crown Solicitor, although there was much civil business to be transacted while the criminal court was sitting; And, when it was ended, the civil term commenced almost immediately.*
>
> *The Governor however, seeing the unreasonableness of requiring me to perform double duty, has caused directions to be given to the Attorney General and Crown Solicitor to relieve me from the mere office duties; but, up to this hour, neither of those Gentlemen relieved me from a single duty of my office.*[3]

So strapped were the government's legal services that Plunkett was even required to prosecute a member of his own household staff. On Boxing Day 1833, while the Plunketts were out, two of their servants got into an argument, and one of them, Bryant Kyne, who was an assigned convict, shot the other, killing him.

Realising the impropriety of prosecuting a member of his own staff, Plunkett arranged for his old Trinity College friend, Roger Therry, who was practising in Sydney as a private barrister, to conduct the trial. However, part-way through the case, Therry was required to appear in another court, and Plunkett was forced to step in. This raised an obvious conflict of interest, but there was no choice. Plunkett was adamant that he could put aside any feelings of sympathy for his servant and prosecute forcefully and fairly. There was an equally serious danger that in attempting to prove that he was not biased in favour of the accused, he would lean overly the other way. It was a situation that would not be tolerated today, but in the context of a colony with a dearth of prosecutors, society had to place its trust in Plunkett doing the right thing. Kyne was found guilty of murder, sentenced to death and hanged. As Plunkett had a moral objection to the assignment of convicts, he thereafter declined to take any convict staff, preferring to pay for domestic services.

Plunkett repeatedly complained that he received little assistance from Kinchela and that he was forced to perform many of the tasks of the Crown Solicitor; however, his protests fell on deaf ears. Many thought that the workload would crush him – and it would have overcome most other men – but Plunkett survived and indeed excelled. He was later to complain that the four years that he was Solicitor General nearly broke him.[4] Despite the amount of work, Plunkett performed it admirably and even had time to pursue other interests, winning the admiration of everyone, including Governor Bourke. Although Plunkett had a right of private practice, he rarely exercised it, seeing his public duties as having priority over any private clients. As a result, his official salary of £800 per year was virtually his sole income.

Finally, in 1834, Crown Solicitor William Moore was dismissed and in early 1836, with the retirement of Kinchela, to no one's surprise John Hubert Plunkett was appointed Attorney General of New South Wales. However, the position of Solicitor General was left vacant, so again he was forced to perform the work of both roles. Once again he flourished and gained universal respect for his ability, diligence, integrity and professionalism.

***

John Plunkett was a man of medium height, with a slight frame, hunched shoulders and a completely uninspiring countenance, so that many considered him ugly. He smiled infrequently and rarely appeared relaxed. His bulbous eyelids, coupled with puffy bags under his eyes, sometimes gave the impression that he was sleepy, but this was completely wide of the mark. His voice was raspy, and some viewed his advocacy as uninspiring, but nobody doubted his profound ability as a barrister. Above all else, he was a man of impeccable morality, who was incapable of deviating from the direction in which his conscience propelled him. Some viewed this as inflexibility, while others saw it as strength of purpose. While Plunkett was an intelligent, gifted and deeply religious man, filled with determination, conviction and boundless energy, he was not a man who easily encouraged friendship. In fact, apart from Governor Bourke and John McEncroe, Plunkett had few, if any, people in the colony he could call friends. It was not something that he missed or strove for – he had little time for personal connections with anyone, except his wife Maria, whom he loved dearly.

John Plunkett inspired admiration from others, due to his diligence and irrepressible integrity, but his firm stance on a variety of issues often brought him into conflict with people. Rather than being a leader of men, he was very much a loner, who won respect through his superior intelligence, his fierce determination, his dedication to social causes, and his many professional achievements. Perhaps that was why he was such a superb prosecutor, because the job required fierce independence and quickness of decision making. While his deep religious convictions were well known, he made a point of never acting in a partial way in favour of his Church or fellow Catholics. Even those who were members of his Church found him difficult to warm to and sometimes inflexible in his views. He did not shy away from controversy or conflict, and in aspects of his life there were some people who disliked him intensely. He was a man who rarely let his guard down and, unlike countless other men at all levels of society, never succumbed to the vice of excessive drinking. He was socially shy and shunned most community celebrations, other than the annual St Patrick's Day celebration, of which he was the enthusiastic organiser. It was only during that day's activities that anyone would see a more relaxed John Plunkett who would give an inspiring speech about the homeland to rousing applause. Only at that day's gatherings would he allow himself to play the fiddle in front of outsiders.

Maria Plunkett was a completely different kind of person to her husband. She was beautiful and genteel, with a love of social contacts and an ability to connect with people from all walks of life. She had a deep social conscience and a keen intelligence, but her modesty often kept the latter hidden. As a woman of her times, she expected her husband and his work to take precedence in their lives, but when she agreed to marry her cousin in the knowledge that he had already accepted the position of Solicitor General in distant New South Wales, she probably had no idea that they would spend the best part of their lives there or that her husband's professional obligations would take up the vast bulk of his time, thereby restricting their social lives. Neither would she have known that his progressive views on many controversial topics would alienate many people in the colony whose company she would otherwise have enjoyed.

***

John Plunkett's views on the rights of all men, no matter what their standing, financial status, education, faith or origins, clashed with contemporary attitudes in the colony. In particular, the wealthy, propertied landowners who had been born in the colony or had arrived as free men jealously guarded their exalted status and privileges under the law. They were known as the 'exclusives', and because of their wealth they were able to exert undue influence on the Governor, the newspapers, the military, and even the magistrates who held authority over the troopers – mounted police, who were often stockmen whose services were sequestered for individual ventures. The exclusives viewed themselves as the social and political elite, and resented any moves towards equality by those who had been convicts and then freed by completing their sentences or being granted tickets-of-leave or being pardoned. These former convicts were known as 'emancipists', because they had presumably been emancipated by their terms as prisoners and were now upright citizens. The non-convict population was deeply divided along these lines, and only a few of the exclusives were enlightened enough to press for the civil rights of emancipists. In the early years of the colony, only the exclusives were owners of large parcels of land, which gave them wealth, power and influence. However, as the number of emancipists grew, and as some of them began successfully engaging in businesses, mercantile activities and farming, their prosperity increased, and so did their demands for social and political recognition. The divisions in society became more pronounced.

It was the wealthy landowners among the exclusives who were represented on three of the most important legal institutions in the colony: the Executive Council, the Legislative Council and civilian juries. The Executive Council, which was appointed by the Governor and included military and judicial officials, had, since 1825, fulfilled the role of the Governor's cabinet and was the pre-eminent administrative organ of the colony. The Legislative Council had, since 1824, acted as the Governor's source of advice on lawmaking. Initially constituted with five members appointed by the Governor, it grew in number until, by 1829, there were ten to fifteen. Many of the Council's recommendations were thoroughly considered by Select Committees, consisting of various combinations of its members, which would research a topic and present a detailed report to the Governor and his Council.

***

Soon after John Plunkett's arrival in the colony in 1832, he became acutely aware of two areas in which there was an urgent need for legal reform. His first concern was that all serious criminal trials were decided by juries comprised of seven military officers, which was quite different to anything he had encountered in England and Ireland. His second observation was that there was no opportunity for Aborigines to give evidence in the courts. Seared into his memory was the fate of his illustrious ancestor, Archbishop Oliver Plunkett, who had been convicted in not dissimilar circumstances to those operating in the colony: he had been convicted by a jury selected from a very limited section of society at a trial in which he had been deprived of the ability to call witnesses in his defence. Plunkett set himself the task of ameliorating these two iniquities in the colony.

***

Prior to 1824, criminal trials were decided by a panel of seven military officers. While this was an appropriate measure for a penal establishment, as the colony developed and the number of free men increased, it became increasingly inappropriate to use military officers to decide important criminal cases involving civilians. Between 1824 and 1828, a choice was available between a jury of military officers and a civilian jury consisting of those who were wealthy property owners and had never been convicts. However, in 1828 the *New South Wales Constitution Act* abolished civilian juries. Within a year of his arrival in 1832, John Plunkett drafted for Governor Bourke the *Jury Trials Act* of 1833, which granted accused persons in the Supreme Court and Quarter Sessions[5] a choice of trial by a jury of twelve citizens or a panel of seven military officers. The Act enlarged the potential pool of jurors by setting the property qualifications lower than they had been before, to match the level set in England.[6] In order to remove any doubt about whether or not this included the emancipists, Bourke approached the three Supreme Court judges for clarification.[7] Their judgement, delivered on 9 August 1833,[8] unequivocally declared that all emancipists were entitled to serve on juries in England, and hence also in New South Wales. One of the many legal restrictions on emancipists had been removed; however, the property qualifications still excluded many of them. All jurors had to be: male; between twenty-one and sixty years of age; British subjects; holding a personal estate of at least £300 or an income from land of at least £30 per annum; and not having been disqualified by the commission of certain serious crimes.

The newspapers took predictable positions on the issue of civilian juries and the inclusion of emancipists. The conservative *Sydney Herald* was resolutely opposed to civilian jury trials in criminal cases, and constantly attacked the notion that former convicts could serve as jurors. *The Australian*, which was more progressive, was firmly in favour of both. John Plunkett frequently complained to the Supreme Court that many free settlers were not turning up for jury service because they refused to sit with emancipists. The *Herald* was in constant conflict with Plunkett on these issues. In 1838, Plunkett successfully moved to extend the operation of the 1833 Act for another five years in the face of the opinion of some colonists that 'it was a judicial monstrosity which has never yet been paralleled in any other part of the world'. In 1839, the military jury panels were abolished.

***

John Plunkett was affronted by the fact that Aboriginal inhabitants could not give evidence in courts, because they were not permitted to take an oath to tell the truth. This was because their spiritual beliefs were so foreign to Europeans. It was considered that the native population did not understand the concept of a supreme being who imposed divine judgement – or at least the Judeo–Christian version – and that they had no belief in 'a future state of reward and punishment' – an accounting for one's sins in the afterlife.[9] Hence, it was thought that an oath to tell the truth had no meaning for them, because there would be no spiritual consequences for lying. If they could not take the oath, the law insisted that they could not give evidence. This had the effect that Aborigines could be brought into court as defendants, but they were unable to give evidence themselves or to call evidence from other Aboriginal people in their defence. Aborigines were subject to the law, because they were considered British subjects, but they had no ability to derive any real benefit or protection from it. This grossly offended John Plunkett's sense of justice and fairness and his concept of equality before the law. He was only too aware from the history of his homeland that oaths could be misused to restrict rights, reduce opportunities and create grave injustices. He also knew of cases in New South Wales, some prosecuted by himself, in which Aboriginal defendants had been unable to call Indigenous witnesses to give evidence, and hence only one side of the story had been told.[10] One of the most significant cases to highlight this deficiency in the law was prosecuted not by Plunkett, but by his fellow barrister Roger Therry.

In May 1836, two Aboriginal men, Jack Congo Murrell and Bummaree, were put on trial for the murder of another Aboriginal man – one of the first cases of its kind.[11] It was argued on behalf of Murrell and Bummaree that the colonial courts had no jurisdiction because the case concerned interrelationships, customs and practices between Aborigines, however, the full Supreme Court decided otherwise. Barrister Richard Windeyer was called to defend Murrell and Bummaree at the last moment, because another counsel had fallen ill. The accused wanted to assert that they had been attacked earlier by the deceased and that their customary law called for 'pay back', which exonerated them for the death. At the commencement of the trial, Murrell asked through his counsel for a jury of 'blackfellows', which, predictably, was denied. At the close of the prosecution case, Richard Windeyer submitted to the Chief Justice:

> *The prisoners have nothing to say and have no witnesses to call, as the only witnesses they could call are Blacks like themselves, who cannot be sworn, as they do not believe in a future state.*

The Chief Justice replied that this point had not been decided, because it had never been raised before, and he declined to say whether or not the evidence of Aboriginal witnesses could be admitted as evidence until the question formally came before him. Mr Windeyer then indicated his intention to call an Aboriginal man named McGill to give evidence of the customary laws and practices of the Aborigines. The judge said he could not admit evidence of that kind because Aboriginal customary law could never be a defence to a charge under New South Wales law. He invited Mr Windeyer to call other witnesses as to the facts of the case, but Mr Windeyer did not call any.

The Chief Justice, in his summing up to the jury, very fairly explained the disadvantages under which the Aboriginal accused men were being tried:

> *This is a most important case, being the first of the sort ever brought before the Supreme Court of New South Wales, and which will be a precedent for future proceedings in like cases; until recently it had been the general opinion of the Public and of one or two of the Judges, that the Aboriginal Blacks are not amenable to British law, excepting when the aggression was made on a white man; but the case has lately come under the consideration of the Judges, who have decided that by the Act of Parliament, in strict terms, the Court has jurisdiction of them, and they are amenable to British law. The Jury are legally in charge of the prisoner. If the prisoner, however, is amenable to British law, he is equally entitled to the protection of the law, and to all the advantages that the law gives to other subjects; and although it has been stated in evidence that the Blacks are generally considered as beasts of the forest, he, in the presence of the Almighty God declares, that he looks on them as human beings, having souls to be saved, and under the same divine protection as Europeans. With respect to their admission as witnesses, the law which requires them to answer for offences, allows them to defend themselves in the best way they can;*

> *and if witnesses of their own nation cannot be put on their oaths, yet evidence might be obtained from them in the best manner possible.*

The Chief Justice seemed to be hinting strongly that he would have allowed Aboriginal witnesses to give unsworn evidence of their direct observations of the offence, even though the law had not previously permitted this. After the judge completed his summing up, the jury retired for a few minutes, and returned with verdicts of not guilty.

Despite the fact that the Chief Justice seemed to appreciate the disadvantages of Aboriginal defendants under the law, there was very little support in the colony to ameliorate this situation. John Plunkett was determined to correct it as soon as possible and to establish some way for Aborigines to have equal access to the courts, but he knew he faced major obstacles in convincing the Legislative Council to pass suitable laws. There was also a serious hurdle in that the laws of evidence in England insisted that an oath on the Bible had to be taken before a person could give evidence in court, so an amendment to change that law in the colony might well be struck down by the Colonial Office in London as repugnant to English law. The ineligibility of Aborigines to give evidence in the courts was to play a major role in John Plunkett's most significant trial several years later.

4

MAGISTRATES, BUSHRANGERS AND THE LASH

The magistracy of New South Wales, as in England, was divided into two types: justices of the peace and stipendiary magistrates. The former were unpaid, generally not legally qualified, and often members of the landed gentry or retired military officers. The stipendiary magistrates, also called Police Magistrates, were paid, more competent, and often legally educated. The Governor held the power of appointment and dismissal, and only the Colonial Office in London could override him, but such occurrences were rare.[1] A Governor who wished to foster law and order in a remote district would choose a prominent landowner and invest him with the powers of a magistrate, despite a complete lack of knowledge of the law. These landowners generally possessed their own assigned convict labourers, and hence held a vested interest in perpetuating this slavery-like system and maintaining discipline among their workers. Many of these masters were known to be particularly harsh in ordering floggings of the convicts in their area who had committed infractions – even minor ones. Common offences included 'disorderly conduct' or 'dishonest conduct'. Their power during the early years of the colony was subject to very few restraints, and because of their non-existent or scant legal training, their judgements were often capricious.

The magistrates (including the honorary Justices of the Peace) not only exercised judicial functions, but also administrative ones on behalf of the Governor. They played a major and direct role in the administration of the convict system, including assignment of convicts, convict discipline, the granting of tickets-of-leave (a precursor to the parole system) and the administration of local police. Their judicial role included much more than one associates with magistrates today. They would investigate crimes, collect evidence, arrest suspects and then, if it was not a capital case, act as judge in a summary trial. In capital cases, they would place the suspects under the Governor's authority in Sydney, so that the Attorney General or the Crown Prosecutor could prosecute them in the Supreme Court. In remote areas of the colony, the magistrates represented the Governor, the law, the police, the land-granting authority, the judiciary – in fact every arm of government. The quality of magistrates was very variable, and increasingly after 1832 under Governor Bourke an attempt was made to reduce their excesses and idiosyncrasies and to increase the quality of their output by appointing more stipendiary magistrates and fewer honorary ones. Two of those appointed as paid magistrates were relatives of John Plunkett: his first cousin, Captain

Patrick Plunkett, who became a magistrate in the Illawarra in 1837; and his twin brother, Christopher George Plunkett, who took up a position in Victoria in 1851, the year that it became a separate colony from New South Wales.[2]

Within a short time of his arrival, the new Solicitor General was horrified at the unbridled power of the magistrates, and recognised that it should be restrained and defined. His solution was two-fold. With the encouragement and support of Governor Bourke, with whom he shared many of his enlightened views, he drafted the *Summary Jurisdiction Act*, which defined the offences that could be dealt with by magistrates and set limits on the punishments that they could impose. Most importantly, it provided that only two or more magistrates sitting together could convict people on charges of theft, drunkenness, disobedience of orders, neglect of or running away from work, abusive language and other disorderly or dishonest conduct. This made it harder for impulsive landowners to order or arrange unduly severe punishment of their charges.

The second solution adopted by Plunkett was to improve access for magistrates to legal information and case law about their role, responsibilities and restraints. During the period he was Solicitor General, despite his enormous workload during the day, Plunkett found the time at night to write Australia's first legal textbook *An Australian Magistrate* – a practical, succinct, everyday guidebook on criminal law practice for the many Magistrates, Justices of the Peace and practitioners scattered throughout the colony, and particularly valuable for those who had not been formally educated in the law. For many years this book stood as a bible for those working at all levels of the criminal courts, and in various iterations it was in everyday use until the end of the century.

Plunkett lost no opportunity to demonstrate to the community that the magistrates were as subject to the law as anyone else. He had several chances to do this when magistrates were accused of crimes and he was called upon to prosecute them. One such case attracted the attention of the whole colony for many months. In 1837 – his first full year as Attorney General – John Plunkett prosecuted two magistrates, Henry Donnison and Willoughby Bean, who had been charged with the theft of cattle in Brisbane Water (now the Gosford district). Both defendants had been Justices of the Peace in that area and Donnison was a large landowner. Both were highly regarded by their local community. The Brisbane Water police magistrate, Captain Alured Tasker Faunce, arrested and charged Donnison and Bean on cattle-stealing charges and gaoled them in leg irons in the local lock-up before sending them to Sydney for trial. As Attorney General, Plunkett had the task of prosecuting both Donnison and Bean at a trial in March 1837. It was clear to all that Faunce had acted on completely inadequate evidence in arresting them and sending them for trial, but Plunkett was determined to ensure that this case was treated in the same way as any other, despite the high profile of the defendants. In his opening address, he declared that he would approach the case without any undue deference to the defendants' position, telling the jury that:

When a prima facie [basic] case appeared upon the depositions, a gentleman was no more entitled to respect than a poor man, and he hoped the time would never come when it could be said of this Colony, as an eminent lawyer, Lord Redesdale, had once said of Ireland, 'there is one law for the rich, and another for the poor'.[3]

Without even retiring to the jury room, the jurors returned verdicts of not guilty. Donnison and Bean subsequently sued Faunce for misusing his office and were awarded huge amounts in damages. The Governor refused to use public moneys to pay the amounts, and Faunce was obliged to pay them from his own pocket.

After the verdict, the Governor moved Magistrate Faunce to another district, which caused the editor of the *Sydney Gazette*, George Cavenagh, to publish these strong words:

The Brisbane Water cases have excited too much of the public attention and aroused too much of the public feeling for us to consider it necessary to enter yet more fully into particulars; it is impossible for any man to view with coolness the brutal treatment, to which a British magistrate and British gentlemen, were subjected at the mere caprice of a holiday military captain. The most charitable conclusion that any one on a review of the circumstances can come to is, that the man himself must be the victim of extraordinary mental imbecility. If we do not come to such a conclusion, it is absolutely dreadful to contemplate the depraved state of feeling which could wantonly urge on its possessor to such extreme length.

And second, what are we to think of the Governor or Government, who after such a disclosure of the utter inefficiency, to use the very simplest word in our power, of Captain Alured Tasker Faunce, have entrusted him with the protection or the guidance of any being whose life or liberty is of more value than that of an old stock horse, and who have marked their censure of his conduct in another way than by removing him to another and more distant district, where as he will be further from the influence of the press, he may again be able to play such fantastic tricks before High Heaven as make the angels weep.[4]

In the next chapter of this colonial saga, Faunce sued editor Cavenagh for libel. Once again the colony was mesmerised. The Chief Justice heard the case with a jury. He commented that:

This was a case of considerable importance to the public, inasmuch as the character of a magistrate of the Colony was involved on the one side; while the liberty of the press was said to be attacked on the other.

After retiring for three-quarters of an hour, the jury returned and announced a verdict in favour of Faunce for the amount of one farthing. The jury had starkly declared how much they thought Faunce's reputation was worth, and many in the community agreed with them.

***

The convict population of New South Wales lived under precarious conditions in which, at best, they were assigned as servants to benevolent settlers to use as free labour, and at worst, subject to severe disciplinary action from capricious, sadistic masters – some of whom were honorary magistrates and a law unto themselves. The prospect of a ticket-of-leave or a pardon, or even completing a sentence and assuming a place in society, kept most of the convicts from absconding or retaliating against abusive employers.[5] A pardon was the most beneficial way of being freed, because it effectively expunged the conviction, but most pardons were conditional on the recipient never returning to Great Britain, so they were effectively forced to remain in the colony. For many persons pardoned, this was no hardship, because their opportunities in the new land were far greater than back in the home country that had been responsible for their incarceration and transportation.

Some convicts, however, were so badly mistreated that their only choice was to abscond and attempt to survive in the rugged bush. Very few of them had the requisite skills to live in the bush unaided and hence they often survived on the fringes of society by robbing travellers, coaches and outlying houses. Such desperate, escaped convicts were known as 'bushrangers', and they were much feared by the population – even by other convicts. Occasionally, bushrangers were aided by local sympathisers who, at risk of severe punishment, provided them with supplies and information to assist in avoiding the mounted police. Some of these escapees lived with Aboriginal tribes and learnt their languages and acquired some of their skills in bushcraft. Parties of mounted police headed by a magistrate and often aided by Aboriginal trackers[6] would scour the countryside searching for these dangerous men. If apprehended and brought to trial, sentence of death was the inevitable and swift outcome. As a result, many of them preferred to die in a hail of bullets during a shoot-out with the mounted police, rather than be taken prisoner and brought to Sydney for trial and public execution.

***

During his four years as Solicitor General, John Plunkett was involved in two significant, high-profile trials that exemplified the unique conditions prevailing in the colony of New South Wales. One of those cases involved a group of convicts who claimed to have been severely abused by their employer, James Mudie, and who as a result had risen up and struck back at their tormentor. This case reminded Plunkett of the many defendants he had represented in Ireland who had committed crimes out of sheer frustration and abject poverty. The other case involved the murder by some escaped convicts of a prominent Sydney citizen, Dr Robert Wardell.

***

James Mudie was a landowner in the Hunter River district who had developed a successful farming property called *Castle Forbes* at Patrick's Plains (Singleton). In 1830, Governor Darling appointed Mudie a Justice of the Peace at the court in Maitland, which gave him power over the punishment of convicts in the area. Mudie and his overseer, John Larnach, who was also his son-in-law, treated many of their assigned convicts with relentless brutality and kept them on rations that were so meagre that their charges sometimes had to resort to crime just to avoid starvation. Mudie and Larnach were well known in the area for the frequency with which they flogged their convicts. As a magistrate, Mudie had the responsibility for issuing tickets-of-leave to convicts, but he would often improperly delay issuing the required documentation in order to get the most out of his workforce.

When the benevolent and progressive Governor Richard Bourke arrived in the colony in December 1831, he limited lashings to a maximum of fifty for any single offence. His views about convict discipline caused him to come into conflict with some of the landowning employers of convict labour, and none more so than the settlers of the Hunter River Valley, including James Mudie. They believed that Bourke's soft attitude to convicts endangered discipline and ran counter to the intent of transportation. The population of the colony and the newspapers divided sharply on this issue.

In 1833, one of Mudie's convicts escaped from *Castle Forbes* and came to Sydney to complain to the Governor about the treatment meted out by his master and the overseer, Larnach. The Governor listened to his complaints, expressed sympathy, and gave him a letter of comfort to take back with him to *Castle Forbes.* On the convict's return, Mudie had the man arrested and tried before a Bench of his magistrate friends, who ordered the man to serve the remainder of his sentence in an iron gang – one of the harshest forms of punishment in the colony.

On 5 November 1833, driven to desperation by the frequent floggings and inadequate rations at *Castle Forbes*, four of the convicts assigned to Mudie broke out and took to the bush, later freeing two other convicts. The six came back to his property and entered his house, intending to kill him in retaliation for the incessant brutality. Mudie was absent, and instead they found his daughter, Emily, who was Larnach's wife, whom they held captive for several hours. Something decent in the escaped convicts prevented them from doing Emily any physical harm. They left her at the house, taking numerous items with them, including three horses, a silver plate, a double-barrelled gun, a single-barrelled gun, a fowling piece, two muskets, two pistols, a tomahawk, a quantity of supplies to sustain them and several sets of clothing belonging to James Mudie, which they hoped could be used to disguise themselves.

They continued searching the property for John Larnack and found him at a sheep run. Seeing the six convicts approaching, Larnach dived into a nearby swamp. As he did so, one of the convicts fired three shots at him, but missed, while another called out, 'I'll take care you shall never punish another man,' and, 'I'll make you remember flogging.' Larnach managed to escape and went to a neighbouring property that belonged to Hunter Valley landowner Henry Dangar. The six convicts then disappeared into the bush with their booty. During their time on the run, they became known as the *Castle Forbes Gang* of bushrangers. They robbed another property and flogged a local overseer known for his brutality. The gang was recaptured at Lamb's Valley, north-west of Maitland, about ten days later, after a dramatic shoot-out with a group of mounted police led by Magistrate Robert Scott. Robert Scott was a well-known, wealthy landowner in the Hunter River Valley who was politically influential in the colony and had a fearsome reputation for organising posses that would track bushrangers and either kill them or bring them to Sydney, where they would be tried and hanged.

John Plunkett prosecuted the six bushrangers from *Castle Forbes* at two trials on successive days for 'stealing in a dwelling-house and putting in bodily fear', and for 'the attempted murder of John Larnach'.[7] Roger Therry defended them. The trials took place on 9 and 10 December 1833 before Chief Justice Forbes and two military juries. During the trials, the prisoners all made statements about the atrocious conditions at *Castle Forbes*, and 'they attributed their present awful state, to the ill-treatment, floggings, bad provisions, and short weight received of their masters, which had driven them to desperation'. It should be noted that at this time there was a rule of procedure that an accused could not give sworn evidence in his or her own case, and could only make an unsworn statement to the court. This was to remove the temptation to tell lies on oath in one's own defence and thereby condemn oneself to eternal damnation in hell. One of the accused told the jury that conditions at *Castle Forbes* were so abhorrent that he would prefer death to returning there. The main defendant, Anthony Hitchcock, asked the court to allow the men on trial to show 'their lacerated backs to the public gaze to show what tortures they had endured'; however, the Chief Justice would not allow them.[8] Nor would he allow further corroborating evidence to be led of their treatment because he did not consider that it raised a valid defence to the charges. All six men were convicted,[9] and five of them were sentenced to death, while the sixth was sentenced to transportation for life to Norfolk Island. Three were hanged in Sydney, while the other two were returned to *Castle Forbes* in an open, horse-drawn cart, sitting on their coffins. When they arrived, the remaining convict servants were forced to watch their execution to deter them from similar misconduct.

The executions caused an uproar in the community because of what were said to be the intolerable conditions under which these convicts had been forced to live. A newspaper campaign was commenced by the *Sydney Gazette*, edited by a former convict, William Watt, and read largely by convicts and emancipists, calling for an investigation into Mudie and Larnach. Governor Bourke agreed to hold an enquiry, and appointed Solicitor General John Plunkett, and Superintendent of Convicts Frederick Hely to conduct it.[10]

Plunkett and Hely's report excited intense public interest throughout the colony.[11] Their findings partially exonerated Mudie and Larnach; however, they found that about half of the convicts at *Castle Forbes* had been lashed at some time, which was higher than the average. They criticised Larnach for abusing the law by bringing a man twice before a magistrate on the same day for the same offence so that he would receive a hundred lashes rather than the maximum of fifty. Governor Bourke responded to the report by appointing a resident stipendiary magistrate at Patrick's Plains to replace the honorary magistrates, like James Mudie, and by failing to reappoint Mudie as a Justice of the Peace.

Mudie and Larnach were greatly angered by the allegations that had been made against them and the subsequent report, and prepared a joint protest, which they asked Governor Bourke to forward to the public servants in London who had decision-making powers in the colonies, but he refused. In September 1834, they printed their own response to the findings in Plunkett and Hely's report, which they sent to the Colonial Office in London.[12] At the same time, William Watt, the ticket-of-leave former convict employed as editor at the *Sydney Gazette*, attacked Mudie for his cruelty to his charges in an anonymous pamphlet entitled 'Party Politics

Exposed'. Mudie suspected that Roger Therry was behind the pamphlet, and retaliated in the newspapers against him and Watt. He also alleged that Governor Bourke's undue favouritism towards convicts had rendered discipline almost impossible and been largely responsible for the uprising at *Castle Forbes.* The dispute between Mudie and the authorities was a major point of controversy in the colony for months, with opinions deeply divided according to social status – the emancipists and convicts sided with Bourke and the free landowners supported Mudie and Larnach.

Disgusted with the way he had been treated, James Mudie sold *Castle Forbes* and sailed to England where, in 1837, he published *The Felonry of New South Wales,*[13] a highly inflammatory, self-serving account of the state of the distant colony and its administration. In it he argued that Bourke's leniency towards convicts had encouraged the rebellion at *Castle Forbes,* however, the publication was so extreme in its views that it was largely discounted by the Colonial Office. Mudie also gave evidence before the House of Commons Select Committee on Transportation, where he was questioned by the chairman, Sir William Molesworth, on floggings in the colony. Mudie made no attempt to conceal his reputation as a 'flogger', and with no sense of shame or embarrassment described the jubilant reaction of convicts to his removal from the bench of magistrates the previous year.[14] The Molesworth report, in August 1838, relied heavily on the system of flogging in drawing an analogy between transportation and slavery.

Mudie returned to Sydney in 1840 to find that he was universally loathed because of his caustic publication in England. Some little time after his return, he was publicly attacked with a horse whip by John Kinchela, the son of the former Attorney General, who had also been denigrated in *The Felonry of New South Wales*. Mudie sued Kinchela Jnr for assault and was awarded £50, which was immediately collected by contributions from members of the public in court – so unpopular was Mudie.[15] Accepting his predicament, Mudie finally retired to England in 1842.

The enquiry into conditions at *Castle Forbes* gave John Plunkett the opportunity to see the system of convict assignments to private masters at close quarters, and although he partly exonerated Mudie and Larnach, he became convinced that it was infused with abuse and injustice, and should be abolished. Too many masters had mistreated their convict labourers, and there were now a sufficient number of freed convicts to service the colony's need for workers.

***

The other major case involving bushrangers that John Plunkett prosecuted in his early years in the colony was the trial in September 1834 of two convicts charged with the murder of Dr Robert Wardell, one of the best-known personalities in the colony.[16] Once again, this case attracted the attention of every echelon of colonial society. Robert Wardell was an English barrister and London newspaper editor who had arrived in the colony in 1824 on the same ship as his fellow legal practitioner William Charles Wentworth. Wentworth had enticed Wardell to come to the colony to set up legal practice and to act as editor of the first independent newspaper in the colony. On them both being admitted as barristers in Sydney, they petitioned the Supreme Court to prevent attorneys (solicitors) from doing the advocacy work normally done by barristers, in accordance with the traditional roles that existed in England. Due to the shortage of qualified barristers in the colony, Chief Justice Francis Forbes refused the application; however, in 1829 he agreed to an order that divided the legal profession into two distinct categories – barristers and solicitors – in a form that has been maintained until today.[17]

Soon after arriving in the colony, Wardell and Wentworth began publishing their own local newspaper, *The Australian*.[18] The paper supported the emancipist causes, and pushed for an elected Legislative Council, the abolition of military juries and freedom of the Press. Wardell clashed repeatedly with the authoritarian Governor Darling, and was twice prosecuted by him for criminal libel, but on both occasions the jury were unable to agree. Darling was to say that Wardell and Wentworth: 'keep the Court and the Bar by their effrontery equally in subjection'.

Wardell was one of the most sought-after barristers in Sydney and he made a handsome living. Despite Darling's ill feelings towards him, he was so highly regarded as a lawyer that he was sometimes retained as counsel for the government.

By 1834, Robert Wardell was a wealthy man, due to his prowess as a lawyer and some prudent land acquisitions. His main estate was at Petersham, where he ran a successful farm with wheat and timber and on which he had constructed a home called *Sara Dell*. On Sunday, 7 September at about 1pm he left his house on his distinctive white horse to ride around his estate. About three-quarters of a mile from *Sara Dell*, in bush near to the Cook's River, he spotted a rudimentary bark hut, from which emerged three white men: John Jenkins, Thomas Tattersdale and eighteen-year-old Emanuel Brace, who were convicts unlawfully at large. Jenkins, the leader of the three, had escaped from an iron-gang working on public roads and buildings in the Georges River district. He had been transported after being convicted of fifteen offences in England and had already been punished twice for misconduct in New South Wales. The three convicts had committed several robberies and thefts in an attempt to survive in the bush around Petersham, which was then on the outskirts of Sydney.[19] Upon Wardell unexpectedly discovering these three escaped convicts, he urged them to give themselves up, an idea that was vigorously opposed by Jenkins. Jenkins then produced a musket that he presented at Wardell. Tattersdale remonstrated with Jenkins, suggesting that he should not harm the man who had discovered them. There was then a verbal altercation between Wardell and Jenkins during which Jenkins shot Wardell. The shot caused Wardell's horse to bolt, but he managed to cling onto it until, weak from his wound, he fell to the ground, crawled to a tree trunk, rested against it, and died.

Wardell's disappearance was noted on the Sunday night after his horse returned home, but it was not until early the following morning that a search party was organised, led by Chief Magistrate Colonel Wilson and containing a large number of 'gentlemen from Sydney'. Wardell's disappearance caused great consternation, because he was a well-known identity throughout society. His body was found later that day, causing a wave of grief in the community. The three convicts were arrested nearly a week later. The youngest of them, Emanuel Brace, immediately confessed to the Chief Magistrate and offered to become an 'approver' (informer) against the others in return for immunity from prosecution. His evidence was critical to the prosecution case against the remaining two.

John Plunkett realised that the success of the prosecution depended entirely upon the informer giving evidence, and he was most concerned that the informer might be threatened or harmed, such that his evidence would be lost. He therefore approached the Supreme Court on Saturday, 20 September 1834 to request an urgent hearing of the trial the following week. The Court could see no justification for such a speedy hearing, and so Plunkett had to wait until 7 November for the trial to commence.

On the morning of the trial, the Chief Justice enquired who was representing the two accused men, and a Mr Kinsman announced that he was. Mr Kinsman had until a short time before been an attorney (solicitor), so Plunkett objected to him representing the accused, but Mr Kinsman assured the Chief Justice that he had recently been admitted as a barrister. So little did Plunkett think of Mr Kinsman that he stated in open court that after the trial he would ask for the man's name to be removed from the roll of barristers.

Emanuel Brace was the star witness. His account of the incident was this:

> *I heard the sound of a horse's feet, and looking up to see who it was, I saw a gentleman on a white horse, who asked me who I was, but I made no answer; Jenkins looked up, and on receiving the same question answered, 'I am a man'; he asked, who are the other two? when Jenkins answered, they are men; the*

gentleman then stooped a little from his horse, and took up a small stick which was leaning against a tree, and flourished it over his head as if beckoning for assistance; he said, you are only three poor run-aways, you had better come along with me; he pranced about the hut, and Jenkins dodged him and took up a rock-stone and told him to go away, but he would not; I heard Jenkins whisper to Tattersdale, to go and fetch the musket, when I said, we need not do that, it would be better to go and receive fifty lashes than to risk our lives; Tattersdale moved towards the bush and got the musket, when Jenkins took it out of his hands, which, on the gentleman observing, he said, Oh, for God's sake don't do that, Jenkins answered – By G-d I will! The horse was prancing back and Jenkins proceeded up to the gentleman, presented the piece and fired. When the gentleman said 'Oh dear, I'm killed', the horse turned short round, and started off at full speed, and went a great distance, over some rocks.

In the defence case, Jenkins wanted to call three character witnesses, but on their names being called outside the court, none of them were present. Jenkins then called a most unsatisfactory alibi witness, convict William Smith. It is not clear from the trial transcript whether Mr Kinsman had left the court, but Jenkins himself questioned the witness. Jenkins asked Smith whether he had seen Jenkins and Brace together on 7 September, the day of the murder. This interchange then took place:

Smith: I heard of the murder of Dr Wardell. I don't remember the day it took place. I don't remember the 7th of September. I never remember seeing you and Brace together on that day or any other day.

Jenkins: Come now Bill, you have nothing to be afraid of. Speak up like a man. No harm can come to you. Was not I and Brace in your company together on that day?

Smith: I never saw Brace before the present time in my life. I never saw you and Brace together. You were never in my company.

Jenkins: (with the most fiend-like expression of countenance) I see it's no use to ask him any further questions. He's afraid to speak the truth on my behalf. No witnesses present. No one can come forward for Jenkins. Never mind, I can do it like a dog.[20]

The Chief Justice in his summing up to the jury explained how the evidence of the informer, who was also an accomplice, was corroborated by many other witnesses, as required by law. Both Jenkins and Tattersdale were found guilty. The prisoners were then asked in the traditional way whether they had anything to say before sentence (of death) would be pronounced. Jenkins stood up and loudly proclaimed that he had a good deal to say on the subject. He considered that he had not had a fair trial, stating that:

That bloody old woman [defence counsel, Mr Kinsman] has been shoved upon us for the purpose of leading us to our destruction. I could have conducted my own case with a better chance of justice. The Jury were not out a second, when they brought in guilty; but I did not care a bloody damn for either Judge or Jury, or the whole bloody Court, whom I would shoot with the greatest pleasure if I had my gun here.[21]

He then struck the dock with his hand in an infuriated fashion.

Tattersdale, on the other hand, while expressing his innocence of the crime, because he had urged Jenkins not to shoot Wardell, begged to be allowed a few days' respite of the sentence to make his peace with God. His Honour refused the application, saying that he did not have the discretion to delay the execution and fervently exhorted him to make the best use of his few remaining hours.

His Honour then passed sentence of death on them both and had scarcely finished when Jenkins turned towards Tattersdale and ferociously lunged at him, striking him two violent blows. This took everyone in court by surprise, and it was several moments before the police rushed into the dock and with much difficulty secured Jenkins. The newspapers reported Jenkins' extraordinary behaviour in great detail.

At the gallows on 10 November 1834, in the presence of assembled felons and official witnesses, Jenkins 'ascended the ladder with the greatest expedition, and on arriving on the scaffold went over to one of the ropes suspended from the fatal beam and struck it with his hand in a playful manner'. Jenkins then addressed those in the yard, telling them that he had informed the Governor of the gaol of details of other offences he had committed, so that no one else would be blamed for them, and then gave this remarkable farewell to the assembled crowd:

> *Well, good bye my lads, I have not time to say much to you; I acknowledge I shot the Doctor, but it was not for gain, it was for the sake of my fellow prisoners because he was a tyrant. And I have one thing to recommend you as a friend, if any of you take to the bush, shoot every tyrant you come across, and there are several now in the yard who ought to be served so.*[22]

***

Governor Sir Richard Bourke left Sydney in December 1837, having sent his resignation to London earlier that year. John Plunkett was deeply sorry to lose not only a Governor whom he greatly respected, but also a friend. Upon the arrival of the new Governor, Sir George Gipps, in early 1838, the relationship with his Attorney General quickly became cordial and mutually respectful, as the Governor, like his predecessor, had a benevolent attitude towards the underdogs of this society – the convicts, the emancipists and the Aborigines.

The new Governor was keen to restrict and eventually abolish the convict assignment system. In this regard, he had the overwhelming support of his Attorney General. One of Gipps's first acts on taking up his appointment was to prohibit the assignment of convicts for domestic service in homes in Sydney and the larger country towns. Over the next three years, assignments were progressively abolished, so that the last assignments were in 1841. From 1840 to 1843 the number of assigned convicts shrank from 22 000 to just over 4 000. This created improved employment prospects for free settlers and emancipated convicts, and was an important stepping stone in the lengthy process of abolishing transportation and transforming the Colony from a penal settlement into a self-governing society of free men and women.

5

CHURCH AND STATE

By 1836, the free citizenry of New South Wales outnumbered convicts by 49 300 to 27 800. Sydney was a city of 18 000 pcoplc. In that year, upon his appointment as Attorney General, John Hubert Plunkett became a member of the Legislative Council. In this capacity he was given opportunities to introduce reforms that would shape the colony and its legal structures for decades to come, and indeed have a lasting effect on the democratic institutions and conventions that were established when the six Australian colonies federated into a nation more than sixty years later. As Attorney General and a member of the Council, Plunkett had the opportunity to fight for the civil rights and egalitarian conditions that he so strongly believed in as he strove to create a society that avoided the discrimination and impediments that had plagued his native Ireland for centuries.

One of his first projects as a member of the Legislative Council was to be his most enduring legacy.

When the First Fleeters landed on the shores of what would become New South Wales in 1788, they brought with them the laws of England and the institutions of British government and justice. This included both British statutory law and the judge-made common law.[1] Over time, local laws were introduced that differed from the equivalent English laws, and there was an uneasy balance between them based on two legal principles: the 'doctrine of paramount force' and the 'doctrine of repugnancy'.[2] The doctrine of paramount force provided that any English Act was also in force in the colony, depending upon the local circumstances being appropriately similar. This allowed for different laws to be passed in the colony to account for divergent circumstances to the mother country. For example, in England a person convicted of a felony had no standing in the courts. In the colony, there were so many convicts that this was impossible to accommodate, and so within six months of the arrival of the First Fleet the principle was established that convicts had access to the local courts. Two convicts successfully sued the master of the ship that had brought them to the colony for the loss of their baggage on the voyage.[3] This marked a radical departure from the laws of England because of the differing circumstances in the colony.

The second principle, the doctrine of repugnancy, stated that colonial legislation was void if it contradicted the equivalent English law. Any law enacted in the colony had to be remitted to London for vetting and was liable to be rejected if considered repugnant to English law and if the conditions in the colony did not warrant a different approach. The Colonial

Office in London therefore had an effective power of veto on any laws passed in New South Wales.

The contradiction between these two doctrines is self-evident and the local courts were kept busy trying to balance them. The question of whether conditions in the colony were sufficiently dissimilar to warrant laws divergent from the mother country was sometimes difficult to determine.

Because New South Wales was an outpost of the British Empire, all the institutions of government in the homeland were adopted to the extent that they were applicable. The most fundamental institution of all was the Monarchy, under which came all other institutions of government. The English Monarch represented the source not only of all temporal – secular – power, but also all religious authority. The King or Queen of England was not only the head of state of Great Britain and Ireland, but also the head of the Church of England, which was the official religion of state. There was no division between church and state in England, which is a situation that still exists in form today, where the Queen is both the Monarch and the head of the Church of England. At the founding of New South Wales (and the other five Australian colonies), the King's status as head of state and head of the official state religion was automatically transferred to the colony.

***

In Ireland, John Plunkett had seen first-hand the negative effects of the unity between church and state, and he had experienced discrimination derived from religion interfering in the business of government. He was determined that the religious divisions that had riven his homeland for so many centuries would not be allowed to infect the colony, and that the solution was to create a division between church and state – to secularise the state and all its institutions. Plunkett, the intensely religious man, saw religion as having no legitimate role to play in government or its institutions and believed that faith should be an entirely private affair. His solution was the *Church Act* of 1836.

The enactment of the *Church Act* arose from one of the most remarkable partnerships for reform in the history of colonial Australia. It involved three men: Governor Sir Richard Bourke, John Hubert Plunkett and Roger Therry. Each man had originated in Ireland, although Bourke was a member of the Anglican aristocracy, while Plunkett and Therry were from the oppressed Catholic majority. All three were reformist by nature, believing in the equality of all men before the law, and were determined that the colony should avoid the religious sectarianism that had plagued their homeland. They realised that a direct move in the colony to remove the Church of England from its central role as the church of state would inevitably be met by a declaration of repugnancy in London. They had all been impressed by the non-sectarian system of public, government-funded schooling that had been established in Ireland in 1831 under a Board of National Education at the instigation of Lord EG Stanley, then the Chief Secretary for Ireland. The Irish system provided that children of all denominations were to be admitted to schools receiving government grants and that their instruction was to include religious teaching of an undogmatic kind. Bourke, Plunkett and Therry were keen to set up something similar in New South Wales.

The seemingly impossible task of changing the status of the Church of England in the colony involved a carefully orchestrated manoeuvre – combining an attack from the flanks disguised as a cost-saving measure and a wide reading of instructions from London. On 30 September 1833, when Plunkett was still Solicitor General, Bourke sent a letter to Lord Stanley, who by this stage had become the Secretary of State for the Colonies, seeking approval from London to expend government moneys in New South Wales on *any* of the Christian religions that wished to build a house of worship and employ a clergyman. His letter explained this unusual request in these terms:

> *I would observe that the Inhabitants of this Colony are of many different religious persuasions, the followers of the Church of England being the most numerous; but there are also large bodies of Roman Catholics and Presbyterians of the Church of Scotland, besides Protestant Dissenters of many different denominations having separate Places of Worship ...*
>
> *I would observe that, in a New Country to which Persons of all religious persuasions are invited to resort, it will be impossible to establish a dominant and endowed Church without much hostility and great improbability of its becoming permanent. The inclination of these Colonists, which keeps pace with the Spirit of the Age, is decidedly adverse to such an Institution; and I fear the interests of Religion would be prejudiced by its Establishment. If on the contrary support were given as required to every one of the three grand Divisions of Christians indifferently, and the management of the temporalities of their Churches left to themselves, I conceive that the Public Treasury*

might in time be relieved of a considerable charge, and, what is of much greater importance, the people would become more attached to their respective Churches and be more willing to listen to and obey the voice of their several Pastors ...

I would propose that, wherever a moderate congregation can be collected throughout the Colony, and that a subscription shall have been entered into for Building a Place of Worship and Minister's dwelling amounting to Sum not less than £300, upon application an equal Sum shall be issued from the Colonial Treasury in aid of the undertaking ...

I cannot conclude this subject without expressing a hope, amounting to some degree of confidence that, in laying the foundations of the Christian Religion in this young and rising Colony by equal encouragement held out to its Professors in their several Churches, the people of these different persuasions will be united together in one bond of peace, and taught to look up to the Government as their common protector and friend, and that thus there will be secured to the State good subjects and to Society good men.[4]

Bourke received no reply from Lord Stanley, and had to wait until a new Whig Colonial Secretary, Lord Glenelg, replied more than two years later, in a letter dated 30 November 1835, with these words:

His Majesty's Government are deeply sensible of the importance of the subject thus brought under their consideration. They fully concur with you in the opinion that in no part of the World is the general Education of the People a more sacred and necessary duty of the Government than in New South Wales ...

I am disposed, therefore, to commit to the Governor and the Legislative Council the task of suggesting and enacting such Laws and Regulations for the distribution and appropriation of the Funds applicable to the general purposes of Religion and Education, as they consider best adapted to the exigencies of the Colony …

Attached as I am, in common with the other Members of the Government, to the Church of England, and believing it, when duly administered, to be a powerful Instrument in the diffusion of sound Religious Instruction, I am desirous that every encouragement should be given to its extension in New South Wales, consistently with the just claims of that large portion of the Community, which is composed of Christians of other denominations. In dealing with this subject, in a case so new as that of the Australian Colonies, few analogies can be drawn from the Institutions of the Parent state to our assistance. In those Communities, formed and rapidly multiplying under most peculiar circumstances, and comprising great numbers of Presbyterians and Roman Catholics, as well as Members of the Church of England, it is evident that the attempt to select any one Church as the exclusive object of the Public Endowment, even if it were advisable in every other respect, would not long be tolerated.[5]

Glenelg also approved of Bourke introducing a system of education based on the Irish national system.

By the time Glenelg's response had been received in New South Wales,[6] John Plunkett had secured his place as the preeminent legal adviser to the Governor. With their equal zeal for reform, the Governor and his Attorney General had cemented a close personal friendship that was to last until Bourke left the colony.[7] John and Maria Plunkett were frequent guests at Government House. The relationship between Plunkett and Therry was more problematical, but even longer lasting. Plunkett and Therry had been students at Trinity College and King's Inn at the same time. Therry had preceded Plunkett in coming to New South Wales when he was appointed as Commissioner of the Court of Requests, a position that gave him freedom to practise as a private barrister. When Plunkett arrived as Solicitor General, he ranked above Therry. There was clearly a sense of competitiveness between these two men, whose careers overlapped for several decades.

Bourke and Plunkett viewed the response from Lord Glenelg in London as an open invitation to press for far more than had been requested in the original letter or approved in the Colonial Secretary's reply. They saw it as an opportunity to move in the direction of their real, underlying objective: to provide that the colony should have no established religion and that there should be neutrality between all faiths – Christian or otherwise. At Bourke's request, Plunkett drafted a Bill to give legislative effect to Bourke's original letter, but it went much further, in that it extended the benefits of state funding to all religions, including Baptists, Methodists, dissenting Protestants, and Jews. The next step was to present the Bill to the Legislative Council. However, before doing so, Bourke took steps to increase the odds of the Bill winning majority approval. Firstly, he appointed Plunkett as a member of the Council. Next, he prevented Bishop William Broughton from voting, on the pretext that he had only recently been appointed to the position of Anglican Lord Bishop of Australia, and until the appointment had been confirmed in London, Broughton should not take up his seat on the Council. In the meantime, the third member of the triumvirate, Roger Therry, agitated in favour of the Bill in the newspapers and in public in a manner that would have been inappropriate for the Governor or the Attorney General. The aim of this exercise was to convince swinging voters on the Council that the Bill had support from a wide spectrum of the community.

After Plunkett's appointment, at the first meeting of the Legislative Council on 2 June 1836, Bourke tabled the exchange of letters with London and two Bills that had been drafted by Plunkett: one to provide multi-denominational funding to all religions for their houses of worship and their clergy; and another to set up a National School System along the lines of the Irish model. There was much public debate in the newspapers and many petitions were sent to the Governor opposing both Bills. The most vociferous opposition was to the Bill that would establish a secular school system. A protest meeting was held at the Pulteney Hotel in Sydney on 24 June 1836, under the Chairmanship of Bishop Broughton, that was attended by the Episcopalian, the Presbyterian, the Independents, the Baptists and the Wesleyans. A resolution was passed opposing 'any system of general education, which shall be founded on the principle of interdicting [i.e. excluding], either wholly or in part, the use of the Holy Scriptures according to the Authorized version'.[8] These church representatives favoured a system of allocating state grants to religious schools under their own denominational authority, rather than the establishment of an independent school system outside their control. Only the Catholic clergy supported the proposals. A majority of the newspapers also opposed the schools proposal. At the core of the opposition were the conservative Anglican landholders and churchmen. No real assessment was made of the merits of a public education system, nor analysis of whether the successful Irish system would work well in the colony. The opposition was based on ignorance and a fear of the religious leaders losing control. So great was the ensuing public opprobrium of Bourke's plans for a new school system that he realised that the secular Irish model was fraught with dissension in the colony, rather than generating sectarian peace and goodwill,[9] so he withdrew the proposal from consideration.[10]

On 27 July 1836, the Legislative Council met again to consider the *Church Bill.* It now referred only to state financial support for church buildings and stipends for the clergy, and made no mention of setting up a new school system. Apart from the Governor, there were twelve other members of the Council. The acting Chief Justice, James Dowling, was a fellow Anglo-Irishman, who was reform minded, like the Governor. There were two members of the Church of Scotland; two Presbyterians; two military officers; three traditional, conservative, Anglican pastoralists; a member of one of the non-conformist Christian churches; and John Plunkett – the only Catholic. The provisions extending the benefits of the *Church Act* to non-Christian religions were defeated, however, a majority of eight to four approved the legislation to provide equality of funding to Anglicans, Catholics and Presbyterian churches. Although the *Church Act* did not set up Bourke and Plunkett's new state school system, the Council did vote at the same meeting to approve £3000 for schools.

The *Church Act* was received with almost universal approval by the local Press, and the *Australian* noted the high quality of the speeches that had been made in the Council by Attorney General Plunkett and Chief Justice Dowling.

In putting forward the *Church Act*, Bourke and Plunkett took an enormous risk. To detract from the status of the Anglican Church not only ran the risk of alienating the hierarchy of the Church in Australia, and its local adherents, but also the top echelons of the Church in England and the Colonial Office in London. Although on its face it was purely a fiscal measure, its true effect was to disengage the Church of England as the church of state in the colony by putting it on the same footing as the other Christian churches. This was entirely repugnant to a host of English laws that had been adopted over centuries to cement the Church's role in the mother country at the centre of religious, political, legal, administrative and educational life. It could not be said that the circumstances in New South Wales were so different as to render these laws inapplicable to the colony, so there was every possibility that a law that had the effect of diminishing Anglicanism as the religion of state in the colony would be rejected by London under the doctrine of repugnancy. That it wasn't is a tribute to Bourke and Plunkett's negotiating and legal skills.

While the *Church Act* was a limited provision that nominally provided only for equal state funding of the various religions, it had an effect far greater than that. It was immediately viewed in the colony as a bold statement of the equality of all religions. From 1836, it became an accepted convention that the colonial government would never intervene in matters of religious belief and that it would maintain strict neutrality between the various religions. For many years, public money was allocated to supporting denominational schools of all the Christian religions. Without even mentioning the status of the Church of England, Bourke, Plunkett and Therry had effectively rendered New South Wales a secular colony without an official state religion. By a masterstroke of tactics, they had achieved a separation of church and state at a time when those two institutions remained inextricably bound together in the home country. The measure irretrievably changed the relationship between the state and religion in all the Australian colonies.

By the time Bourke left the colony in December 1837, the merit of his educational policies had become more evident to those who had opposed the new school system. When he departed, he was accorded tributes from every section of society, including Catholics, Protestants, Dissenters and Jews. It would be much later, well after Bourke had returned to Ireland, that Plunkett would be instrumental in setting up a public school system in New South Wales.

In 1839, the *Church Act* was extended to apply to Methodists and other dissenting Christian religions. It was not until 1858 that the *Jews Relief Act* was passed in the United Kingdom, followed soon after in New South Wales.

***

The *Church Act* of 1836 is the reason why the Commonwealth of Australia that was established in 1901 was, and still is, a secular country with no religion of state. It is one of the great strengths of the nation, and, like the United States of America, one of the reasons so many migrants from diverse parts of the world have come over many decades, creating a peaceful, prosperous, democratic, multicultural society in which plurality and diversity are some of its foremost strengths. Meanwhile, in England, the Monarch is still the head of the Church of England. There is still a law that any member of the Royal Family who converts to Catholicism automatically renounces any right to the throne, and it was only in 2011 that the British Monarch could marry a Catholic. Australia owes a great debt to Bourke, Plunkett and Therry; because of the work of these men, the nation has been able to avoid the most blatant discriminatory measures on religious grounds that were a feature of so many European countries in their time.

6

SANCTUARY

During the early 1830s, hot on the heels of the great explorers such as John Oxley, Charles Sturt and Major Sir Thomas Mitchell, cattle and sheep graziers appropriated large swathes of fertile land along the major rivers of the Liverpool Plains[1] in the New England district of northern New South Wales, including what is now known as the Gwydir River, but was then called the Big River. The deep narrow valleys of the Big River offered ideal conditions for the grazing of cattle. There was an abundance of trees and steep mountains along the sides of the river, so that cattle could safely be contained with little effort, because cattle do not wander far from their drinking water and are not mountain climbers like goats or sheep. The nearby mountains also protected the verdant grassy floor from violent storms. The large pastoral landholdings, known as 'stations' or 'runs', had originally been covered in bush and used for millennia by the local Aboriginal inhabitants, the Gamilaroi, who would set fire to the low scrub near the river in order to encourage the growth of grasses that would attract the native wildlife, which formed the basis of their diet.

With the arrival at the Liverpool Plains of white 'squatters', whose occupation of the land had no legal foundation, bush areas were cleared using assigned convict labour. The introduction of sheep and cattle had a devastating effect on the native animals, and hence on the local Aborigines. A flock of sheep or a herd of cattle could reduce a waterhole to polluted mush in a matter of weeks, depriving people and all native animals of clean water. This would quickly reduce the wildlife available for hunting and therefore the amount of food available to the Aborigines diminished, and starving tribes would soon resort to the cattle or sheep as a readily available source of sustenance. This soon established a source of conflict for resources between whites and blacks. The Aborigines had a number of unpalatable choices. They could relocate to areas where they could live on meagre charitable handouts of basic food from the whites. They could be employed on subsistence wages – often just food and a place to camp – on white stations, or as Aboriginal police trackers. They could live in the bush, surviving on the occasional sheep or cow, and run the risk of brutal retaliation from the far-better-armed whites. Especially in times of drought, which occurred with monotonous regularity, the competition for resources between whites and blacks became particularly intense, and the conflicts more vicious on both sides.

Once the white settlers' stations were established with the building of small workers' huts and basic cattle or sheep yards, they were predominantly staffed by assigned convicts or ex-convicts, while the landowners lived in far greater comfort in Sydney or larger country towns. In the bush, the prisoners were given far greater freedom of movement than those in the more populated areas of the colony. Many of them worked on their master's property virtually unsupervised, other than by an appointed manager, known as the superintendent, who was often himself an assigned convict or ex-convict. The ability to live and work without supervision by a master or his non-convict overseer was often preferred, particularly when it meant that a ticket-of-leave – the right to live as a free, emancipated citizen before the expiry of one's sentence, to occupy and farm one's own land, and to move more freely about the colony – might come sooner. It was far preferable to work as a stockman in the remote bush than it was to be part of a convict gang in irons constructing roads, bridges or public buildings in the more settled parts of the colony under the watchful eye of military guards and ruthless overseers. The rural convict workers in colonial New South Wales therefore tended to be more resourceful, trustworthy and dynamic than some of their Sydney counterparts.

Since 1829, the colony had been divided into those areas over which colonial administration applied and those outside. The dividing line was known as the 'limits of location'. It was bounded by the Manning River to the north, the Lachlan River to the west and the Moruya River to the south. In 1829 Governor Darling divided the area of settlement into nineteen counties. Within these established counties, which constituted the area of the colony over which the law prevailed, all ownership of land derived from Crown grants in the name of the Governor. These were recognised by the issuing of official title deeds, which meant that ownership of the land could be transferred.

The system of Crown grants as the sole source of ownership of land was seriously challenged in 1835 when John Batman – grazier, entrepreneur, and explorer from the island settlement of Van Diemen's Land (Tasmania) – crossed the Bass Strait to explore the area of Port Phillip Bay on the south-eastern tip of the Australian mainland, more than 500 miles distant from Sydney. When Batman discovered the current site of central Melbourne on the Yarra Yarra River, he noted in his diary that 'this will be the place for a village' and promptly named it 'Batmania'. He attempted to take advantage of the absence of government presence outside the limits of location by engaging in a treaty with the Wurundjeri leaders of the Kulin nation. Under the treaty, Batman agreed to give them 40 blankets, 30 axes, 100 knives, 50 scissors, 30 mirrors, 200 handkerchiefs, 100 pounds of flour and 6 shirts as an annual payment for 600 000 acres of their land. Governor Bourke could not allow this unbridled assertion of private interest to go unchallenged, as it would create a precedent for land ownership that bypassed Crown grants. With the support of the Colonial Office in London, he issued a Proclamation on 10 October 1835 that declared:

> *Whereas, it has been represented to me, that divers of His Majesty's Subjects have taken possession of vacant Lands of the Crown, within the limits of this Colony, under the pretence of a treaty, bargain, or contract, for the purchase thereof, with the Aboriginal Natives; Now therefore, I, the Governor, in virtue and in exercise of the power and authority in me vested, do*

hereby proclaim and notify to all His Majesty's Subjects, and others whom it may concern, that every such treaty, bargain, and contract with the Aboriginal Natives, as aforesaid, for the possession, title, or claim to any Lands lying and being within the limits of the Government of the Colony of New South Wales, as the same are laid down and defined by His Majesty's Commission ... is void and of no effect against the rights of the Crown; and that all Persons who shall be found in possession of any such Lands as aforesaid, without the license or authority of His Majesty's Government, for such purpose, first had and obtained, will be considered as trespassers, and liable to be dealt with in like manner as other intruders upon the vacant Lands of the Crown within the said Colony.

The Proclamation established the principle of '*terra nullius*' in Australia – an assertion that the land belonged to nobody prior to the British Crown taking possession of it, and hence any treaty with the Indigenous population was null and void. This effectively negated Batman's treaty and compelled white settlers who were pushing into remote areas beyond the limits of location, including those in northern New South Wales, to negotiate with the Crown for land ownership rather than with the Indigenous owners. Any Europeans who occupied land without a Crown grant were incapable of passing title to it and at risk of being classified as trespassers – hence they became known as 'squatters'. The doctrine of *terra nullius* was to prevail throughout Australia until the 1992 High Court decision of *Mabo v State of Queensland (No 2)*.

The division of New South Wales into nineteen counties was also used for other administrative purposes, including police and courts administration. Outside the nineteen counties, however, no courts operated, no police patrolled, and no Crown grants of land were issued, so that ownership derived from mere possession, force of arms, and an unspoken convention among the squatters in a district. After 1836, a degree of legitimacy was given to the squatters when a law was passed partially validating their holdings on payment of £10 for a squatter's licence.

It was primarily in these remote areas, outside the limits of location and beyond the reach of the law, where the most atrocious murders of Aborigines occurred. Their occupation of the land was forcibly terminated by those whose claim of right depended solely on the superiority of their arms and their willingness to engage in brutal suppression. Many of the landholders ruthlessly dispossessed Aboriginal tribes and disposed of their surviving remnants by driving them from their traditional hunting grounds, polluting or poisoning their waterholes, or just plain murdering them. White colonists had a euphemism for the sustained, systematic pursuit and murder of rural Aborigines: 'the big bushwhack'.[2] Much of the work of dispossession, dispersal and disposal was done by hired hands and assigned convicts working for distant landholders living in Sydney or the larger country towns, who may not have visited their holdings for months or years at a time. The lowly rural workers and their convict charges thus became the instruments of genocidal pillage of land and clearing of the native bush on behalf of wealthy, absent landowners.

Both free men and convicts were generally armed with firearms when they moved around in remote bush areas between pastoral properties, because of the perceived threat of attack from the Aboriginal inhabitants. It was a common complaint by landlords and their assigned or hired station hands that a group of Aborigines had 'rushed' their cattle or sheep, or had caused 'depredations'[3] to their stock or property. The Indigenous people, having had their traditional hunting grounds expropriated or disturbed, attempted to preserve their source of food and ceremonial grounds by dispersing the invading colonists and their livestock.

As the colony had only just managed to avoid starvation in the first decade after arrival in 1788, any activity that increased the security of the food supply was rigorously pursued and tacitly supported by the various Governors that were posted to Sydney by the Colonial Office in London. In 1815 the first road over the 'Blue Mountains' to the west of Sydney was built and it was only in 1836 that the Great North Road was completed by convict labour, linking Sydney with Newcastle and the fertile Hunter River Valley. Further north, there were only scant, rough tracks leading to the lush grazing grounds around the Big River, requiring a journey of many weeks. With scarce and stretched police and military resources, the Governor and his administrators were unable to exercise any viable restraints on the squatters, and so these illegal graziers were tacitly given a free hand to do whatever they wished, unimpeded by the law or any agent of the Governor. Most inhabitants viewed the squatters as pioneers in whose hands the future viability and prosperity of the colony depended. It was soon realised that these remote, new areas were ideal for the grazing of sheep, and the wool trade soon became the financial backbone of the colony.

At the same time, a powerful humanitarian movement had arisen in Britain, and this culminated in the abolition of slavery in 1833. Philanthropic organisations were established in both Britain and the colonies, dedicated to advancing the welfare of the Indigenous inhabitants of the Empire. In London, a Select Committee of the House of Commons on Aborigines in the British Settlements concluded that:

> *Too often their territory has been usurped; their property seized; their numbers diminished; their character debased; the spread of civilisation impeded … It might be presumed that the native inhabitants of any land have an incontrovertible right to their own soil; a plain and sacred right however, which seems not to have been understood. Europeans have entered their borders uninvited, and, when there, have not only acted as if they were undoubted lords of the soil, but have punished the natives as aggressors if they have evinced a disposition to live in their own country.*[4]

The report was particularly damning with regard to the plight of the Australian Aborigines:

> *In the formation of these [penal] settlements, it does not appear that the territorial rights of the natives were considered, and very little care has since been taken to protect them from the violence or the contamination of the dregs of our countrymen.*

The solutions suggested by the Committee in its 1837 report were:

- the reservation of lands so that Aborigines could continue as huntsmen until tilling the soil ceased to be 'distasteful' to them
- education of their children
- increased expenditure for missionaries and for 'Aboriginal Protectors'
- and, if necessary, the prosecution of the whites responsible for massacres.

In January 1838, Lord Glenelg, the British Secretary of State for the Colonies, sent the report to the New South Wales Governor, Sir George Gipps. The report recommended that Protectors of Aborigines should be appointed as soon as possible; they would be required to learn the Aboriginal languages and watch over their rights, guard against encroachment on their property and protect them from acts of cruelty, oppression and injustice. The first Protector of Aborigines was George Augustus Robinson, who was appointed Chief Protector at Port Phillip (Melbourne) in 1839. His claim to the position was that he had single-handedly rounded up what was thought to be the approximately 300 remaining Aborigines in Van Diemen's Land (Tasmania) and relocated them to Flinders Island. He succeeded in doing this with the assistance of Truganini, a female Tasmanian Aborigine. However, once removed from their traditional lands, the indigenous community quickly deteriorated and Truganini was the last original member of her tribe to die there.

Closer to Sydney, in 1826 Reverend Lancelot Threlkeld, a missionary of the London Missionary Society, established a mission house for Aborigines at Bahtahbah (Belmont) on the eastern side of Lake Macquarie. Threlkeld learnt the local Aboriginal language and began the task of translating the Bible, thinking that 'the word of the Lord would travel [Aboriginal] Australia' by this means. The Society abandoned him in 1828 due to the exorbitant cost of maintaining the mission, and he moved, courtesy of a government grant, to a large reserve on the western side of Lake Macquarie at present-day Toronto. Threlkeld played a significant role in relations between the whites and the blacks because he was one of the few who learnt to speak an indigenous language. He provided spiritual comfort and translation services for Aborigines who were defendants in the white courts, so that they had a chance to understand the proceedings and the evidence led against them. A typical example is the following from 1835:

> *In August last, I was again subpoenaed to the Supreme Court in consequence of an outrage having been committed by the Aborigines in the vicinity of Williams River; when another Black named Charley was found guilty of murder, which he did not deny, even when arraigned, but pleaded in justification the custom of his nation, justifying himself on the ground that a talisman, named 'Mura-mai', was taken from him by the Englishman, who, with others were keeping a Black Woman amongst them, was pulled to pieces by him, and shown to the Black Woman, which, according to their superstitious notions, subject all the parties to the punishment of death; and further, that he was deputed with others, by his tribe, to enforce the penalty, which he too faithfully performed. It was deemed necessary, for the tranquillity of those disturbed Districts, that Charley should be executed at a place called Dungog.*[5]

By 1838, the mission house at Lake Macquarie had closed because most of the Aborigines from that area had disappeared. According to Threlkeld:

> *All the lake blacks are now employed at Newcastle where there is plenty of work for them, fishing, shooting, boating and carrying wood and water.*

The reality was that most had died or been displaced and were leading miserable lives in Sydney and Newcastle.

Successive British governments were acutely aware of the sad plight of the Indigenous people of New South Wales, and Colonial Office Secretaries issued instruction after instruction directing the Governor to exercise restraints on the illegal activities of pastoral landholders in disrupting and dispersing the Aboriginal inhabitants. In the bush, however, the edicts of London and the good intentions of the Governor in Sydney were often disregarded.

***

By 1838, most of the stations beyond the nineteen counties in the north-west of New South Wales were still semi-cleared bush and, apart from occasional stockyards, there were few fences to keep cattle secured, so losses were frequent. The area was severely affected by a devastating drought that had begun the year before, and the colony was in the grip of an economic recession. There had been clashes with local tribes for years involving occasional attacks on whites and massive retaliatory raids – big bushwhacks – to punish them. During times of drought, when there was increased pressure for survival on the whites and the blacks, violence by both sides became more prevalent.

At that time and in those districts where the agents of law and government were distant, it was common for marauding gangs of white stockmen to slaughter any Aboriginal people they came across in the bush in retaliation for attacks on the colonists' stock or property, or even the occasional murder of a white. According to Police Magistrate Edward Denny Day, who was the closest magistrate to the Big River at his faraway base in Invermein,[6] around mid-1838 a war of 'extirpation'[7] was waged all along the river whereby Aborigines in the district were repeatedly pursued by parties of mounted and armed stockmen. Day claimed that a great number of them had been killed at various locations. Dispossessed remnants of clans, often desperate for food and seeking refuge from roaming gangs of vengeful, armed, mounted whites, would sometimes descend on stations seeking sanctuary and miserly rations in return for manual work cutting bark or gathering wood.

Early in 1838, a contingent of twenty-three mounted police and an Aboriginal interpreter under the leadership of Major James Nunn was ordered by acting Governor Colonel Kenneth Snodgrass[8] to proceed to the Liverpool Plains district, where several white colonists had been murdered late the previous year. The expedition led to the massacre of between 200 and 300 Aborigines in retaliation for the deaths of the few whites. The worst of the murders was on Foundation Day[9] in 1838 – the fiftieth anniversary of the founding of the colony. On the day when almost everyone in Sydney was enjoying the colony's first public holiday, and people crowded the foreshore of Sydney Harbour to see a regatta, Major Nunn and his mounted troops in the north of the colony drove a large group of the Gamilaroi into a swamp and picked them off one by one with gunfire. Because Nunn was a veteran of the Napoleonic campaigns, the swamp was later named 'Waterloo Creek'. By the time Major Nunn returned to Sydney and presented his report of the incident, the newly arrived Governor, Sir George Gipps, had replaced Snodgrass in February 1838. Gipps had a completely different approach to the Aborigines, and he had been given firm instructions in London to respect the rights of the Indigenous people of the colony and to treat them as British subjects. Gipps was horrified by Nunn's report and determined that a repetition would not occur.

***

Myall Creek Station was a medium-sized station on the banks of a tributary of the Big River[10] about 350 miles from Sydney. The local indigenous people called the area 'Bingara'.[11] The 'owner' was Henry Dangar. By 1838, Dangar was already one of the wealthier property owners in New South Wales and an aggressive squatter on two stations in the Big River district: *Myall Creek Station* and *Pond's Creek Run*.

The term 'station' was a misnomer for the *Myall Creek Station*, because the only structures on the property consisted of three makeshift wooden huts in a large cleared area within sight of some waterholes of the Myall Creek and some basic cattle yards about half a mile to the west. The three huts had been built to house Dangar's employees and their stores. The men were:

- William Hobbs, a twenty-six-year-old free settler from Somerset, who was Henry Dangar's superintendent at both *Myall Creek* and *Pond's Creek*. He had been in the colony since 1825.
- Charles Kilmeister, a convict stockman, aged twenty-three from Bristol, who had been assigned to Dangar. Under the name Charles Kilminister, in 1832 at the age of seventeen he had been sentenced to transportation for life for 'stealing in a dwelling house' as a member of a gang of three. Prior to his trial he had been a rope maker.
- George Anderson, aged twenty-four from Middlesex, the hut keeper, who had been transported for life in 1833 at the age of nineteen for robbing his master, and assigned to Henry Dangar. Prior to transportation, he had worked as a 'lath renderer' (someone who worked in the building trade as a plasterer's assistant, applying the first layer of plaster to laths, which were strips of wood used mostly for interior walls and ceilings). Early in 1838, Henry Dangar had him flogged with a hundred lashes for leaving his post. He was then sent to *Myall Creek Station* as the hut keeper, a lower position than a stockman.
- Andrew Burrowes, a twenty-five-year-old stockman from County Sligo in Ireland, who in 1835 at the age of twenty-two had been transported for life for highway robbery. He had previously been a groom and indoor servant.
- Charles Reid, thirty-year-old stockman from Antrim, Ireland. He had been sentenced to transportation for life after a conviction for house robbery and had arrived in the colony in 1826.

- William Wall, a shepherd, who had been born at Waterford, Ireland, in 1800. He arrived in Australia in about 1835, and was employed by Henry Dangar, initially at Gostwyck near Uralla, then Koloona, which was part of *Myall Creek Station.* Dangar's sheep were kept at Koloona, twelve miles away from the huts on *Myall Creek Station*, and Wall only came to the huts once or twice a week to collect food.

These six men were attended by two young Aboriginal men, brothers Davy (Yintayintin) and Billy (Kwimunga), who were aged eighteen and fourteen respectively. Davy and Billy were trusted and had a good command of English, because they came from a different area – the Peel River district in the Northern Tablelands – where a diminished number of local Aborigines were living in imposed harmony with white settlers.

***

It was in this context in May 1838 that a group of more than forty Aboriginal men, women and children of the Wirrayaraay tribe of the Gamilaroi nation, obviously emaciated and hungry, walked out of the bush and descended into the clearing around the huts at *Myall Creek Station.* The arrival of such a large group of Aborigines initially caused apprehension among the whites at the station, but it soon became apparent to Kilmeister and Anderson that the blacks were peaceful and seeking refuge to set up camp in sight of the apparent safety of the huts. For many months this tribe had been camping at *McIntyre's Station* and *Wiseman's Station*, but had moved away because of fear of attack from roving groups of mounted white stockmen.

The leader of the tribe was a man who had been given the name 'King Sandy' by local white settlers, and he wore a brass breastplate bestowed on him by Daniel Eaton, overseer at Peter McIntyre's station, *Byron Plains*, near present-day Inverell,[12] as a mark of his acceptance by white society.[13] King Sandy had a seven-year-old son called 'Charley' who spoke a good deal of pidgin English and showed an unusual lack of shyness in the presence of the whites, and would converse with them and play around them. The oldest member of the tribe was an enormously tall man – the tallest anyone had ever seen, either black or white – who had been given the name 'Daddy' and was described by Hobbs as the doctor of the tribe.

When the Wirrayaraay sought to establish camp near the huts on *Myall Creek Station*, manager William Hobbs was initially hesitant to allow them to do so, mainly because he feared that his employer, Henry Dangar, would disapprove. However, stockman Charles Kilmeister urged him to allow the blacks to make camp, pointing out that Dangar was not expected to visit the property for many months and that by the time he was due, the Aborigines would have long since gone. In light of their poor appearance and their obvious predicament, Hobbs took pity on them and gave them permission to set up camp.

Over the next four or five weeks, the condition of the Wirrayaraay improved. Hut keeper George Anderson became enamoured with an attractive, young Aboriginal woman called Heppita, who, despite the fact that she had a tribal husband, spent more time with Anderson than with her husband. After finishing work, Kilmeister would frequently dance and sing with the Wirrayaraay, and Charley became one of his favourites.

On Monday, 4 June or Tuesday, 5 June 1838, Burrowes and Reid left Myall Creek to drive a herd of cattle to Dangar's other station, *Pond's Creek.* Several days later, while on the way to *Pond's Creek,* they arrived at *Bell's Station,* where they found a group of stockmen from other stations who were awaiting the arrival of John Henry Fleming, a free man and station manager at *Mungie Bundie Station,* to lead them on a hunt for blacks responsible for depredations in the area. Burrowes and Reid casually mentioned to John Russell, the superintendent at *Bell's Station,* that a large group of Aborigines was peacefully camped at *Myall Creek Station.* The following day, while continuing their droving, Burrowes and Reid met Fleming on his way to *Bell's.*

On Thursday, 7 June 1838, William Hobbs left Myall Creek to check on Burrowes and Reid, and to proceed with them and the herd to *Pond's Creek.* This left stockman Charles Kilmeister and hut keeper George Anderson, as well as the two Peel River Aboriginal young men, Davy and Billy, as the only employees remaining at *Myall Creek Station.* Kilmeister and Anderson had a lot in common: they were both around the same age, being twenty-three and twenty-four; they had both come from England, where they had lived about a hundred miles apart; they had both been transported to New South Wales for life; they both worked for Henry Dangar; and they had both interacted closely with the Wirrayaraay during the weeks the tribe had been camped at their station. However, this is where their similarities ended. In character, they were very different, and this was to play a major role in events just three days later.

On Saturday, 9 June, when the Wirrayaraay tribe had been at Myall Creek for nearly five weeks, Thomas Foster, the superintendent at nearby *Newton's Run,* came to *Myall Creek Station* and offered employment cutting bark to the most able-bodied men of the Wirrayaraay. Early the following morning, ignorant of the fact that a band of whites was on the warpath heading for Myall Creek, ten of the strongest Wirrayaraay men, including King Sandy, accompanied Foster to his property about fifteen miles away. This left about thirty members of the tribe, being older men, women and children, at Myall Creek under the leadership of Daddy and in a very vulnerable state. The stage was set for a great tragedy.

***

One of the larger stations in the Big River district was known as the *Mungie Bundie Station*. It was owned by Joseph Fleming, who also had another 56 000-acre run called *Mundowey*[14] and a 47 000-acre run called *Orrabar*. The *Mungie Bundie Station* was managed by Joseph Fleming's younger brother, John Henry Fleming. The Fleming brothers had been born free men in the colony. Their father, Henry Fleming, was one of the earliest native-born, free settlers, having been born on 28 August 1791 on board the ship that brought his parents to the colony as it arrived in Sydney Cove as part of the third Fleet, carrying more than 2000 convicts and desperately needed provisions for the starving colony. Henry's father, also Joseph Fleming, was a sergeant in the New South Wales Corps whose wife, Mary, had accompanied him on the journey to Sydney.[15] In 1810, Henry Fleming, then eighteen, married Elizabeth Hall at St John's Church, Parramatta. Henry and Elizabeth spent the early years of their married life on land on the Hawkesbury River near the junction with Bardonarrang Creek, and their first two children were born there. Between 1815 and 1819, Henry built an inn on land he had acquired at the new township of Pitt Town,[16] forty miles north-west of Sydney, and it was here that his third child, John Henry Fleming, was born in 1816. In 1828, Henry and Elizabeth moved to 250 acres at Lower Portland Head,[17] where Henry remained a farmer for the rest of his life.

By 1838, twenty-two-year-old John Henry Fleming was working as superintendent of the three properties his older brother Joseph owned in the Big River district in northern New South Wales. It was unusual for a superintendent in such a remote area beyond the limits of location to be a free man, let alone a native-born son of a native-born free man, and this gave John Fleming unrivalled status and authority among the whites in the district and unparalleled freedom of movement. The Fleming stations were at the frontline of the battle to push back Aboriginal occupation of their traditional lands, and frequent depredations of cattle had occurred that were viewed as a challenge to possession of the land by white squatters. John Fleming knew that he had the support of his elder brother to take whatever steps were necessary to protect the family's possessory rights to their stations, as well as their stock and stockmen.

In early May 1838, the whites on *Mungie Bundie* were enraged by the discovery of speared and dying cattle in the bush, and there had been attempts to spear two of their men who had been camped in the bush minding the cattle.[18] This led John Fleming to the formation of a large group of mounted stockmen with the object of wreaking vengeance for these attacks and taking action to prevent it happening again. Fleming got together ten convicts and former convicts to form a posse to locate, round up and punish the blacks who were responsible.

The possibility of extermination of what was referred to as the 'black menace' was never openly spoken of, but it was implicit in the minds of all those who agreed to accompany Fleming in his action. Nine of the posse were of European extraction and one, John Johnstone, was an African.[19] They were armed with muskets, pistols and swords, and Fleming had a fowling-piece.[20]

It can be seen from the identity of the ten men who accompanied Fleming that they represented a large cross-section of the squatters in the Big River district. There were five former convicts who had either received tickets-of-leave or served their sentences, and five assigned convicts working as stockmen. They were:

- John Russell, thirty-five years old from Tipperary in Ireland, free by servitude, who was the superintendent at *Bell's Station* at Bengari. Russell had been transported for seven years for stealing saddles and brushes. He had arrived in the colony on the convict ship *Eliza* in 1827 at the age of twenty-four. Prior to his sentence he had been a servant by occupation. After seven years in the colony his Certificate of Freedom was granted on 25 April 1834.
- George Palliser, a twenty-seven-year-old colleague of Russell at *Bell's Station*, who was a free man after serving his sentence in the colony. Palliser came from the County of York, West Riding, in England where he had worked as a farm labourer and stockman. He had been sentenced to seven years for stealing a coat, arriving in the colony in 1831.
- James Lamb, a thirty-six-year-old ticket-of-leave man from Middlesex, who was the overseer at James Cobb's run, *Gravesend*, and had been with Major Nunn during

his campaign against the Aborigines earlier in 1838. He had arrived in the colony in 1825, making him the former convict who had been in the colony the longest. In 1826 he had been one of seven men charged with the gang rape of an elderly white woman in the Hunter River district, but they had all been acquitted because the victim failed to identify them.

- William Hawkins, a twenty-eight-year-old ticket-of-leave man from Buckinghamshire, who was a stockman at Andrew Blake's run, *Mosquito Creek*. He had arrived in the colony in 1828 after being convicted of stealing and sentenced to transportation for fourteen years. He had previously been a tool cleaner and scraper.
- John Johnstone, a twenty-eight-year-old African from Liverpool, described as a 'half-caste'. He had been sentenced to seven years for house robbery, and arrived in the colony in August 1829. He had been freed by servitude, and was the superintendent at George Bowman's run at Moree.
- John Blake, twenty-seven, from County Meath in Ireland, an assigned convict stockman at James Glennie's run, *Gineroi*. He was the only married man among the group and had two children. A butcher by trade, he had been transported for life to New South Wales in 1834 for stealing sheep.
- Charles Toulouse, a thirty-year-old from Worcester who was also assigned as a convict stockman to James Glennie at *Gineroi*. Originally sentenced to death at seventeen for stealing a pair of women's shoes from a shop, he had been saved because of a petition by his parents to the King that resulted in the sentence being commuted to transportation for life. He arrived in the colony in 1827. In Worcester,

Charles had been sentenced to 'three months exercise on the treadmill' for riding a horse in a public field.

- James Oates, twenty-five, who was a convict stockman at Thomas Simpson Hall's run, *Bingara*[21]. Also known as 'Hall's Jemmy', Oates was, like John Plunkett, a man from Roscommon in Ireland. In 1829, at the age of nineteen, he had been sentenced to transportation for life for assisting in a robbery.
- James Parry, twenty-four, from Shropshire, who had been a private solider in the 1st Royals. He was a convict stockman for Daniel Eaton at *Binguy*. He had arrived in the colony in 1835 after being sentenced to seven years for stealing silver and coins from a Sergeant in his corps.

  and:
- Edward (Ned) Foley, twenty-six, from Queen's County, Ireland. He and his brother, John, had been farm servants and were sentenced to transportation for life for 'assault of a habitation' and 'assault by levelling' (a gun) – essentially a home invasion. He arrived in the colony in February 1833 and was assigned as a convict stockman to John Fleming's older brother, Joseph, at *Mungie Bundie*, after previously working for their father, Henry Fleming, at Lower Portland.

John Fleming and his ten mounted stockmen journeyed for some days, visiting many of the stations in the district, looking for any blacks to kill. The fact that the Wirrayaraay at Myall Creek could not possibly have been responsible for the depredations – because prior to taking up residence at Myall Creek they had been living peacefully for many months at *McIntyre's* and *Wiseman's* stations, and that they had had most harmonious relationships with the whites at each of these stations – was of no consequence to the marauding stockmen. As they approached the *Myall Creek Station*, they were in a murderous state of mind, intent on suppressing the Indigenous challenge to white pastoral supremacy.

***

In the late afternoon of Sunday, 10 June 1838, about an hour and a half before sunset, John Henry Fleming and his ten fellow mounted stockmen, armed with muskets, pistols and swords, separated into two groups and approached the ridge to the west of the huts at *Myall Creek Station*. Oblivious to what lay in store, Charles Kilmeister and George Anderson were relaxing in the late afternoon, chatting with Davy and Billy on the verandah of one of the huts at *Myall Creek Station*, while the Wirrayaraay, who were camped closer to the creek, were preparing their evening meal. As the eleven mounted stockmen came to the edge of the clearing and advanced at a gallop towards the Aborigines, the rumble of horses' hooves disrupted the calm domestic atmosphere of the campsite. The Wirrayaraay immediately panicked, the women quickly grabbing their children and most running towards the huts, seeking the protection of the two white men. Two young Aboriginal brothers, John and Jimmy,[22] aged about eight or nine, who were closer to the creek than the main group, dived into the water and escaped from the immediate vicinity. Anderson and Kilmeister were equally frightened by the unexpected arrival of such a large group of stockmen, and overwhelmed by the rush of Wirrayaraay who had retreated inside the apparent safety of one of the huts. Davy and Billy clung to their masters, anxious to know whether they would be treated differently to the Wirrayaraay.

Charles Kilmeister and George Anderson, two young convicts in an isolated bush setting of a remote penal colony, faced an armed and angry mob consisting of an influential, confident and assertive free-born colonist and ten of his henchmen, many of whom were known to them. Kilmeister and Anderson were the only obstacles obstructing the murderous vengeance that the eleven invaders were intent on carrying out. This sudden confrontation was to test Kilmeister's and Anderson's mettle to the limit, and determine the future course of their lives.

7

THE BIG BUSHWHACK

When the Wirrayaraay fled in fear into the workmen's hut at *Myall Creek Station*, it served the purpose of the invaders, because it made the entrapment of the Aborigines easier than if they had run off into the bush. The horsemen rounded towards the huts and stopped in front of where George Anderson and Charles Kilmeister were now standing quite alarmed, on the verandah. Some of the stockmen dismounted, and one of them, John Russell, took a long rope from around his horse's neck and began unravelling it as he walked towards the hut in which the Aborigines were cowering in fear. In the meantime, John Henry Fleming remained on his horse, clearly in command, confidently directing events from his elevated position. It was obvious that these men had discussed beforehand what was to occur.

Anderson, the hut keeper, bravely confronted the stockmen as best he could in the circumstances, asking them their business. John Russell informed him that they were going to 'take them over the back of the range and frighten them' and that they intended rounding up any other blacks they could find. He claimed that they were acting in retaliation for the theft of cattle, although he made no attempt to identify any individuals or even tribe that had been responsible for the theft. Anderson was doubtful that they were merely intending to frighten the Wirrayaraay. Although fearful for himself, he felt an overwhelming sense of responsibility to do all that he reasonably could to prevent whatever it was that these men were planning to do.

In the meantime, Charles Kilmeister, in abject fear, had retreated inside the hut with the Wirrayaraay, where they begged him, as the man who had been largely responsible for allowing them to remain at the station, for help and protection. Russell and a couple of his fellows entered the hut with the long rope and closed the door behind them. Russell took Kilmeister aside and threatened him that unless he joined the mounted whites, Kilmeister would suffer the same fate as the blacks. Kilmeister was petrified by the group of armed stockmen and fully aware of what they were likely to do to the Wirrayaraay. He readily reasoned to himself that if it was a decision between his life and those of the blacks, he had no choice but to join the stockmen. Without speaking, he nodded an acknowledgement to Russell, indicating that he had understood his options, then exited the hut. He walked over to his own hut, where he armed himself with his pistol, which he holstered into his belt, then came outside, saddled his horse, and joined the group of invaders, thereby becoming complicit in whatever it was they had in mind to do.

Inside the hut with the Wirrayaraay, John Russell and his fellows tethered the Aborigines to the rope, while another stockman, Edward Foley, stood outside standing guard with a pistol in his hand. Men and women were tied to the long rope, including 'Daddy'. Those children who were too young to walk were held in their mothers' arms, while older children were allowed to stay next to their mother. All this time, the Wirrayaraay were wailing and crying out for assistance from their two erstwhile protectors.

George Anderson, who had boldly remained outside, refused to join the group of invaders. He was convinced that the men confronting him were about to commit a most egregious crime. While he was not prepared to recklessly risk his own life by physically resisting them, he was firmly resolved not to cooperate with them in any way. Anderson managed to save a little Aboriginal girl by pushing her into a different hut while the adults were being tethered. The two Aboriginal brothers, Davy and Billy, were not touched by the marauding party, because they were viewed as being the property of Henry Dangar, and nobody would dare to cross him. Anderson tried to save Heppita, the striking Aboriginal woman with whom he had been in a relationship for the previous five weeks, by begging for her to be released into his care. To spite Anderson, and clearly with evil intent, John Fleming responded that the gang would keep Heppita, and instead indicated another young woman to be given to Anderson as a token gesture, whom the men thrust aside in his direction. Fleming's intention in doing this was to compromise Anderson, as though he were giving him a consolation prize for not standing in their way, thereby making him complicit in their actions. Another woman was thrust in Davy's direction.

John Russell emerged from the hut with the end of the rope in his hands and hitched it to his saddle. The twelve horsemen – now including Charles Kilmeister – mounted their steeds and began slowly moving away from the huts. Twenty-eight terrified Aborigines emerged, each of the adults secured to the long rope by the wrists and the children either being carried or clinging to their mothers. The stockmen – deaf to the crying and wailing – rode on either side of their tethered captives, prodding them to move away from the huts in a westerly direction towards what was ultimately going to be a terrible outcome. George Anderson, who remained in great trepidation at the huts, lost sight of them after two or three minutes. Once they had disappeared, at Anderson's suggestion, Davy surreptitiously followed the caravan of death at a safe distance, and when the forced march entered a gully about half a mile away from the huts, he hid behind a tree and witnessed the fate that befell the wailing Wirrayaraay.

Fifteen or twenty minutes after being forcibly led away, the captives reached their destination – a wooden stockyard in a shallow gully where they could not be seen from the huts.[1] Once inside the stockyard, John Fleming lined up the majority of his horsemen in a circle surrounding their intended victims, while several of his men remained outside to prevent escape. Many of them had their swords drawn, while a few had guns in their hands. One of them dismounted and untied the terrified Wirrayaraay. Fleming then pointed his fowling-piece in the air and fired two shots to create panic among the Wirrayaraay and to signal the beginning of the massacre. George Anderson, who had remained at the huts, heard only the two shots, and then silence. The mounted stockmen urged their horses forward at the defenceless group in their midst, hacking and slashing their swords down on them, as the men, women and children of the Wirrayaraay ran a murderous gauntlet within the confines of the stockyard. Not one of them made it out. Many of them were felled with swords, while others were trampled under hoof. The stockmen did not need to use their precious ball and powder on their victims when they could just as easily dispose of them by sword or by crushing them. The gully was filled with the screams of the victims and the war cries of the horsemen as a thick cloud of dust kicked up by the horses became intermingled with the blood and mangled bodies of the Wirrayaraay. The stench of death was everywhere. Gradually the noise died down as the Wirrayaraay were killed. When it came to an end, the whites showed exhilaration as they slashed at the last few bodies still writhing on the ground. All but one of the Wirrayaraay who had been led away from the huts were murdered in this manner. The last remaining captive, Heppita, had been kept aside by Fleming as they entered the stockyard, and was 'saved' to service the stockmen's sexual pleasures at a later time.

At the conclusion of this gruesome slaughter, at Fleming's direction the bodies were decapitated and dismembered. He then instructed his men to build a pyre of logs and sticks and to heap all the remains in a pile on top. The collection of body parts caused the men to become even more saturated with the blood of their victims, so that by the end of the process they were almost entirely covered in a thick crust of blood-soaked dust. When all the bodies had been collected, Fleming directed his men to set fire to the logs. They remained at the scene as the bodies slowly burned, and then they left.

George Anderson remained at his hut in great trepidation, desperately hoping against hope that the stockmen would be satisfied with merely frightening the Wirrayaraay and that they would return unharmed. However, when Davy appeared from the vicinity of the gully and told him what had happened, Anderson was filled with horror and regret that he had not done more to prevent the atrocity. He immediately instructed Davy to run to *Newton's Station* to warn the Wirrayaraay men there that they were in terrible danger. At *Newton's*, manager Thomas Foster sent the Wirrayaraay back to Myall Creek by a short-cut over the ranges. The young men rushed back as soon as they could, arriving at *Myall Creek Station* at 10pm that night to find that, other than two women and three children, their families had been murdered. At Anderson's insistence, they left the same night after he explained to them that the killers would probably return. The remaining Wirrayaraay walked to *McIntyre Station*, twenty-five miles to the east. As the night wore on, Anderson grew more and more morose as the reality set in of what had happened. It was not until the following morning that he saw an ominous plume of smoke coming from the gully to the west of the huts.

The twelve stockmen spent the night camped in the bush, drinking, carousing, abusing Heppita, and reminiscing about their latest bushwhack and, for some of them, their previous murderous exploits, until they fell into a drunken sleep. The next morning, Monday 11 June, Fleming and his gang awoke with renewed vigour for further bloodshed. They rode (with Heppita) about sixteen miles to *Newton's Run*, looking to find and kill the younger men of the Wirrayaraay tribe, however, the Aboriginal men they sought were not there. Fleming spoke to Thomas Foster, who observed that there were ten to twelve armed stockmen. He recognised many of them, as well as John Fleming: John Russell, Charles Kilmeister, John Johnstone, William Hawkins and James Oates. Foster observed that they had an Aboriginal woman with them who was tied up and appeared to be in bad condition. Oates asked Foster the location of the Aboriginal men who had been cutting bark, to which Foster merely replied, 'God knows where they are now.' When Foster enquired whether Kilmeister was 'after the blacks', Kilmeister replied, 'They rushed my cattle yesterday,' which Foster knew to be a lie. Hawkins added it was a bad job that the blacks were not in the vicinity and remarked that they must have been moved away in order that they should not be caught. The group of stockmen asked one of Foster's men to look after Heppita while they went looking for the black men, saying that someone would come back for her later, but Foster would not allow his employee to mind the woman. The stockmen left *Newton's*, taking Heppita with them. She was never seen again.

Having failed to find the young Wirrayaraay men at *Newton's Run*, the marauding stockmen proceeded to look for them at the nearby *Dight's Station*. At *Dight's*, they spoke to the hut keeper, John Bates, and again enquired after the blacks, only to be told that they had not been seen there. The group remained at *Dight's* chatting for about an hour. At one point in the conversation, one of the stockmen, James Parry, said that they had 'settled the blacks'. They soon left *Dight's Station* and returned to *Myall Creek Station*, still looking for the men they had missed at *Newton's*, only to find that the Wirrayaraay men were not there. They spent the rest of that day and night camped there.

The following morning, Tuesday, 12 June, John Fleming, John Russell and Charles Kilmeister returned to the massacre site. Fleming saw that the fire had failed to properly burn the bodies, so he re-lit the pyre in an attempt to further destroy the evidence of their deeds. He instructed Kilmeister to maintain the fire for as long as it took to consume the bodies. Meanwhile, back at the huts, Anderson spoke to Edward Foley and asked him if any of the blacks had made their escape, to which he was told that all but one had been killed. Foley showed Anderson his sword, and Anderson could see that the blade was covered in dried blood. The eleven stockmen left Myall Creek later that day, still in search of the ten young Aboriginal men of the Wirrayaraay tribe, leaving Charles Kilmeister at the station to look after the fire.

As soon as the men left, Kilmeister went to the fire and tended it for the remainder of that day. He had every incentive to destroy the evidence of the murders before the return of his superintendent, William Hobbs. However, it proved to be very difficult to completely destroy the bodies. With Hobbs due to return at any time, Kilmeister pleaded with Anderson: 'For God's sake, mind what you say. Do not say that I went with them.' Anderson needed little encouragement to remain silent about the atrocity. He knew that there were eleven men in the district who would be only too ready to kill him if they thought he might reveal what he knew about the identity of the murderers.

Some days later, between thirty and forty Aborigines, possibly including some of the ten or so younger men, two women and three children who had fled from the *Myall Creek Station*, were murdered at *McIntyre's Station*, their bodies also cast onto a large, open fire. Many suspected that the later murders were committed by the same stockmen who had perpetrated the Myall Creek massacre.

8

DAY'S DILIGENCE

Five days after the murders, on Friday 15 June 1838, manager William Hobbs returned to the *Myall Creek Station*. He had already heard rumours about the murders, which were reverberating throughout the district. At the Wirrayaraay's former campsite near the huts he found several baskets containing articles generally used by them. He also found a cap that had been given by a white man to one of the young boys called Joey. Hobbs questioned George Anderson and Charles Kilmeister, both of whom denied any complicity in the murders but asserted that a group of unknown stockmen had taken away the Aborigines. Hobbs had previously been informed that Kilmeister had been seen with the others scouring the countryside for the ten young men of the tribe, so he challenged Kilmeister with this, but Kilmeister advanced the lame excuse that he had been out and about looking for cattle that had wandered off. Hobbs disbelieved him. Anderson was so fearful of reprisal from the group of stockmen that he deliberately failed to inform his manager of the identity of those who had been responsible for the massacre, including Charles Kilmeister, claiming that he had not recognised any of them. Only Davy, the young Peel River Aboriginal man, was prepared to speak openly to his superintendent. He told Hobbs he had witnessed the murders and offered to show him where they had taken place.

That afternoon, Davy led Hobbs to the massacre site. On their way along a regular bush track, despite the fact that it had rained in the meantime, Hobbs could still see the footprints of bare feet, including children's, with horse tracks on either side. He also found a discarded woven basket of the kind used by the Aborigines that contained a piece of possum skin, some pipe clay they used for painting, belts, and a few small crystal stones that the Aborigines greatly valued as they were considered to have 'a charm to cure them when they are sick'. At the site identified by Davy, Hobbs was horrified to find a mass of piled-up, partially burnt, dismembered bodies of men, women and children among the ashes of a large fire. There were numerous bloodstains on the ground and the fencing of the nearby stockyard. He saw the shoe marks seemingly made when people had rolled logs to construct the fire. Hobbs noticed that the footprints of naked feet along the track from the station led only towards the stockyard, whereas the horse tracks indicated movement both towards and away from the vicinity.

The sight before him was so shocking and the stench so

abhorrent that Hobbs was overcome with nausea and dread. Although tempted to leave this scene of mayhem, he was determined to ascertain how many victims' bodies had been burnt in this pyre. He reluctantly and tentatively stirred among the ashes and found numerous severed heads, limbs, torsos and other body parts of adults and children. Those sections of skin that had not been burnt enabled him to be certain that the victims were all Aboriginal. He made several attempts to count the number of bodies, getting a different number each time because most of them had been beheaded and dismembered. The lowest number was twenty and the highest number was twenty-eight, including ten or twelve small heads and bodies of children. Hobbs saw one particularly large torso, which, though totally burnt, he assumed to be the remains of 'Daddy' because of its size, but the head had been removed and the body so extensively burnt that a definitive identification was impossible.

The following morning, Hobbs returned to the massacre site with Thomas Foster, the manager at *Newton's Run*. Foster briefly inspected the pile of partially burnt bodies but made no attempt to count them. Hobbs was so sickened from his previous sighting that he was unable to approach the pile again. Overnight, the bodies had been attacked by dingoes, hawks and other birds of prey. Foster also noticed the horse tracks both towards and away from the site of the murders. By the time of this second inspection, Hobbs had a fair idea that Kilmeister had been involved, so he told his stockman that he thought it was a very cruel thing for him to have sanctioned the murder of these people when he had been on such friendly terms with them. He pointed out that it had been largely because of Kilmeister that the Aborigines had been permitted to stay on the property. Kilmeister still denied any involvement in the murders, but when Hobbs told him that he considered it his duty to report the murders to the authorities, Kilmeister begged him not to do so, lamely adding, 'Not that I had anything to do with it.'

William Hobbs delayed informing his employer and the authorities of the atrocity. However, Hobbs told Frederick Foote, a free settler on a nearby pastoral lease, what had occurred. Foote was appalled at the treatment of the Aborigines in his district, and determined to report the murders. Foote's first attempt – to inform the Police Magistrate closest to the atrocity, Captain Edward Denny Day, who was based in Invermein (Scone) and Muswellbrook, more than 160 miles south of Myall Creek – was unsuccessful, because Day was away on patrol. So, Frederick Foote travelled to Sydney, where he delivered a note to the new Governor, Major Sir George Gipps, who had landed in the colony only four months earlier with strict instructions from the British government to protect the Aboriginal inhabitants of the colony and to prevent unlawful incursions against them. On receiving Foote's note, Gipps wrote a letter of instruction to Captain Edward Denny Day at Invermein instructing him to proceed post-haste to the Myall Creek district with a party of mounted police and, once there, to investigate, gather evidence, arrest those responsible and bring them to Sydney for trial.

In the meantime, William Hobbs sent a letter to his employer, Henry Dangar, and another identical one to Police Magistrate Edward Denny Day reporting the murders. Before sending the letter, Hobbs read it aloud to Kilmeister and Anderson. The letter was as follows:

July 9 1838

Sir,

I beg to acquaint you that about a month since I had occasion to leave Mr Dangar's Station on the Big River for a few days, on my return I saw near the Hut the remains of about thirty Blacks, principally women and children. I recognised them as part of a Tribe that had been at the Station for some time and who had since they first came conducted themselves in a quiet and proper manner. On making enquiry, I was informed that a party of White men had come to the Station, who after securing them, had taken them a short distance from my Hut and destroyed nearly the whole of them. I should have given information earlier, but circumstances having prevented my sooner coming down the country.

I am, Sir,

Your obedient Servant,

W Hobbs[1]

Kilmeister became extremely agitated and attempted to dissuade Hobbs from sending the letter, claiming that those Aborigines had been spearing their cattle, but Hobbs knew that this was a lie. Hobbs pointed out to Kilmeister the indecency with which the bodies had been treated after death, and Kilmeister offered to go to the site and bury the remains. Hobbs replied, no doubt with an appreciation of the irony, that if Kilmeister's protestations of innocence were true, then it could do him great harm to interfere with the bodies in the event of a later investigation.

When Henry Dangar received the letter from his superintendent at Myall Creek, he deliberately took no immediate action.

***

Captain Edward Denny Day had come to the colony from Ireland in 1837 to take up a position as a Police Magistrate. Among the stipendiary magistrates, none was superior to him in diligence or capability. Day was assigned to a huge district on the northern frontier of the 'limits of location', based in Muswellbrook, Merton[2] and Invermein. By the time of the murders at Myall Creek, Denny Day already had a reputation as a thorough and competent magistrate, and was particularly well known for his record in apprehending bushrangers.[3] Day was both brave and physically strong, which were qualities necessary for extensive travel throughout his districts, many parts of which were dangerous, due to the presence of bushrangers and warring Aborigines. He was known to conduct his investigations in a most tenacious manner.

When Magistrate Day received the letter from William Hobbs, he forwarded it to Governor Gipps, who replied with instructions to immediately investigate the incident. Day was provided with a small group of mounted police, and he set off without delay. Many other magistrates would have conducted a cursory investigation, biased in favour of the local settlers and their convict staff, and returned to Sydney empty-handed. Magistrate Day, on the other hand, made a concerted effort to ascertain who had been responsible, to apprehend them, and to collect evidence that would be admissible at their trial in Sydney.

For forty-seven days from 19 July 1838, Magistrate Denny Day interviewed witnesses, questioned them thoroughly if he thought they were withholding information from him, then wrote out their statements in longhand, read them back and obtained signatures or marks attesting to the truth of the facts contained in them. Almost everywhere, Day was met with hostility from and obstruction by most of the settlers and their convict staff. His difficulties were described in this way:

> *Day was received everywhere outside Myall Creek and Newton's very coldly from the first. As he moved west this increased to barely concealed hostility. The length of his stay astonished everybody; feelings became very incensed; shepherds etc hid near an area called Mungi Bundi [and] it is told that a herd of cattle was deliberately stampeded in the troopers' direction (by whites not blacks), which was made an alibi for several shots to be fired.*[4]

On 28 July, Day arrived at the *Myall Creek Station* and, with William Hobbs as his guide, inspected the massacre site. It was immediately apparent that since Hobbs's previous visits six weeks earlier a concerted effort had been made to strip away all evidence of the murders. The vast bulk of the human remains that Hobbs had previously observed had been removed, leaving only numerous small fragments of bone and the remains of a fire. Day expresssed the opinion that the area had the appearance of having been swept clean. The only body parts that Day was able to find and take into possession as evidence of the massacre were a lower jawbone, a child's rib and a few teeth.

The child's rib, no more than four inches in length, was to play a major role later in the case.

Magistrate Denny Day spoke at length to those who were employed at *Myall Creek Station*. George Anderson initially denied having recognised any of the marauding stockmen; however, Day could sense that he was not telling him everything he knew. Day spoke at length to Davy and heard the only first-hand account of the murders. Although he believed Davy's account to be accurate, he did not bother to get a statement from him, as Davy was an Aborigine and hence his testimony was inadmissible in court. Day intensively questioned Charles Kilmeister, who denied any involvement in the murders, but other evidence already collected strongly implicated Kilmeister, so Day charged him and took him into custody. As Kilmeister was leaving the hut where he had been questioned, he could not resist trying to explain his participation in the murders, saying to Denny Day:

> *If you knew what they threatened to do to me, I would not be blamed.*

Day assumed that Kilmeister was disclosing a threat from the Wirrayaraay. This misunderstanding was to have severe consequences for Kilmeister at a later time.

Denny Day next questioned hut keeper George Anderson, who in the meantime had developed a sense of guilt for having failed to report all that he knew. Anderson had told another Dangar employee that he was 'sorry that he had not told the whole affair'. Day suspected that Anderson knew much more than he had previously admitted, so he threatened to charge him with perjury unless he cooperated with the investigation. Anderson then disclosed to Day the identity of eight of the perpetrators, including Kilmeister. He also provided details of some of the victims, including the little boy, Charley. Anderson was terrified of retaliation from the men he had implicated, or their colleagues, and he begged the magistrate to protect him, so Day took him into 'protective custody'. Over the ensuing weeks, Day gathered further evidence, and located and arrested further suspects who, as convicts, ticket-of-leave men, or men freed by servitude, were still in the district. Only one of them, James Parry, expressed any regret for what he had done, but like all the others, he was not prepared to give information implicating any of his co-offenders.

By the end of his investigation, Captain Day had locked up eleven of the twelve perpetrators and charged them with the murders. The only one to escape his roving round-up was the ringleader, John Henry Fleming. Fleming had the advantage that, unlike the eleven convict or ex-convict stockmen who had been rounded up, he had unlimited freedom of movement and extensive family support, not just in New South Wales but also in the settlement at Moreton Bay (Brisbane) and in Van Diemen's Land (Tasmania). His older brother, Joseph, had a residence in Moreton Bay (Brisbane); his father lived in the Ebenezer–Macdonald Valley area;[5] his grandfather and uncles resided in Van Diemen's Land; and his six other siblings were spread throughout the Hawkesbury River district. Day went looking for Fleming at *Mungie Bundie Station* on the Big River, but he was nowhere to be found. It was thought that he may have gone to his father's home in the Macdonald Valley, but enquiries there failed to locate him. The horse that he was supposed to have ridden at the time of the murders was found at Morpeth Wharf on the lower Hunter River, which had probably been left there as a decoy. Magistrate Day considered that Fleming may have boarded a ship bound for Van Diemen's Land, so he caused enquiries to be made of ships' captains on the Sydney–Van Diemen's Land route and for Fleming's description to be circulated among them, but no information on the man's whereabouts was forthcoming. A reward of £50 was offered for Fleming's capture, which was described by the *Sydney Herald* as an insult to those who were native-born, because it was not much more than the £10 offered for the apprehension of absconding convicts.[6]

In fact, evidence obtained much later suggests that Fleming hid on a property at Surat, 300 miles west of the Moreton Bay settlement, where his brother, Joseph, and brother-in-law, Thomas Simpson Hall, owned a large property.[7]

As news spread of the arrest and charging of such a large group of men for the murder of Aborigines, colonial society was split. A clear majority of whites took the position that the Aborigines were 'pests' and 'lawless savages' who needed to be driven off the land so that the colony could continue to expand unhindered. The issue provided a rare focus of unity between many of the free settlers, the emancipists and even the convicts. Only a small minority of people considered this to be an opportunity to achieve justice for the victims of a terrible crime and to establish the rights of Aboriginal inhabitants to live on their traditional grounds without the threat of annihilation.

The eleven men arrested by Magistrate Day were walked in chains and under guard for 200 miles to Muswellbrook in the Hunter Valley. During this march, John Russell managed to escape, but was later recaptured. The prisoners arrived at Muswellbrook on 10 September. From there, they were transported in a cart, still in chains, to Sydney, where a date was set for their trial on charges of murder.

It was at this time that Governor Gipps advised John Plunkett that he wished him personally to prosecute the trial. Realising the significance of the matter, without a moment's hesitation, Plunkett agreed. It would have been open to him to request that the Crown Prosecutor, John Holden, conduct the case, but he entertained no such thought. He was not perturbed by the fact that he would face the enmity of the influential pastoralists whose interests had been advanced by the murders – and who had probably encouraged, if not actively ordered, them. He was not dissuaded by the fact that for the first time since the colony had been established fifty years earlier almost every echelon of this multi-layered society would be behind the accused men. Already, all but one of the newspapers had joined forces in opposing the prosecutions, and a large group of influential property owners had banded together to form an organisation that they sarcastically named 'the Black Association', in order to support the accused men and to raise funds for their defence. Even the convicts, who identified with their fellow prisoners because they were facing the death penalty, saw the prosecution as yet another attempt by their overlords to use the law to oppress and punish them. This would surely be the most unpopular prosecution in the short history of the colony, but such a thought only served to strengthen Plunkett's resolve to follow what his conscience told him – that these eleven men and their leader, who still remained at large, had perpetrated an abomination that had to be punished if Christian values and the rule of law were to prevail in this remote part of the British Empire. Thankfully, he had the full support of the Governor, who was firmly in favour of the trial, not only because of his personal views but also by virtue of his instructions from the Colonial Office in London.

The only twinges of doubt, which Plunkett quickly laid aside, came from his knowledge that his wife, Maria, would be distraught and would pester him endlessly for yet again disrupting her social standing. He contemplated the much greater trials and tribulations faced by his illustrious ancestor, Archbishop Oliver Plunkett, and the far more serious consequences that this martyr had borne. When he returned home at night after discussing the case with the Governor, Plunkett reassured himself by once again taking out the ancient chalice, holding it delicately in both hands, and praying that he would find the strength of mind and purpose to carry out God's will and to achieve justice for those whose lives had so cruelly been brought to an end because of the colour of their skin, their different lifestyles and their distinctive cultural and religious beliefs.

Plunkett immediately began preparing the prosecution case and, realising that it was far more complex and significant than any of his previous criminal trials, he recognised that he needed a junior counsel to assist him. Without thinking twice, he chose Roger Therry. While Therry was less able as a lawyer than Plunkett, he was a most devoted and diligent counsel at the private Bar of New South Wales. They had previously worked together – and more often against each other – and had a history in common going back to Trinity College in Dublin. Plunkett was confident that Therry was one of the few men at the Bar who would be totally unaffected by what other people thought about the case. The only drawback of having Therry as his junior counsel was that, as they were both Irish Catholics, their collaboration would inevitably raise accusations that this was a conspiracy against the Anglo majority, even though the defendants included Anglicans and Catholics, English and Irish, and even a fellow Roscommon man. Plunkett's greatest regret was that John Fleming, the ringleader of those responsible for the massacre, had evaded capture, despite overwhelming efforts by Police Magistrate Captain Edward Denny Day.

9

DANGAR'S DILEMMA

In the 1820s, as an assistant government surveyor, Henry Dangar explored and mapped the Hunter River Valley, and in return was granted 300 acres of valuable grazing land near Patrick's Plains (Singleton), on which he built a homestead, *Neotsfield*, and another 700 acres near Morpeth. In 1827, as a result of a disputed land claim, he was found guilty by a Board of Inquiry of using his public position for private gain and was dismissed from office by Governor Darling. In the early 1830s, he explored the Liverpool Plains district in the north of the colony and made extensive land claims there in the name of his employer, the Australian Agricultural Company. In June 1833 he retired to *Neotsfield* and quickly developed it as a successful grazing property. By this time, he was already a wealthy landowner.

While surveying the Hunter Valley and pursuing his pastoral interests, Dangar had extensive contact with the local Aborigines. He believed that the best way to protect livestock was to reach an accommodation with the Indigenous population, rather than warring with them. Dangar adopted the same approach when squatting on his two properties in the Big River district. Dangar also had an enlightened view of dealing with his employees, for which he was rewarded by long and faithful service. Dangar selected William Hobbs as his superintendent at *Myall Creek Station* and *Pond's Creek Station* because he believed that the man had the capacity and personality to deal with the local Indigenous population in a cooperative and humane manner, and thereby avoid stock losses. He gave Hobbs the choice of which assigned convicts he wanted to accompany him to the Big River, because Dangar knew that his men would have to get along together and have confidence in each other if they were to survive so far from civilisation. Hobbs selected four men from the convicts assigned to Mr Dangar on the basis that he could rely on them to conscientiously attend to the stock and not to needlessly antagonise the local indigenous people.

Dangar heard about the murders at Myall Creek well prior to the receipt of William Hobbs's letter, and by the time he received it, he was already aware that the Governor had ordered Magistrate Day to investigate, and so Dangar did not feel the need to take any immediate action. It was only in early September, after Denny Day had finished his investigation and rounded up the eleven accused men and sent them on their way to Sydney, that Dangar finally felt the urge to go in person to Myall Creek. On the way from his home at Patrick's Plains, he stopped at Muswellbrook to speak to Magistrate Day, who gave him a full report on what he had discovered about the murders. Dangar listened carefully to Magistrate Day, but gave nothing away about his own views. This was a carefully orchestrated fact-finding mission before travelling to his station further north. Dangar then proceeded to Myall Creek, where he spoke at length to his superintendent, William Hobbs. Once again, he was reticent to expose his own views, but interested to hear everything that Hobbs had to say about the matter. It was a case of carefully assessing the situation before forming his own opinion. Dangar was not able to speak to Charles Kilmeister, because the man had already been arrested and taken to Sydney by Denny Day. Nor was he able to speak to George Anderson, who was in protective custody.

Henry Dangar was faced with a serious dilemma: should he support Hobbs and Anderson, who had done the right thing in cooperating with Day's investigation, or should he join the vast majority of landowners in the Hunter River and Liverpool Plains districts, and indeed most white people throughout the colony, in opposing the prosecutions? If he took the former approach, he would alienate his fellow landowners and the vast majority of others who were against the prosecution. If he adopted the latter attitude, he could compromise his reputation as an enlightened employer with a progressive view of dealing with the Aborigines.

By the time Dangar returned from Myall Creek to his principal home at Patrick's Plains, he had made a decision. Instead of supporting his embattled superintendent William Hobbs and his hut keeper, George Anderson, Dangar resolved to go on the warpath on behalf of the accused stockmen, particularly his own, Charles Kilmeister. In coming to this decision, Dangar aligned himself with all the other major landowners in the colony, but he also did great harm to his long-term reputation. He began by dismissing William Hobbs as his station superintendent, with the intention of weakening Hobbs's credibility. Hobbs, who had been an exemplary superintendent for two years, was devastated to be cast aside for having told the truth about the murders. To lose employment in the empire of Henry Dangar was indeed a calamity.

On his return to his home property at Patrick's Plains, Henry Dangar got together with his near neighbour, Magistrate Robert Scott, who was also a wealthy settler, owning properties in both the Hunter and Gwydir River districts. Robert Scott and his brother Helenus Scott owned a property called *Glendon* on the Hunter River near Patrick's Plains. Robert had won a reputation as a bold and daring settler by his involvement in the capture of a number of bushrangers in the area. In 1825, he led a party that captured a gang of bushrangers known as 'Jacob's mob', who had been robbing settlers throughout the district. As mentioned previously, in 1833 he joined John Larnach and a group of mounted police in the pursuit of absconders from James Mudie's property, *Castle Forbes.*[1] They discovered the runaways in a deep ravine near Lamb's Valley, whereupon Scott shot dead one of them, James Henderson, when he refused to lay down his gun, and the others were captured. In 1833, Robert Scott was appointed an honorary magistrate, and he gained a reputation for initiating and supporting efforts to hinder the 'depredations' of Aborigines and bushrangers.

Both Dangar and Scott had direct proprietary interests in the suppression of the Aborigines, and both were implacably opposed to the prosecution of those accused of the Myall Creek murders. They called a public meeting at Patrick's Plains, to which they invited all the local property owners. The meeting was well attended and reported extensively in the newspapers. At the first meeting, they established an organisation that, ironically, they called the 'Hunter River Black Association', in order to raise money for the defence of the eleven charged men. Scott was appointed chairman. The Governor was scandalised at what he considered to be an illegal association to support those who had committed serious crimes, and he was particularly enraged that a serving magistrate was behind it.

The support from the public and the newspapers for the Black Association was overwhelming, and within a short time enough money was raised to pay for the best legal counsel in Sydney to represent all eleven men. Dangar contributed £5 of the total amount of £300 that was raised. Another contributor was John Larnach.[2] The real reason behind the raising of this money was not only to provide the best counsel to represent the men who had been charged, but also to ensure that all eleven would be represented by the same counsel, so that no individual defendant would be tempted to embark on a separate defence by implicating the others. The association also initiated a petition which was sent to Governor Gipps with signatures from many livestock owners in the north-western districts seeking more permanent support against 'renewed Aboriginal aggression'. Henry Dangar was one of the first signatories.

Not everyone supported the accused men. The publicity surrounding the murders at Myall Creek caused colonial philanthropists to rally at two well-attended public meetings in

Sydney in October 1838. These events resulted in the formation of the 'Australian Aborigines' Protection Society', an arm of the British organisation of a similar name. The leaders included John Dunmore Lang, Presbyterian minister, writer, politician and activist; Reverend Lancelot Threlkeld, missionary to the Aborigines; and George Augustus Robinson, who had previously been Protector of the Aborigines in Van Diemen's Land.

A concerted campaign was launched by supporters of the prisoners in an attempt to convince the Governor to release them, however, Gipps held firm in his resolve to make this case a lesson to others. The prominent *Sydney Herald* strongly supported the accused men, and advanced views that were widely held in the community at the time:

> *We want neither the classic nor the romantic savage here. We have far too many of the murderous wretches about us already. The whole gang of black animals are not worth the money the colonists will have to pay for printing the silly court documents on which we have already wasted too much time.*[3]

By far the most important step in support of the eleven men was taken surreptitiously by Robert Scott. As a magistrate, he was able to improperly gain access to them in gaol in Sydney while they were awaiting trial. He informed them that sufficient money had been raised to pay for a team of the colony's best barristers to represent them all. They were so grateful at having their legal fees paid that none of them even considered that in sharing the one team of lawyers some of them might be disadvantaged. Scott spoke firmly to the eleven charged men and assured them that if only they all stood together and none of them broke rank by saying anything in their defence at the forthcoming trial, they would all be acquitted. Scott counselled them:

> *Not to split amongst themselves, saying there was no direct evidence against them, and that, if they were only true to each other, they would not be convicted.*

This was sound advice, and it convinced the eleven prisoners to maintain solidarity as a group by not saying anything that could be used against the others at the forthcoming trial. This approach, however, was to have profound consequences for Charles Kilmeister.

When news reached the Governor of Scott's access to the prisoners and the influence he had had on them, the Governor was so incensed at a magistrate taking a position against the Crown's interests that at the next available opportunity later that year he made a point of not reappointing Scott as a magistrate.

***

As the trial drew near, public agitation intensified. The *Sydney Herald* requested jurors 'not to convict persons on charges originating in collisions with the blacks, except upon the most conclusive evidence of wanton cruelty'.[4] On the morning before the trial, the *Herald* issued this extraordinary challenge:

> *We say to the Colonists, since the Government makes no adequate exertion to protect you, protect yourselves; and if*

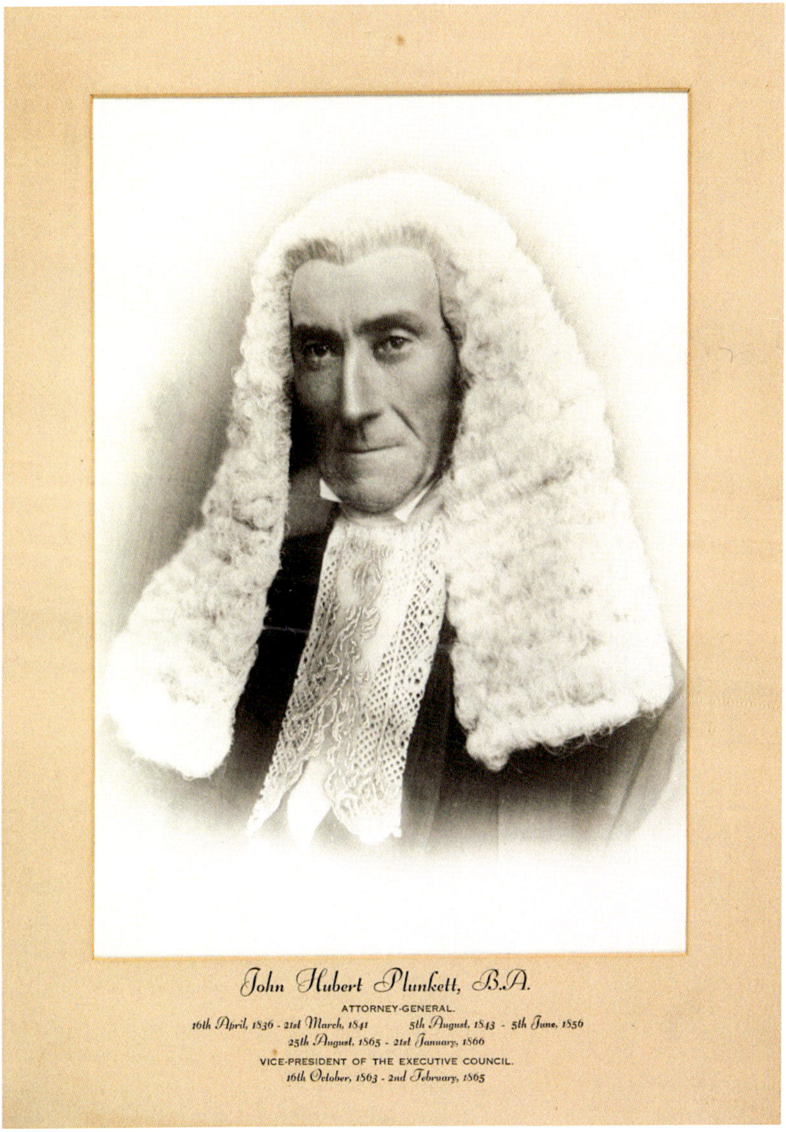
John Hubert Plunkett, B.A.
ATTORNEY-GENERAL.
16th April, 1836 - 21st March, 1841
5th August, 1843 - 5th June, 1856
25th August, 1865 - 21st January, 1866
VICE-PRESIDENT OF THE EXECUTIVE COUNCIL.
16th October, 1863 - 2nd February, 1865

Courtesy of Mitchell Library, State Library of NSW.

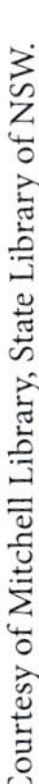

John Hubert Plunkett.

Painting by unknown artist hangs at the Irish College, Rome.

Archbishop Oliver Plunkett (1625–1681).

Painting by Sir Martin Archer Shee, courtesy of Dixson Galleries, SLNSW.

Governor Sir Richard Bourke.

Painting by Richard Read, courtesy of Mitchell Library, SLNSW.

Roger Therry, 1834.

Painting by Henry William Pickersgill, courtesy of Mitchell Library, SLNSW.

Governor Sir George Gipps.

Drawing by John Rae, courtesy of Dixson Galleries, SLNSW.

The Supreme Court (with dome), St James' Church and a barren Hyde Park from Elizabeth St in 1842. The Western Court was approached from the portico on Elizabeth St.

'Danger's Station, Mayal creek' (sic) from *Sketches of Australian scenes 1852–1853* (sic) by JG Sawkins.

Peel River July 9th 1838

Sir

I beg to acquaint you that about a Month since I had occasion to leave Mr Dangar's Station on the Big River for a few days on my return I saw near the Hut the remains of about thirty Blacks principally Women and Children I recognised them as part of a tribe that had been at the Station for some time and who had since they first came conducted themselves in a quiet and proper manner, on making enquiry I was informed that a party of White men had come to the Station who after securing them had taken them a short distance from my Hut and destroyed nearly the whole of them

I should have given information earlier but circumstances having prevented my sooner coming down the country

I am

E D Day Esq
Police Magistrate
Invermein

Courtesy of State Records NSW.

Letter from William Hobbs to Police Magistrate Invermein concerning the Myall Creek Massacre, 9 July 1838.

Police Magistrate Captain Edward 'Denny' Day.

Sketch from *Australian Town and Country Journal*, 27 May 1876.

Image courtesy of National Centre of Biography, Australian National University.

Henry Dangar. Sketch from *Australian Men of Mark*, volume 1, 1889–1890.

Image courtesy of Government Printing Office, SLNSW.

Justice William Westbrooke Burton.

Photograph by Charles Percy Pickering, courtesy of Government Printing Office, SLNSW.

The site of the first Board of National Education school and teacher training facility – formerly a military hospital at Fort St on Sydney's Observatory Hill. It is now the SH Ervin Gallery.

Courtesy of St Mary's Cathedral, Sydney.

The remains of Saint Oliver Plunkett's chalice.

Photograph courtesy of Michael Burge.

Elders and dignitaries at the memorial site in 2015, including (L to R): Rev Dr John Brown, Aunty Sue Blacklock, Kelvin Brown, Prof John Maynard, Uncle Lyle Munro, unknown.

> *the ferocious savages endeavour to plunder or destroy your property, or to murder yourselves, your families, or your servants, do to them as you would do to any white robbers or murderers – shoot them dead, if you can .... As to giving the blacks any support from the state – that is, from the labour of the settlers – not one fraction should have they, unless some means be devised to make them labour in return. Place them, too, in a position where they cannot evade justice – that when murders are committed they may be found and hanged, as white men are when they murder.*[5]

John Plunkett viewed the adverse publicity with dismay, realising that it could well influence the jurors in the trial he was about to commence. With his preparations nearly complete, he was fully aware of the ordeal in front of him: to convince twelve men on the jury to convict the eleven defendants, when the vast majority of inhabitants wanted them acquitted. Plunkett's greatest test of advocacy loomed before him. Never before had he faced a more formidable task. Never before had he been so sure of the need to succeed.

10

TRIAL

As John Plunkett and Roger Therry completed their preparations for the trial, they considered their case was strong, but they also realised that it depended entirely upon circumstantial evidence and inferences. They had heard from Denny Day that Davy, the Aboriginal servant at *Myall Creek Station*, had been an eyewitness to the murders, and that Magistrate Day was convinced the young man had spoken the truth, but they also knew that the law prevented them from calling him to give evidence. Plunkett was outraged that he was precluded from putting Davy – the only eyewitness to the atrocity – into the witness box. Neither was it possible for another person to give evidence of what Davy had reported to them, as this would be categorised as hearsay evidence. It made no sense to Plunkett that an eyewitness who was good enough to work for one of the larger landowners of the colony was not permitted to give an account in court because of the colour of his skin and the differences of his religious beliefs. The injustice of it brought back to Plunkett the travesty that had been perpetrated against his famous ancestor because of the differences of *his* religious convictions. John Hubert Plunkett was determined that this trial – 150 years later – in such a different place and such different circumstances would not be a mockery of justice like the trial of Archbishop Plunkett, but rather a beacon of light to guide others through the storms of bigotry and hatred in the future.

Plunkett and Therry knew that in order to prove the identity of the victims and the perpetrators they would be relying strongly on the evidence of two crucial witnesses: George Anderson and William Hobbs. Anderson would testify to the following facts: the arrival of the group of eleven stockmen; the Aborigines being tied and led away by the stockmen, including Kilmeister, to the west of the huts; the sound of two shots; the return of the stockmen the following day; the admissions made that all but one of them had been killed; and finally the fact that the Wirrayaraay had never returned to their camp or been seen in the vicinity again. William Hobbs would then provide evidence of having gone to the site of the murders and inspecting the burnt bodies, which he had counted. He could also describe the large torso in the ashes, which he assumed to be Daddy. Other witnesses from other stations were available to give evidence of the group of stockmen searching for Aborigines both before and after the murders. There was also a witness from *Newton's Run* who had seen Heppita in the company of the stockmen after the murders. All in all, the evidence to be presented amounted to a good, strong Crown case. But would it be enough?

***

The trial began in the Western Court of of the Supreme Court building on the corner of King and Elizabeth Streets[1] on 15 November 1838. Originally designed by former convict Francis Greenway as the Georgian School, the building plans had been clumsily altered by another, inferior government architect so as to enable the construction of a courthouse for the Supreme Court. Despite efforts to vary the original plan, the courtroom still had the feeling of a converted classroom. The building had only been occupied by the Supreme Court since 1827. The elevated judge's bench sat imposingly over the body of the court, while the jury box was situated against a side wall. Large windows against the western wall behind the judge drew light into the room, and a steep, narrow staircase connected the dock to the cells below. The wood panelling, which had been installed as part of the conversion, still gave off an odour of authority and respectability. In the afternoons, the sun would often stream through the windows behind the judge, making it difficult for counsel to look at the bench without squinting.

The presiding trial judge was the Chief Justice of New South Wales, Sir James Dowling. The jury of twelve were all men of substantial property and wealth. The prosecutors, Plunkett and Therry, and the three defence counsel were cheek by jowl at the small Bar table in the body of the courtroom. The eleven accused men were even more crowded in the dock. The public gallery at the back of the court was full of spectators, most of whom were animated supporters of the defendants. The eleven accused men were represented by the three defence counsel: William à Beckett and his two juniors, Mr Richard Windeyer and Mr William Foster, who had all been carefully chosen by Robert Scott and Henry Dangar using the funds collected by the Black Association. William à Beckett was hired not only for his forensic skills but also because of his charismatic appeal to juries. Scott and Dangar considered that à Beckett was far better as a jury trial advocate than Plunkett, even though the Attorney General might be superior as a technical lawyer. Although Mr Windeyer was a junior counsel, and a young one at that, he was clearly a man on the move who would one day become a senior counsel himself, and who would see his junior role in this case as a significant step on his way up the legal ladder.

The formal part of the trial began with the judge's associate reading out the charges to each of the accused men and asking them to plead guilty or not guilty. Plunkett and Therry had thought long and hard about the charges that should be proferred. They had debated extensively between themselves how many murder charges there should be and how they should be formulated. In order to understand their predicament, it is necessary to explain some aspects of practice in the criminal courts at that time.

***

Today, the eleven accused men would be charged at the one trial with all the murders arising from the one incident. In

Plunkett's day, however, it was unacceptable to have more than one murder case heard at a single trial, so Plunkett was forced to decide which of the twenty-eight deaths he would prosecute at this trial. In 1838, it was assumed that the prosecutor would select his strongest murder case to go to trial. If he succeeded, the penalty was death, so there was no point proceeding with any other charges at another trial. If he failed, it was assumed that the prosecutor would give up and not proceed with the other charges, as he had already failed to convince a jury on his best case.

It was then, and still is, a requirement of the law that a criminal charge must identify with some specificity the offence that the accused is charged with. It is necessary that the victim of a murder charge be particularised in a way that enables the accused to know the precise offence that he or she is charged with. While it is not essential for the victim's name to be stated, because in some cases it cannot be known, the identity of the victim still needs to be specified in some way. This precision may be established by reference to a body (or body part) that has been found, or in some other way that makes it clear exactly which victim is referred to in the murder charge. Where there have been a number of people killed at the same time, it was, and still is, not permissible to make a general allegation of murder without stating with a degree of specificity the identity of the victim. It was not sufficient, for example, to allege that an accused person had murdered 'one of the Wirrayaraay', and to leave it to the jury to decide which one of them had been killed. John Plunkett and Roger Therry were therefore obliged to make a decision which one of the twenty-eight Wirrayaraay they would nominate as the victim in the forthcoming trial of the eleven accused men. Their choice depended upon being able to specify the identity of the victim with some particularity. This proved to be a most difficult decision, because very few, if any, of the bodies had been identified.

Plunkett and Therry decided to focus on the death of Daddy, because it was his unusually large corpse that arguably had been the only one that Hobbs had been able to identify when he first saw the burnt bodies. However, Plunkett was only too aware that Hobbs could not conclusively state that the large torso seen by him had been Daddy's. The solution to this problem was to frame the murder charge in the alternative. Plunkett decided that the indictment – the document containing the charges presented by the prosecutor at the trial – would have two alternative approaches to the identity of the victim: one would identify the alleged victim as Daddy and the other would specify the identity of the deceased with the description 'an Aboriginal male to the Attorney General unknown', being the man with a large torso seen by Hobbs – whoever he was. This approach of describing the victim in alternative ways was perfectly acceptable in those times. It meant that the indictment would have two alternative charges against each accused man, with each charge expressing the identity of the victim in a different way, and the jury would have to decide which alternative version they found proven. Plunkett considered that this dual approach to the identity of the victim should cover any shortcomings or ambiguities in the evidence as to the identity of the victim.

Plunkett faced an even more difficult task in this case, in that the exact mode of death of each individual Wirrayaraay at Myall Creek was unknown. The possibilities were: by gunshot, by sword, by fire or by being trampled to death by horse. Today, it is not necessary to specify in the indictment the method of causing death, or the weapon used to kill. This is a detail that, where known, can be disclosed in the Crown Prosecutor's opening address. However, in 1838 the mode of death was considered an essential ingredient of the charge that had to be specified in the indictment. For this reason, where, as here, there were multiple possibilities of how a victim had come to die, it was necessary for a prosecutor to include an alternative charge in the indictment for each possible mode of death. Plunkett was therefore obliged to include four alternative charges in the indictment, each alleging a different mode of death, and for each of the two descriptions of the victim. This approach meant that there were eight alternative charges in the indictment against each of the eleven accused men, making a total of eighty-eight charges, which took the judge's associate more than an hour to read, despite the fact that the prosecutor was essentially charging each of the eleven men with the murder of a single person: the man who had been known as Daddy whose body had presumably been seen by William Hobbs.

***

In his opening address to the jury, John Plunkett summarised the evidence to be led in the Crown case. He explained that George Anderson, the hut keeper, had initially been too afraid to say anything, knowing that 'so many men at various stations in the district had collaborated together for the destruction of the natives'. He warned the jury about the activities of the Black Association and the risk of prejudice from newspaper articles:

> *I am sincerely glad to see prisoners defended by counsel. I am glad to see the present prisoners in that situation, but a rumour has gone abroad that this defence is made at the insistence of an association illegally formed for the purpose of defending all who may be charged with crimes resulting from any collision with the natives. I say that if such an association exists, that if there be men who have joined together for the purpose of defending such men as these, the object of that society is to encourage bloodshed and crime of every description. Gentlemen, I have too high an opinion of you, and of the discrimination of the public at large, to think for a moment that any blood article appearing in any paper or papers will at all influence you in the verdict which you are to give this day. Gentlemen, it has been promulgated from the bench by the judges of the land that the black is as amenable for his evil acts as the white men, and therefore as much entitled to protection by the laws.*

Our record of the evidence in the trial is not in the form of questions and answers, like the official court transcripts today, because court reporters in those days worked for the newspapers and recorded a summary of the evidence. Plunkett called Hobbs to give this evidence of what he had discovered when he returned to *Myall Creek Station* to find the Wirrayaraay had gone:

> *From what Davy said to me, I asked him to go with me and he took me about half a mile from my house in a westerly direction. There had been a shower of rain and the tracks of horses and of naked feet were quite discernible. It was a regular*

track; there were children's footsteps; the horse tracks were on either side and the track of the naked feet were in the middle; they were in the same direction as the horse tracks. I arrived at a spot where there were a great number of dead bodies, but the stench was so great that I was not able to be accurate in counting them. I endeavoured to count them and made more of them sometimes than others. The most I made was 28. The skulls which had been burnt were easily discernible. The last number I counted was 20. I will undertake to swear that there were the remains of above 20. I saw some of the bodies. They were very much disfigured. I cannot say how many.

Hobbs also gave evidence of the personal consequences for him of bringing this matter to the attention of the authorities: his employment with Henry Dangar had been terminated for no other apparent reason.

The main problem faced by Plunkett during the trial was that, because of the condition of the bodies, he could not produce any witness, including William Hobbs, who could swear that Daddy was definitely one of the victims. During his evidence-in-chief,[2] when Hobbs was asked about this issue, he said:

I did know Daddy. He was an old man. He was the largest man ever I saw, either white or black. I saw a large body there, but the head was gone. From the size of the body I think it was his. I left Daddy on the station. I could not swear that it was Daddy's body. I am perfectly satisfied within my own mind that it was the body of Daddy. It was lying on its back. There was no head and the fire had destroyed nearly the whole of the flesh. I believe to be the body of a man – the body of Daddy.

In cross-examination[3] by defence barrister Mr Foster, Hobbs said:

I saw the large body. The legs and arms were gone. I could not swear that it was a male. It was a large frame. I could not swear that the Black called Daddy is not now in existence.

In re-examination[4] by the Attorney General, Hobbs testified:

I could not swear that Daddy is dead. I have not seen him since. I never saw a female so large as that frame. I never saw any of those persons who were on the station since. I have made enquiries for them.

The main Crown witness was undoubtedly George Anderson, who was well aware of the significance of his testimony. While he gave his evidence in a forthright manner, he was clearly fearful of those in court – both the accused and their supporters in the public gallery. Of all the people in the courtroom, he had the most to lose if the accused men were found not guilty. He gave evidence that about ten horsemen had arrived at the station armed with muskets, swords and pistols. He identified them by name[5] and gave evidence of what happened next:

The Blacks on seeing them ran into the hut. The men then got off their horses, the prisoner Russell took a rope from his horse's neck, and commenced undoing it. While he was preparing his rope, I asked what they were going to do with the Blacks. He answered me that they were going to take them to the back of the range and frighten them. Russell went into the hut, and the Blacks were brought out tied [up]. I heard the Blacks crying out for assistance. The mothers and children were crying, and the little ones that could not walk. Russell brought out the end of the rope that they were tied with, and gave it to one of the men on horseback. They then started taking the Blacks with them. The man who took the rope from Russell went in front. They were tied; one black was handcuffed; their hands were all tied with the palms to each other. The rope was a very long one. They took all the Blacks away, except two boys that jumped into the creek as the men were coming up. They left one black Jin with me in the hut; they left another black Jin with Davy; a little child was at the back of the hut while they were tying the Blacks; instead of allowing her to go with the party, I pulled her into the hut and kept her there.

The oldest of the lot was called 'Old Daddy'. He was a very old, big, tall man. They went towards the west from the hut. Kilmeister got his horse while they were tying the Blacks. He went with them, and took the pistol with him. I was frightened. They had a great many pistols. I saw the swords in the distance. Kilmeister went with them. I did not keep them in sight more than a minute or two. About a quarter of an hour afterwards I heard the report of two pieces, one after the other, in the same direction as they had gone.

The women and children who were left with me I sent away with the ten Blacks who had left our station with Mr Foster. It was a moonlit night. I turned them all away the same night, because I did not want them to be killed by those men whom I knew to be out after the Blacks.

I saw the same men the night after. They came back to my hut whence they had taken the Blacks. They all came except Kilmeister. They stopped there all night. On the next morning, they went out on the same road as they took the night before. I asked Foley if any of the Blacks had made their escape. He said none that he saw; they were all killed but one. I saw the smoke a short time after. Fleming told Kilmeister to go up by and by and put the logs together and to be sure that all was consumed. Kilmeister did go in that direction almost immediately, and remained nearly the whole day. I never went to the spot. Davy went.

In cross-examination, Anderson admitted that initially he had told Mr Hobbs that he did not know the identity of the stockmen who had come to the huts. He denied that he had been offered his freedom in return for his evidence, stating that he had only asked for protection. He admitted that Magistrate Day had threatened to commit him for perjury if he did not tell him the truth about everything he knew. He said that it was only after that warning that he made a serious attempt to recollect and tell Mr Day everything that he knew about the murders. He tearfully told the court that he had wanted to save Heppita, because of his special connection with her, but she had been forcibly taken away with the others.

The Attorney General called a number of other witnesses in his case, and when he had completed presenting his evidence the judge invited the defence to present their cases. At this point in a trial in 1838, an accused person might make a statement to the jury from the dock. It was not permissible for him to give sworn evidence as it was considered that this would present a guilty person with an irresistible temptation to tell lies on oath in an attempt to avoid a conviction, and thereby condemn his soul to eternal damnation.[6] The solution provided by the law was to permit an accused person to make an unsworn statement to the court. In this case, however, not a single one of the accused men did so. Instead, they all maintained the solidarity that Robert Scott had urged upon them, and remained silent. The defence merely called a number of character witnesses to express how unlikely it was that each of these men of good character and prior good record in the colony would commit such a heinous crime. Counsel for Charles Kilmeister called Henry Dangar to give evidence of his good character. In those days, the most serious challenge that could be made against a man's honesty and integrity was to say that one would not believe him 'on his oath'. As the oath was taken in the name of God and on the Bible, a deliberate lie under oath was considered to place the person at risk of eternal damnation and relegation to hell in the afterlife. Dangar gave evidence against George Anderson that he had been a troublesome and unreliable assigned servant who was 'addicted to lying', and that Dangar would not believe him on his oath. On the other hand, Dangar gave a glowing account of the honesty and reliability of his stockman Charles Kilmeister.

Plunkett's cross-examination of Henry Dangar was rather lame and timid. One can only conclude that he was concerned that Dangar was such a well-known and influential personality in the colony and that he might have a friend or business associate on the jury who would take a dim view of a rigorous challenge by the prosecutor. Plunkett secured from Dangar an admission that he had provided funds for the defence of the eleven accused men. Dangar denied that he had dismissed Hobbs as station manager because of his letter to the magistrate, and explained that Hobbs's service had ended merely because the term of his contract had expired. This, of course, hid the real fact that Dangar had dismissed him in retaliation for bringing the murders to the attention of the authorities. Plunkett did not ask him why he had taken so long to make enquiries about the murders, or why he had not immediately gone to *Myall Creek Station* to investigate. Plunkett did not attack Dangar's evidence by challenging *his* reputation, which he could have done by questioning him about the circumstances in which Dangar had come to be dismissed as government surveyor some years earlier. Neither did Plunkett challenge Dangar's personal interest in having the Aborigines removed from an area where they were challenging his pastoral interests. Finally, Plunkett did not ask him any questions about the more underhand activities of the Black Association, and particularly whether he supported the approach that Robert Scott had made to the prisoners in gaol. All of these lines of enquiry would have exposed Dangar's bias in favour of the accused. Perhaps Plunkett felt that the jury would already know of this, so there was no need to labour the point, or maybe he feared that there was a good chance that the jury felt the same way as Dangar and he did not want to exacerbate their prejudices by a vigorous cross-examination of someone with whom they sympathised.

Unusually for its time, this trial went into a second day. On resumption the next morning, the Chief Justice summed up the case to the jury at considerable length and in an exemplary and balanced manner. In those days, there was no right for counsel to give a closing address to the jury, so the judge's summation of the evidence was the only overview that the jury heard.[7] The Chief Justice told them this:

> *It is clear that a most grievous offence has been committed; that the lives of nearly 30 of our fellow creatures have been sacrificed. In order to fulfil my duty, I must tell you that the life of a Black is as precious and valuable in the eyes of the law as that of the highest noble in the land.*
>
> ...
>
> *The point you have just to determine is whether Daddy was the unfortunate man who lost his life as set forth in the indictment, or whether a man whose name is unknown to the Attorney General came to his death by violent means from the prisoners' hands.*

The judge recapitulated the whole of the evidence, before sending the jury out to consider their verdict.

Plunkett and Therry thought that the trial had gone well for them, and that the evidence of guilt was overwhelming, but they also knew that there was a tremendous amount of discontent in the community at the prosecutions. The *Sydney Herald* had actively campaigned against a conviction. Although Daddy had undoubtedly been part of the tribe that had been camping at *Myall Creek Station*, this was not necessarily sufficient to prove beyond a reasonable doubt that his body was the large one that had been inspected by Hobbs. Unless the jury were satisfied beyond a reasonable doubt that that body had in fact been Daddy's, they were obliged to acquit on those charges that alleged that Daddy was the victim. However, this still left open the alternative charges of the murder of 'an Aboriginal male to the Attorney General unknown', being the person whose large body Hobbs had seen on the pyre. Would a group of twelve wealthy, propertied jurors, most of whom had come to the colony as free men, convict eleven convicts or former convicts of the murder of an unnamed Aboriginal man?

A mere fifteen minutes after retiring to the jury room to consider their verdicts, the jurors returned to court and gave Plunkett and Therry the answer to this question by announcing verdicts of *not guilty* on all charges. One of the jurors was alleged to have said later: 'I knew well they were guilty of the murder, but I for one would never see a white man suffer for shooting a black.'[8]

Plunkett was gutted by the verdicts. Although he had been fully aware of the evidentiary weaknesses in his case, he was so overwhelmed by the enormity of the crimes that he had convinced himself that the jury would convict. At this point, Plunkett was faced with one of the most difficult decisions of his career. In several moments the judge would ask him whether the eleven men who had just been acquitted should be released from custody and returned to their former places of work. If he gave the expected response and answered in the affirmative, it would mark the end of these proceedings and the murders would go unpunished. If, instead, he departed from the usual practice and answered in the negative, it would signal his intention to place the men on trial again for one of the other murders arising out of the same incident. Plunkett realised that he would have no additional evidence to lead at a second trial. Would he accept the jury's verdicts, or would he insist on another trial on the same evidence? Would he bow to society's views about this case or would he pursue what his own conscience insistently demanded: that these men had committed a most horrid crime for which they should be punished? He had to make a decision on the spur of the moment, and it was one that, once announced, would be irrevocable. It seemed to Plunkett that this was the defining moment of his life – when he would call on all the moral lessons that he had learned to reach a decision in just a few seconds. It was like a runner who has trained for a year in order to run a defining race over a hundred yards. He was aware that his announcement would be the yardstick by which his entire career, and maybe even his whole life, would be judged. He had no opportunity to discuss it with his junior counsel, Roger Therry, who was seated beside him, let alone with the Governor whose offices were several blocks away, but Plunkett knew that the Governor's sympathies and objectives were aligned to his own. With only a few, long moments to turn over the conflicting issues in his mind, he reverted to what he had done on numerous previous occasions when he had not known what to do: he asked himself what his noble ancestor, Oliver Plunkett, would have done. What came to him was the revelation that this case was a unique opportunity to demonstrate to all and sundry that the law values the life of an Aborigine as much as that of a white.

John Plunkett slowly raised himself to his feet and announced to the assembled court that there would be another trial on fresh charges, and then requested the judge to remand the eleven accused men until the following Monday week, 26 November, when he would present a fresh indictment.

The reaction in the courtroom was immediate and intense. It was almost unprecedented in the short history of the colony that a prosecutor had failed to heed the clear message of an acquittal by a jury on a murder charge. A sense of unfairness overwhelmed the defendants, their counsel and their supporters in the public gallery. Their venom was directed at the Attorney General, whom they believed had embarked on a prosecutorial vendetta from which he was not to be deterred. The reaction in the public arena and the newspapers over the following days was equally hostile.

11

AN OFFER REFUSED

In preparation for the second trial, Attorney General John Hubert Plunkett gave much thought to the defence tactics that had won the accused men acquittals at the first trial. He realised that by putting all eleven on trial at the same time he had enabled them to close ranks and defeat justice by withholding any account of their evil deeds. As the prosecutor, Plunkett had the right to decide which of them would be included on the indictment at the next trial. He decided that in order to strengthen his case and encourage some of them to give evidence against the others, he would charge those against whom he had the most evidence and offer the remaining ones immunity from prosecution in return for their testimony. He selected the four against whom he considered he had the weakest cases, based on the evidence that had been led at the first trial, and made them the offer. He was astounded and most perplexed when they declined his invitation to avoid the gallows in return for their cooperation.

In fact, the men who were offered this deal did not even have to think about it before rejecting it. They were loath to assist a prosecutor to secure convictions against men they knew well and felt affinity towards, but, most importantly, they realised that if they did cooperate, their future lives would be forever plagued by bitter hatred and the threat of retaliation from other convicts and ex-convicts. Those who were still serving terms would eventually be returned to their previous assignments, where they would have to face their fellows and account for any deal they had struck with the evil prosecutor. In any age, in gaol communities around the world, the worst breach of trust among prisoners is to cooperate with the authorities against a fellow prisoner.

Despite the rejection, John Plunkett maintained his decision to put on trial only the seven worst offenders, namely: Charles Kilmeister, John Russell, Edward Foley, James Oates, John Johnstone, William Hawkins and James Parry. Some hypothesised that Oates had only been included because he was a Roscommon man and therefore nobody could complain that favouritism had been shown in the selection of the seven defendants by virtue of their origins. There was an even spread of Protestants (Kilmeister, Hawkins, Johnson and Parry) and Catholics (Russell, Foley and Oates). The second trial of the seven men was set down for Monday, 26 November – less than a fortnight after the previous acquittals. Meanwhile, the retrial of the remaining four was adjourned to an undetermined future date and they remained in custody – the Attorney General still hoping that the threat of facing their own second trial at some time might cause them to change their minds about cooperating with him.

Having failed to convince a jury of the murder of Daddy, Plunkett once again had to decide on the identity of the victim for the second trial. The conclusion he reached was that the most likely path to success was to prosecute for the murder of the young child whose rib bone had been found by Magistrate Denny Day months after the massacre when he inspected the scene with William Hobbs. While it was possible, because of its size, that the rib bone had been part of the body of the boy Charley, Plunkett realised that, once again, he was not in a position to definitively prove the identity of the deceased. Indeed, he was unable to prove that the rib bone had once been part of a boy or a girl. He therefore formulated the charges with two alternative versions of the victim's identity. It was the murder of either: an unknown Aboriginal child (whose rib had been found by Magistrate Day), or Charley. Once again, there were four alternative scenarios of the mode of death, making a total of eight charges against each accused man – but all essentially referring to the murder of the child whose rib bone had been found by Police Magistrate Denny Day. Plunkett's rationale was that a fresh jury could not fail to be sympathetic to the murder of a child, and he had the advantage of a physical exhibit from the body of the victim. He knew from experience that jurors did not like to convict where there had been no body, or body part, found. Magistrate Denny Day had not observed the remains of Daddy, but he had seen and taken into possession the rib bone of a child.

As the day for the second trial drew closer, the Attorney General became increasingly concerned at comments that appeared in the Press – especially the *Sydney Herald*, which was once again calling for an acquittal, no matter what the evidence. On the morning of 26 November 1838, the day the second trial was due to commence, the *Sydney Herald* published a report of some Aborigines who had driven away cattle on the Big River. Although it made no direct mention of the Wirrayaraay killed at Myall Creek, the article was clearly designed to influence jurors in the forthcoming trial:

> *How long are the settlers to endure outrages such as are here detailed? ... We say the government must interfere, or the settlers will set the government at defiance by taking the law into their own hands – by executing summary justice. To this it will come at last, in spite of all the ranters that ever lived.*

Plunkett was convinced that adverse publicity had played a role in the previous acquittal, and he was determined to take action to prevent a fresh jury being tainted by comments in the newspapers. That morning, 26 November, he appeared in court before Justice William Westbrooke Burton, who had been allocated to preside over the second trial, seeking redress in the form of an adjournment of the trial and a court order prohibiting any further public comment on the case – the latter being rarely applied for and even more rarely granted. In fact, both sides requested an adjournment: the defence for one day only to consider the multiple charges in the new indictment, which had taken an hour and a half to read; and the prosecution for an indefinite period because of the prejudicial effect of material in the newspapers, particularly the *Sydney Herald*. Plunkett railed to Justice Burton against those newspapers attempting to sway the decisions of jurors, saying that he had only seen the *Sydney Herald* that morning and that in his view the publication tended to pervert the course of justice. Applying for a postponement of the trial, he advanced the argument that:

> *If the case was brought on and tried now, that it could not have a fair and impartial consideration by a jury who must, in a certain degree, be biased by what they had heard out of the Court.*[1]

He stated his intention to apply to the Court for an order prohibiting any mention of the case during the trial, but Justice Burton cautioned him against making such an application, so Plunkett abandoned it lest he needlessly antagonise the judge prior to the trial.

Justice Burton agreed to the matter going over for a single day to accommodate the defence request and, in response to Plunkett's concerns about prejudicial publicity he assured everyone of his firm opinion that the Court and its jurors would not be affected by outside influences. According to *The Australian* the next day:

> *Mr Justice Burton said that the Attorney General could take what course he thought proper, but he would advise him not to be hasty in his application, nor in the course he intended to adopt. For in his [Mr Justice Burton's] opinion, he thought, and he said so with confidence, that the course of public justice would never be perverted when a case came before a Jury and a Judge of New South Wales. He thought there was too much honour in the Supreme Court of New South Wales, to*

> *ever bias a case that might come before the Court ... However wicked persons might attempt, by their writings, to sway the course of justice, he would never admit that the moral state of the Colony was so bad as had been represented, and that the course of justice could be perverted by anything that was said out of the doors of the Court.*[2]

Burton's confidence in the resistance of the court and its jurors to any prejudicial pre-trial publicity in the Press was not shared by the Attorney General. Plunkett was irate that the newspaper proprietors and editors had used their privileged positions in an attempt to manipulate the outcome of the trial.

***

The defendants and their counsel were still smarting from the almost unprecedented actions of the Attorney General in forcing them to undergo a second trial. On the reading of the fresh indictment, defence counsel submitted to the court that some of the charges in it were legally barred because they alleged the same offences for which the accused had already been acquitted at the first trial. This is known to lawyers as a claim of '*autrefois acquit*' – or 'I have previously been acquitted'. Today this question would be decided by the trial judge before empanelling a jury; however, in 1838 the procedure was for a special jury to be empanelled to decide this issue before the commencement of the trial.

The following day, 27 November 1838, just prior to the commencement of the second trial, the defence argued before Justice Burton and a specially empanelled jury that at the first trial they had been charged with, and acquitted of, the murder of 'an Aboriginal male to the Attorney General unknown', and that they could therefore not be put on trial again for the murder of 'an Aboriginal child to the Attorney General unknown', because the former offence necessarily included the latter one. The defence argued that an unknown Aboriginal male necessarily included all of the male bodies that had been discovered at Myall Creek. As the child whose rib bone had been found by Denny Day could be male, this retrial impermissibly challenged the acquittal that had been delivered at the last trial. They correctly alleged that the prosecutor was intending to lead exactly the same evidence against them at this trial as he had led in the previous one, thereby demonstrating only too clearly that this was an impermissible rehearing of the same matter.

At one stage, Justice Burton asked the Attorney General this pointed question:

> *How is it possible that [the Crown] can prove whether one person stated to be unknown is or is not the same as a person set forth a second time also unknown?*

Plunkett submitted that the previous trial had been about the murder of the large man, probably Daddy, whose torso had been observed by William Hobbs when he first examined the pile of burnt bodies, whereas this trial was about the murder of a child whose rib bone had been found at the same location by Magistrate Day. He argued convincingly that the two victims were necessarily different people and that the charges did not overlap in any way, making it permissible for the Crown to put the accused on trial again for a completely different murder. The fact that the evidence would be similar or the same at the second trial did not challenge the previous acquittals.

After vigorous legal argument and an explanation of the law by Justice Burton, the special jury retired to deliberate. More than an hour later (which was a long time in those days), after hearing nothing from them, Justice Burton brought them back into court and told them that perhaps they did not understand exactly what they had to consider. He sought to summarise and simplify the issue by explaining:

> *The prisoners say they have been tried for the crimes alleged against them in this information; it is for you to consider whether they have or not.*

The jurors again retired, and returned to court a few minutes later to announce their decision in favour of the Crown. The second trial was ready to proceed in front of a fresh jury. Plunkett had overcome the initial hurdle in putting some of the men on trial again. He was relieved to have won this first round, but realised only too well that the next one would be far harder and, if anything, more controversial. He was well aware of the overwhelming hostility to the prosecution in the general community and much of the Press. Plunkett and his junior, Roger Therry, acknowledged to themselves and each other that their court advocacy would need to be extraordinary to overcome the public sentiment against this prosecution.

***

Plunkett's tactic of putting the seven defendants up for trial again by charging them with the murder of another victim in the same incident would never succeed today, and even in 1838 he was fortunate to have had his way. The first jury had made a decision to acquit, presumably based on the fact that the prosecutor had failed to prove the identity of the victim because of the state of the bodies. A retrial would challenge that finding. If the previous jury could not be satisfied beyond a reasonable doubt that Daddy had been one of the victims of the massacre, how could this jury conclude that Charley was one of them? Surely, such verdicts would be inconsistent. If there was a reasonable possibility that Daddy had just wandered off into the bush and disappeared, didn't the same possibility also apply to Charley? If the first jury were – however bizarrely – unable to conclude that the eleven accused stockmen had murdered the Aborigines who had been tied up and led away from the huts at *Myall Creek Station*, then surely the retrial was seeking to canvass that same issue now – in clear breach of the law. While Plunkett's approach to the second trial would not be successful today, in 1838 it was perfectly acceptable, because of the practice that only one murder could be tried at a time.

Plunkett's tactics were bold and clever, and he had succeeded in convincing a special jury to allow him to go to trial again. Justice Burton had shown no inclination to stand in his way of asking another jury to come to a different conclusion on essentially the same facts. Plunkett had won a second chance for the Crown.

12

RETRIAL

On 29 November 1838, the second trial commenced before Justice William Westbrooke Burton, who had a different character to the Chief Justice and a more assertive approach towards the right of Aborigines to the protection of British law.[1] Several incidents at the commencement of the trial caused John Plunkett to have grave concerns about the integrity of the proceedings. On the morning of the hearing, an unusually large number of men who had been called for jury duty failed to appear. Only twenty-eight of the forty-eight who had received jury notices arrived at court, making it impossible to select a jury of twelve, because of the rights of both parties to challenge jurors. This hurdle demonstrated in a most pointed way the distaste that many people felt for the case, and prompted Plunkett's ire and disgust, because he was convinced that the

Black Association had succeeded in encouraging or intimidating jurors to stay away.[2] He requested the judge to severely punish the absent panel members, and Justice Burton issued heavy fines against ten of them.

As a result of the absent jurors, the judge was obliged to direct the Court Sheriff to '*pray a tales*', which meant pulling a sufficient number of (male) passers-by in the vicinity of the court off the street and into court to make up the numbers on the jury.[3] It was in this context that the second incident occurred that morning that caused Plunkett great concern. He was deeply suspicious of Mr William Humphreys, one of the men who had been brought into court off the street by the sheriff, feeling that he may be a stooge or plant, deliberately positioned outside the court by some associate of the accused, with a view to Humphreys being chosen to serve on the jury so that he could then influence the outcome of the trial. When Humphreys' name was called, the Attorney General ascertained that he had in fact been a member of the jury at the first trial. On discovering this, and realising that his suspicions were justified, he rather rudely challenged him by calling out, 'You may walk off', which earned a rebuke from the judge.

Another incident at the commencement of the second trial confirmed Plunkett's view that the Black Association was making every effort to subvert the trial process. That morning, shortly before the commencement of the trial, a sheriff's officer arrested William Hobbs on the pretext of having failed to pay his debts. Undoubtedly, it was an attempt to intimidate Hobbs and remove him on that critical day so that he would be unable to give evidence. Plunkett immediately made arrangements to have him released.

The jury panel sworn to try the case comprised: Mr George Sewell of Sydney, foreman; Mr William Knight, a publican of Castlereagh Street; Mr Francis King, soap boiler, King Street; Mr John Little, publican, King Street; Mr Richard Leeworthy, tailor, George Street; Mr Henry Linden; Mr Benjamin Lee, landholder of Parramatta; Mr Edward Hyland, landholder of Richmond; Mr William Johnson; Mr Alexander Long, publican, York Street; Mr John Leary, publican, York Street; and Mr William Johnstone, a blacksmith of Pitt Town.

Plunkett began his opening address to the jury by seeking to overcome the prejudice that had been engendered by the extensive publicity in the newspapers. It was reported that he told the jurors:

> *He was aware that considerable feeling and excitement had prevailed in the public mind on the subject; and on his head he might receive blame for not having, at the close of the last trial, obtained an order from the court to prevent the publication of the trial before the matter was finally terminated, as well as the comments that appeared in some of the public prints ... The trial appeared fully in the public prints and was commented on generally by every portion of the press according to the different opinions of the case. He did, however, hope that the jury came into the box uninfluenced and unbiased by any feeling but that of a determination to strictly observe the oaths they had taken, and conscientiously to perform that duty which the stern Justice of the country, and the sacred obligation of their oaths, demanded at their hands.*

He then sought to explain to the jurors the enormity of the crime that had been committed:

It could not be concealed, as it had already been disclosed in evidence, that 28 human beings had lost their lives in a manner which was sufficient to move the most hardened and obdurate heart; it was not his intention, nor was it his wish, to bias them against the prisoners now put on trial, but it was his duty as well as his custom to bring before them the enormity of the crime, and to paint it in its most debasing colours.

Plunkett then launched his surprise tactic, which caused great discomfort in the defence camp because it was something that the prosecutor had not been able to do in the first trial. According to *The Australian*, he told the jury that they would have noticed that only seven of the alleged offenders were on trial and four of them were not, and he suggested that:

It would be competent for the prisoners to put those four persons into the [witness] box, to relieve them from the charges of which, having all been in company, they could not be ignorant. If they do not avail themselves of this, it is presumptive proof of their guilt, as they can call those who were present to establish their innocence.[4]

Not a single objection was voiced to this proposition, either by defence counsel or the judge, thereby indicating that, by the standards of the day, it was quite permissible.

***

By these words in his opening address, John Plunkett threw down the gauntlet and challenged the defence to call the other four offenders, or face the inevitable inference that they had not been called because they were all guilty. He was, in effect, requiring the accused men to prove their innocence by calling the other four prisoners. This tactic revealed that his decision to split the defendants into two groups and to present an indictment against only seven of them was a blatant tactical manoeuvre. Plunkett knew perfectly well from the first trial that the defence would not call any of the stockmen to the witness box, because their evidence would implicate them all. So instead he adopted an approach that he thought would appeal to the common sense of the jurors. In his frustration at being denied the opportunity to call some of the men to give evidence against the others, he had contrived a situation where the defence would suffer an inference of guilt from *their* failure to call them.

Today, John Plunkett's tactic would be completely unacceptable, because it infringes two of the most basic rights of an accused person: the presumption of innocence and the right to silence. The presumption of innocence entails the proposition that an accused is entitled to be considered innocent unless and until the prosecution has proven guilt during a trial. The onus of proving guilt always falls upon the prosecution; an accused has no burden of proving his or her innocence. The right to silence, as it exists today, dictates that the failure of an accused person to answer questions or to give *or call* evidence in court cannot be used to infer guilt. It would be quite unacceptable now for a prosecutor to suggest that the defence should call a witness or witnesses to prove their innocence, and if a modern-day prosecutor made a similar suggestion in an opening address, the trial would immediately come to an abrupt end and the prosecutor would be severely rebuked and probably disciplined for professional misconduct. However, in 1838, although both the presumption of innocence and the right to silence had been acknowledged by the English courts, they were not as clearly defined and strictly applied as they are today.[5]

In 1838, the right to silence varied in its application from place to place, from time to time, and from judge to judge.[6] At its highest, it meant that the jury could not use the failure of an accused to provide an account to an investigating magistrate or to make an unsworn statement at trial as a sign that he was guilty. However, there was nothing to stop a defendant calling another person as a witness who *could* give sworn evidence. The jury was entitled to conclude that the failure of any party – including the accused – to call a witness was because that witness would not have assisted the party who would normally be expected to call that witness.[7] This approach was not viewed as infringing the right to silence, so the failure of the defence to call a witness *could* at that time be used to draw an inference of guilt against the accused.[8] That is why the transcript of the second trial does not reveal any objection by Justice Burton or the defence to this part of Plunkett's opening address.

Plunkett had devised this tactic in response to the dirty tricks of the Black Association: their access to the defendants in gaol to convince them to stand firm as a group; their raising of funds for the defence legal costs; the voluminous amount of adverse publicity against the prosecution in the newspapers; and the attempt to infiltrate the jury at the second trial. John Plunkett knew that he would never get another opportunity like this one to establish that the law valued the sanctity of Indigenous lives to the same extent as non-Indigenous ones. Since the founding of the colony, there had been so many Aborigines massacred, and only one group of perpetrators charged – this one – so Plunkett believed there was an overriding, urgent need to deter future murderers.

***

Once again, Plunkett had the problem of proving the identity of the victim. The best he could do at this trial was to call William Hobbs to say that, from the size of the burnt and dismembered heads and bodies, he could say that there had been ten to twelve children killed; and then to call Police Magistrate Captain Edward Denny Day to explain how he had found the rib bone of a child in the same locality. Would the jury accept that the rib bone must necessarily have been from the child known as Charley? Possibly not. Would the jury convict the seven accused men of the death of an 'Aboriginal child to the Attorney General unknown', being the child whose rib bone had been located? Plunkett desperately hoped they would.

***

Although the evidence called by the Crown in the second trial was substantially the same as at the first trial, in his opening address Attorney General Plunkett identified one piece of evidence against Charles Kilmeister that had not been previously led. He told the jury:

> *There is one circumstance, which has come out since the former trial, which will clearly implicate Kilmeister, and show that he,*

at any rate, was actuated by malice in the share he took in the matter. It is his having, when spoken to of the motives which could have induced him to commit such a deed, replied that if it was known what the Blacks had threatened to do to him, he would not be blamed.

The actual evidence given on this point at the second trial by Denny Day was as follows:

In the course of the examination [i.e. his questioning of Kilmeister], or rather at the close of the examination, and just as Kilmeister was leaving the room, I said that I was more surprised at Kilmeister than at any of the others, on account of his great intimacy with them [the Wirrayaraay], when he turned round and said, 'If you knew what they threatened to do to me, you would not be surprised.' I did not make any further remark at the time. I did not state this on my former examination [at the first trial], but when the Chief Justice was summing up, I recollected the circumstances, and told the Attorney General of it at the time.

***

It is quite clear from the evidence given by Magistrate Day at the second trial that Kilmeister had not been referring to a threat from the Aborigines who had been peacefully camped at the station for weeks, but rather from the mounted stockmen who had precipitously arrived at the huts. Not only did Magistrate Day misconstrue what Kilmeister had said, but Plunkett repeated the same mistake. Because Kilmeister did not make a statement at either trial, he was unable to correct this fundamental misunderstanding of why he had joined the stockmen. If properly understood, Kilmeister had been suggesting to Magistrate Day that he had only joined the murderous venture because his own life had been threatened by one or more of the eleven stockmen who had arrived at *Myall Creek Station*. This was a clear assertion of what is known today as the defence of duress.

The defence of duress is available if an accused can show that he has committed an offence because of a threat that death or serious violence would be inflicted on him if he refused to commit it. The threat must be so serious and so proximate to the offence that a reasonable person in the position of the accused would have yielded to it.[9] Duress was, and is, unavailable as a defence to murder by a person who has been directly involved in the actual killing (a principal in the first degree), but it was, and is, available as a defence to a person who was 'aiding and abetting' in the vicinity of the murder.[10] Plunkett was not in any position to prove that Kilmeister had been directly involved in the killings, as he had no eyewitness that he could call, so any evidence of duress would have been highly relevant to Kilmeister's case at the trial.

If Kilmeister had raised the defence of duress during an unsworn statement to the jury, setting out the threat to his life that had been made by Russell inside the hut, he may well have been acquitted. Evidence of the threat, supported by the overwhelmingly intimidating arrival of the eleven stockmen at the huts before the murders, could have influenced the jurors to accept that he was under an intolerable risk to his own life that any person would have succumbed to, and therefore that he was entitled to raise the defence of duress. Alternatively, the jurors may have had compassion for him, in which case they may have acquitted him out of sheer sympathy. His situation was clearly different to the other defendants who had ridden for days in search of the Wirrayaraay before arriving at *Myall Creek Station*. On the other hand, Kilmeister's actions in maintaining the fire to burn the bodies for several days after the murders demonstrated a form of assistance called 'accessory after the fact', and there was no evidence of an imminent threat to his life at that point. In addition, it could be said that Kilmeister's continuing involvement with the other stockmen when they later went in search of the young Wirrayaraay men after the murders at *Myall Creek Station* would have gone against him, and possibly convinced the jury that fear for his own life had not been his only motivation.

Because of the misinterpretation of Day's evidence and the fact that Kilmeister did not say anything at his trial, he was deprived of the real opportunity of an acquittal. Instead, his confession to Denny Day was misused as evidence of some hostility towards the Wirrayaraay and a motive to kill them. It is incomprehensible that his barristers did not confront Denny Day in cross-examination during the prosecution case and put to him that he had misunderstood what Kilmeister had said. One can only think that the defence counsel did not want to treat differently any of the seven defendants they were representing in court, because they were expecting a sympathetic jury to acquit all the accused, as had happened at the first trial.

***

Plunkett called the same witnesses at the second trial to give virtually identical evidence they had given at the first trial. After the prosecution case had finished, all seven accused once again declined to say anything in their defence. Needless to say, not a single one of the remaining four prisoners was called in the defence case. Once again, various character witnesses were called. Henry Dangar again gave evidence on behalf of Charles Kilmeister, singing his praises and denouncing George Anderson as being of general bad character and addicted to telling lies. This time, however, Plunkett launched a withering cross-examination of Dangar that challenged his honesty and attempted to put before the jury evidence of his overwhelming bias in favour of the prisoners.

Dangar admitted that he had not gone to *Myall Creek Station* until after Magistrate Day had been there, despite receiving a letter from William Hobbs about three or four weeks after the murders. He attempted to explain that he had not believed that twenty-eight Aborigines had really been murdered. Plunkett cross-examined Dangar about the fact that he had been dismissed as a government surveyor some years earlier. In response, Dangar insisted that he had merely been suspended, rather than dismissed. At one point, Dangar became so exasperated by the penetrating questions from the prosecutor that he asked Justice Burton whether he had to answer the question, to which Burton replied that he was bound to respond. The questioning went like this.[11]

Plunkett: Were you not dismissed from your situation?
Dangar: I was suspended.

Plunkett: Were you not dismissed. I say, sir? You know what I mean.

Dangar: I was suspended.

Plunkett: Answer me without equivocation, sir! Were you not dismissed, and not suspended, as you want us to believe?

Mr Dangar addressed the Court, wanting to know whether he was bound to answer that question.

Mr Justice Burton replied that he was bound to answer the question.

Dangar: I was a surveyor; I did not ask to be reinstated; perhaps the Secretary of State might have given orders that I was not to be reinstated; perhaps I received a public intimation; it is ten or twelve years ago, and I don't recollect the contents of a letter of so remote a date; I was suspended.

Justice Burton: Mr Dangar, if you were not dismissed, you can have no hesitation in stating so without equivocation.

Dangar: A suspension was tantamount to a dismissal. The Governor ordered my suspension, and perhaps the Secretary of State might have ordered that I was not to be reinstated.

Plunkett also cross-examined Dangar on the fact that he had dismissed William Hobbs after receiving his letter about the massacre, to which Dangar again replied in an equivocal manner, which prompted another response from the judge:

Plunkett: Did you dismiss Mr Hobbs from your employment?

Dangar: Mr Hobbs is not to remain in my service; his time is expired.

Justice Burton: When an answer is given to a question, it is to be fully given without reservation. Was that the only reason of his leaving your service?

Dangar: No, your Honour, and I was going to add, he has not given me satisfaction in the case of my property; that is the only cause.

Plunkett: Was that the only reason?

Dangar: That is the only cause.

Plunkett: Did you ever express any dissatisfaction at Mr Hobbs's conduct in this case?

Dangar: No. I expressed my dissatisfaction at his keeping me in town the other day.

Plunkett: Did you ever tell him or anyone else that you were dissatisfied at his bringing this case forward?

Dangar: No. If this case had not happened I would still have discharged him. I had an intention six months ago of putting an end to his [work] agreement.

Plunkett: Did you tell him that?

Dangar: I did not state so to him.

Plunkett: How long had he been with you?

Dangar: He had been with me two years.

Plunkett: When did his term with you expire?

Dangar: I believe his term expired in October, and I gave him notice in October.

Plunkett: When did you make up your mind to discharge him?

Dangar: I made up my mind six months ago.

Plunkett: Did you tell anyone?

Dangar: I communicated that determination to my own family, but not to him.

Plunkett: When you were going up to your station the last time, [on the way] did you state to Mr Day that you were well pleased with Mr Hobbs?

Dangar: Yes.

Plunkett: When was that?

Dangar: That was in September.

Plunkett: How long was that before you gave him notice that you would terminate his agreement?

Dangar: It was a month before I gave him notice.

Plunkett: Did you tell Mr Day that Hobbs was a man of truth?

Dangar: No, I did not. I said that Mr Hobbs was a respectable young man.

Plunkett: What else did you say to Mr Day?

Dangar: That I was very glad that Mr Day had found my station so regular.

Plunkett: Why didn't you give Mr Hobbs notice of termination of his employment?

Dangar: When Mr Hobbs agreed for [employment for] a year, it was not imperative on me to give him notice. If he had asked me, I should have told him.

Plunkett: Didn't you renew his contract for a second year?

Dangar: I did not come in contact with him in the second year as I did in the first, when I renewed his agreement.

Plunkett then questioned Dangar about the fact that William Hobbs had been arrested on a pretext that very morning for failure to pay his debts:

Plunkett: Were you about the court this morning?

Dangar: Yes.

Plunkett: Did you know that Mr Hobbs was arrested at the court this morning?

Dangar: Some person told me he was arrested, but I did not know that he was to be arrested.

Plunkett then questioned him about the shortage of jurors that morning and the attempt to plant a defence supporter among them:

> *Plunkett: Did you know that there was a scarcity of jurors this morning?*
>
> *Dangar: No.*
>
> *Plunkett: Did you speak to anyone this morning who came for jury service?*
>
> *Dangar: I swear I did not speak to anyone.*
>
> *Plunkett: Did you advise anyone to come to court to get on the jury?*
>
> *Dangar: No.*
>
> *Plunkett: Did you suggest to anyone that he might sit on the jury?*
>
> *Dangar: No, I did not ask anyone why he did not sit on the jury and I did not say to anyone, 'Why did you not sit on the jury and why did you refuse?'*

Plunkett next questioned Dangar about his financial support for the defendants:

> *Plunkett: Have you defrayed any of the expenses of the defendants?*
>
> *Dangar: No, I have not. I subscribed £5 in the month of July or August to defend my servant, who is a faithful one.*
>
> *Plunkett: Why did you subscribe money to defend your servant?*
>
> *Dangar: It was simply because Kilmeister was my servant that I subscribed.*

Plunkett: Would you have subscribed if he had not been your servant?
Dangar: I won't swear that I would not have subscribed if he had not been my servant.
Plunkett: When you subscribed, had you heard the particulars of this matter?
Dangar: No, I had not.

These lines of cross-examination were so effective at destroying Dangar's credibility that the jury would not have given the slightest weight to his evidence supporting Kilmeister or denigrating Anderson. It was quite clear from the judge's interjections that he was singularly unimpressed with Dangar's evidence.

After Dangar had finished, and other witnesses had given character evidence for the other prisoners, William Hobbs was recalled in reply by the prosecutor[12] to say that Anderson had been under his immediate control at all times that he had been at the Big River, and that from his general character he would believe Anderson on his oath. He concluded by saying that Anderson was as good a servant as he had ever met.

***

John Plunkett was extremely bold in taking on Henry Dangar in the way that he did. Dangar was one of the richest and most powerful men in the colony. He had an extensive network of friends and supporters, and the consequences of challenging him in the way that Plunkett did must have been obvious. Plunkett did not hesitate to do so on this occasion, believing that it was essential in the conduct of the trial to demonstrate to the jury how unreliable Dangar's evidence was in supporting Kilmeister's character and detracting from Anderson's. Plunkett's fearlessness in his cross-examination of Dangar was in the best traditions of the Bars of England and Ireland.

At the conclusion of the evidence at 11pm, Justice Burton refused to adjourn the trial until the following day and insisted on commencing his summing up to the jury.

***

Trial procedure in 1838 was quite different to what it is today. At a modern-day trial, at the conclusion of all the evidence, counsel for both sides have the opportunity to make submissions to the jury during closing addresses in which they can suggest how the jury should view the evidence and why a verdict should be reached in their favour. The persuasive power of closing addresses cannot be overstated. However, it was not until October 1840 – nearly two years after the Myall Creek murder trials – that counsel in New South Wales were permitted to address juries at the conclusion of the evidence, despite the fact that it had been permitted in England since 1836.[13] Juries in New South Wales at this time therefore relied very heavily on the judge's summation of the evidence.

***

The tone of Justice Burton's summing up was different to the Chief Justice's at the first trial. He began by suggesting to the jury that they might have the same view as him, which was that 'there was no doubt but a great crime had been committed by someone'. He warned them:

> *Opinions had been formed, and inferences drawn from what had appeared in print, but the jury were, in the solemn situation in which they were then placed, between God, their country, and the prisoners, separated from the community; and they, as well as himself, were bound to hold themselves responsible to God and their country, and not to public opinion.*

He reminded them that the Aborigines were 'equally under the protection of God and the law', and that as jurors they were obliged to maintain 'a rigid regard to the laws of God, and the laws of the country'. He cautioned them:

> *He knew how pleasant it was to have the goodwill of friends, and of the public, but in the conscientious discharge of the duty now imposed on them by the solemn oath they had taken to administer justice, they must discard all private feeling, and guard against the semblance of being biased by any consideration.*

So far as the facts were concerned, Justice Burton impressed upon the jury the enormity of the crime that had been committed:

> *The circumstances of the case presented a fearful barbarity which perhaps had rarely been equalled. Several persons had*

been tied together and shot, and cut and burned, in the most barbarous manner.

He stressed how important it was that everyone was entitled to the protection of the law:

I hope I need not impress on your mind that it matters not in the sight of God or of the law whether that creature has a white or black skin. They are equally liable to the protection of the law.

He reminded them that the Wirrayaraay had done nothing to warrant the attack on them, and hinted not too subtly that proprietary interests had been at stake:

I cannot help noticing (and I have waded through the evidence to find it, if possible) that in this case there had not been the shadow of provocation given by the unfortunate Blacks. If the pecuniary interests of gentlemen [i.e. landowners] require that their servants should go armed, it ought to be impressed upon them that nothing but extreme necessity will warrant their using those arms against their fellow creatures. If the community should ever become so depraved that lives of human creatures are of so little value, and that the Blacks might be indiscriminately killed wherever they are seen, then it would be no wonder that the Colony should be visited by the displeasure and heavy visitations of God. If outrages had been committed by other Blacks down the [Big] river, this tribe has been represented as peaceable. They were in constant contact with the whites and they were peaceably encamped for the night when they were led away to slaughter.

Burton clearly insinuated his own view that Anderson was entirely believable and that Dangar had shown himself to be utterly unreliable:

> *With respect to the evidence of the man Anderson, it has been impeached strongly by Mr Dangar, who from some frivolous cause has stated that he would not believe him on his oath. But if it were allowed that men charged with some trifling disobedience of orders or neglect were to be incapacitated from giving evidence, I am fearful that many crimes, and murders amongst the number, would go unpunished. However, you have heard Mr Hobbs's character of Anderson, and you have also heard Mr Dangar's reason for impeaching the credit of Anderson. You have heard circumstances relative to the misappropriation of land, and you have seen the manner in which Mr Dangar has conducted himself in the box. It is for you to judge whether Anderson's testimony has been impeached or whether Mr Dangar's testimony has not rather been impeached by himself. In any event, Mr Dangar has shown the bias of his mind. He has shown that his opinion had already been formed and that he came before the court prejudiced.*

The judge's summing up concluded at 1am on 30 November. Perhaps in an attempt to encourage the jury to come to a quick decision, Justice Burton insisted on sending them out to consider their verdicts at that hour of the night. They returned to court at 2am and were asked for their verdicts. The extraordinary events that followed were probably a result of the jurors' tiredness after a full, tension-filled day and most of the night in court. The foreman, George Sewell, stood and, in response to the first group of charges – those relating to the murder of an unknown Aboriginal child – he announced verdicts of *not guilty*. The seven defendants heaved a sigh of relief and their counsel looked knowingly at each other and at their clients; this was what they had predicted. Their trial tactics had once again been vindicated. Because these were the charges on which the jury was most likely to convict, Plunkett was gutted by the fresh set of acquittals. However, within a few seconds of these verdicts being announced by the foreman, one of the other jurors, William Knight, jumped up and informed the judge that the foreman had delivered the wrong verdicts and that the correct verdict on each of those charges was *guilty*. After a suitable enquiry of the foreman to confirm that a mistake had in fact been made, the judge entered verdicts of *guilty*. The seven prisoners, who had precipitously lurched from anticipating their freedom to facing their execution, looked pleadingly and in confusion at their representatives at the Bar table, hoping that their counsel could somehow retrieve the previous situation and rescue them from this unexpected nightmare. Plunkett felt an enormous sense of relief, but also a feeling of fragility at how close this jury had come to delivering yet another miscarriage of justice from the point of view of the murdered Aborigines.

The sentencing of the seven convicted prisoners was delayed until after the appeal five days later in front of three Supreme Court judges, who reviewed the decisions of law that had been made before and during the second trial. On 5 December 1838, Chief Justice Dowling and Justices Burton and Willis heard argument from counsel, after Mr Justice Burton assured the court that he had fully explained to his brother judges the nature of the points of law that had been decided during the trial.

This procedure is very different to what happens in an appeal today. A modern-day judge would not sit on an appeal from a trial over which he has presided. That only happened in 1838 because of the shortage of judges. Furthermore, an appeal court today would not rely on the trial judge for an explanation of the points of law that had been raised at the trial, but instead would refer to a transcript of the trial and require written submissions from the parties in advance of the appeal hearing. The three judges had no difficulty confirming the correctness of Justice Burton's decisions of law and, most importantly, determining that the pre-trial, special jury's decision that had allowed the second trial to proceed was not able to be challenged.

After the three judges dismissed the appeal, his Honour Mr Justice Burton put on 'the black cap'[14] and delivered lengthy remarks on sentence. He used the opportunity to make observations that he hoped would have a salutary effect on the wider community of New South Wales.

His Honour said (in part):

> *The circumstances of this murder were marked with a singular atrocity, and I am persuaded that the prisoners, long ago, must have anticipated such a result to their trial. It is not a case of the murder of a single individual – it is not a case of death ensuing from violence committed in a drunken quarrel, many of which has been tried this session, when it appears that blood has flowed and intermixed with the damning liquor. This is not a case where any provocation has been given, which*

might have been pleaded in excuse for the deed. This was not a case where the property or lives of individuals have been attacked, and force has been resorted to, to repel the attack. The murder was not confined to one man, but extended to many, including men, women, children, and babies hanging at their mothers' breasts, in numbers not less than 30 human souls – slaughtered in cool blood. This massacre was committed upon a poor defenceless tribe of Blacks, dragged away from their fires at which they were seated, resting secure in the protection of one of the prisoners. Unsuspecting harm, they were surrounded by a body of horsemen, 12 or 13 in number, from whom they fled to the hut, which provided the mesh of destruction. In that hut the prisoners, unmoved by the tears, groans, and sighs, bound them with cords – fathers, mothers, and children indiscriminately – and carried them away to a short distance, when the scene of slaughter commenced, and stopped not until all were exterminated, with the exception of one woman. I do not mention these circumstances to add to the agony of that moment, but to portray to those standing around the horrors which attended this merciless proceeding, in order, if possible, to avert similar consequences hereafter. It appears that extraordinary pains have been taken by the prisoners, or by some persons deeply interested in the concealment of their crime, to prevent the murder from coming to light. But, it has pleased Almighty God to conduct a person to that heap of human remains, to be a witness of the scene, before the heap was taken away bit by bit, as it evidently had been, to remove every vestige of the murder. The crime was, however, committed in the sight of God, and the blood of the victims cries for vengeance.

> ...
> *The crime was conceived, and not suddenly executed whilst imaginative injuries acted on their minds. It was premeditated, and coolly planned, as appeared by their being seen some time before it was perpetrated at a station further down the river preparing straps, and burnishing their swords. They had called the Saturday previous at* Newton's Station, *avowedly seeking the Blacks, and on the Sunday evening they came on them, thus closing a hallowed day by the perpetration of murder, thus doubly offending their God by selecting His holy day for the commission of this unheard-of barbarity.*

His Honour then passed sentence of death on all seven prisoners. The following day, the *Sydney Gazette* noted:

> *The judge was deeply affected – to tears. His honour was listened to with the deepest attention by a crowded court, and we trust that the remarks which fell from the bench will have the effect they were intended to produce on the audience – of showing them that the black man, like the white man, has a soul to be saved, and that any outrage on the former by the latter will be as soon avenged as would be an outrage on the white man by the black savage.*

***

The public reaction to the sentences was vociferously hostile, and particular venom was directed at the chief prosecutor, John Hubert Plunkett. An editorial in the *Sydney Herald* sought to demonstrate that the law had been applied unfairly because numerous whites had been killed by blacks without any consequences:

> *The men found guilty of the alleged murder of certain aboriginal natives have received sentences of death. Will the Executive government cause that sentence to be carried into execution? This, whatever may be urged on the other side, is a most important question at the present juncture. A contemporary of Thursday last announces his intention to go, at an early day, into a full discussion of what he terms 'the whole aboriginal question'. It needs no discussion: it may be summed up in a few brief sentences: 'Are we to have equal laws? Are the white settlers and their servants, to be protected against the outrages of the blacks? Are blacks to be hanged for murder as well as whites? And if so, what steps have been taken to apprehend and hang the scores of black murderers who have shed the blood of white British subjects?'*[15]

The *Sydney Herald* listed the murders of whites by Aborigines in the Liverpool Plains District that had occurred in recent times without anyone being charged, and then commented on the death sentences passed on the seven whites:

> *The men may be guilty – they may be innocent; but take which view of the case we may, the principle for which we contend is in no way altered. The law is unequal, and while it is so – while the murder of so many whites has been unavenged, it is nothing short of legal murder to take the lives of white men for the alleged slaying of blacks. Upon the heads of the various governments of this Colony all this shedding of blood will fall.*

> *No attempt has been made, by means of a properly organised force on the frontiers of the Colony, to keep the blacks in subjection, by means, simply, of intimidation; and thereby protect the white settlers and their servants.*

The twelve jurors who were responsible for the convictions faced hostility from the community and even from their families. George Sewell was told that he was 'a bloody rogue for finding the prisoners guilty' and that William Knight, the juror who had alerted Justice Burton to the incorrect verdicts, 'ought to have had his brains knocked out' for standing up in Court.[16]

Three petitions calling for mercy were submitted to the Governor and the Executive Council, which had the power to remit the sentences. The first petition was from eleven of the jurors who had served at the first trial, and the second came from ten of the jurors at the second trial. The latter, who had been responsible for the convictions, expressed the view that 'the ends of justice have been satisfied by the prisoners' condemnation and long imprisonment'. A third petition had been signed by about 450 residents of Sydney, Parramatta and Windsor. Membership of the Executive Council included the Anglican Bishop of Australia, William Broughton, and the Chief Justice, James Dowling, who had presided over the first trial. The Council met on 14 December and rejected the petitions.

There was so much agitation on behalf of the condemned men that the Governor thought there might be civil unrest on the day of the executions, and so he made special arrangements with Mr Henry Keck, the gaolkeeper at the Sydney Gaol in George Street, in case there was a need to 'repress any violence, should any be attempted on behalf of the condemned men by the mob, which was not deemed improbable, on account of the degree of excitement which the case had occasioned in the public mind'.[17] Right up until the morning of the executions, there was public conjecture that the condemned men would receive a reprieve from the Governor – but none was forthcoming.

On the day of the executions, Tuesday, 18 December 1838, shortly before 9am, a guard of eighteen men of the 59th regiment under the command of Lieutenant Sheaffe arrived at the gaol and immediately afterwards the Sheriff, Thomas Macquoid, appeared. The seven condemned men – Charles Kilmeister, John Russell, Edward Foley, James Oates, John Johnstone, William Hawkins and James Parry – who ranged in age from twenty-three to thirty-five, had already spent time with their religious advisers, who comforted them and received their confessions. The Protestants were attended by Reverend Mr Cowper and Mr Hyndes and the Catholics by Reverend F Murphy. When the clock struck nine, the procession began to move towards the scaffold. It was reported that:

> *Russell was much agitated, and he was obliged to cling to the Priest's coat for support … Foley, who was the youngest of the culprits, requested [the Sheriff] Mr Thomas Macquoid for permission to embrace his companions, and the request being complied with, they kissed and shook each other's hands and with eyes streaming with tears, bade each other a last adieu. They shook hands with Mr Keck and embraced Mr Hibbs, the turnkey, and then knelt down and proceeded with their devotions, at the close of which they mounted the scaffold, attended by the clergymen who continued to exhort them while the final preparations were being completed. These done, the Rev*

> *Gentlemen and the executioners descended from the scaffold, and in the short interval that followed previously to the falling of the drop, the cries of the men to God for mercy were distinctly audible, and they were soon launched into eternity.*[18]

One of the many witnesses to the hangings was a Mr JH Bannatyne, who was so shocked by the experience that, on returning home, he immediately wrote a note to a friend saying:

> *I have just returned from seeing the seven men all launched into eternity at the same moment. It was an awful sight and has made me feel quite sick – I shall never forget it.*[19]

It was later reported to the gaolkeeper, Mr Keck, and through him to Governor Gipps, that all seven men had confessed their guilt to their respective religious advisers.[20] Their confessions, however, were qualified by a disturbing, but no doubt truthful, explanation. Mr Keck informed the Sheriff that:

> *Frequently, during their confinement here, they each and all, at different times, acknowledged to me their guilt, but implied that it was done solely in defence of their Masters' property, that they were not aware that in destroying the Aborigines they were violating the law, as it had, according to their belief, been so frequently done in the Colony before.*[21]

13

CONSEQUENCES

The press and public reactions to the hangings of the seven stockmen for the murders at Myall Creek were in the main overtly hostile to the prosecutor, John Hubert Plunkett, who was looked upon as the perpetrator of a crime worse than what had occurred at Myall Creek.[1] The *Sydney Herald* accused him of placing the prisoners 'twice in jeopardy on the same charge', and called on him to resign. Sir George Gipps was petitioned to remove Plunkett from office in order to avoid any further 'miscarriage of justice'; however, the Governor stood by his Attorney. The most common view about the case among whites of every class and status was that no white person should ever hang for the murder of a black. Plunkett was the object of hatred from many, diverse sections of the community, but none more so than the squatters beyond the limits of location. This antipathy endured for years.

For many months after the second Myall Creek murder trial, the fate of the four remaining prisoners – James Lamb, John Blake, George Palliser and Charles Toulouse – hung in the balance. In late December 1838, following the execution of the seven from the second trial, Plunkett applied to have the trial of the remaining four postponed until the next sitting of the Court in early 1839. The basis of his application was an affidavit from William Hobbs that stated that an Aboriginal boy named Davy, who was now nineteen, had told him that he had stood behind a tree and witnessed the murders of the Aboriginal men, women and children. The affidavit further stated that Davy could speak English and, in the opinion of Hobbs, might be 'sufficiently instructed so as to become a competent witness'.

The problem was that Davy, as an Aborigine, was legally disentitled to give evidence unless and until he had been given some 'instruction in the ordinances of religion' so as to be able to take an oath on the Christian Bible. This entailed a basic education in a belief system of rewards and punishments in the afterlife and the dire spiritual consequences of lying under oath. It was submitted to the court by the Attorney General that, if the trial was adjourned, there would be sufficient time for the instruction of Davy to take place. The application for an adjournment was granted.

The *Sydney Herald* predictably criticised Plunkett for his intention to put Davy in the witness box:

> *Will a young savage, who must be instructed as a parrot would be instructed, be admitted to give evidence in a case*

of life and death? Does any rational man suppose that such evidence be anything but one-sided? ... We trust that should any such witness be pushed into the witness box, that the Counsel for the defence will probe his competency to the quick, and not permit the possibility of four men's lives being frittered away upon the statements of a young black savage, possessing no more idea of ultimate responsibility than a baboon.[2]

Two months later, on 14 February 1839, the four remaining prisoners appeared before Chief Justice Dowling. Plunkett informed the Court that Davy was an essential witness for the Crown, and although two months had elapsed Davy had not yet been instructed in the nature of an oath. Upon the Chief Justice enquiring whether there was any chance of Davy being sufficiently instructed, Plunkett admitted that he knew of no instance in which an Aboriginal person had been sufficiently instructed to the point of being able to appear as a witness in a trial. He acknowledged that there was insufficient evidence against John Blake and that he should immediately be freed. So far as the other three prisoners were concerned, Plunkett had no objection to them being granted bail pending a further adjournment to allow Davy to be instructed. Chief Justice Dowling freed Blake and, realising that it was unlikely that the other three would ever face trial, released them on bail and added this salutary addendum:

If you are not brought to justice, there is still that small voice which will without fail admonish you. If your conscience does accuse you, I hope you will repent and atone to God for any part that you might have taken in the bloody affray with which you have been charged.

***

The reality behind the failure to 'instruct' Davy was that the young Aboriginal man had disappeared without trace and was never to be seen again. Missionary to the Aborigines, Lancelot Threlkeld, was of the view that Henry Dangar had arranged for Davy 'to be put out of the way'.[3] In all likelihood, Davy was murdered by one of Dangar's henchmen. Plunkett felt a terrible sense of guilt that, having informed the Court that he would rely on Davy as a witness and having admitted that he had no case without him, he had effectively signed the man's death warrant.

Plunkett faced a severe dilemma. Without Davy as a witness to the murders, he would have the same challenge as before to prove the identity of another victim. The public mood was firmly against any further prosecutions. Governor Gipps had been affected by the public hostility to the convictions and executions and had lost enthusiasm for a further trial. Plunkett acknowledged to himself that if he went to trial again, the defendants would undoubtedly raise the issue of their prior acquittals, and another special jury might find that the four remaining prisoners were entitled to rely upon the earlier verdict. Even if he won the right to put them on trial again, he would likely face a hostile jury reluctant to convict in light of the seven earlier executions. Having won the second trial, the last thing he wanted was a contradictory verdict of acquittal at a third trial that would challenge the correctness of the earlier convictions. Plunkett felt that he had adequately made his point that Aboriginal lives were as valuable as white ones, and he did not want to run the risk of diminishing that message by failing to get convictions on the same evidence at a third trial.

Plunkett was recorded as saying that he could not 'risk public justice'. From this remark, it is apparent that he acknowledged, if only to himself, that the convictions in the second trial were fortuitous and unlikely to be repeated. If a trial of the remaining four stockmen were held, he could hardly rely on the same tactic of suggesting an unfavourable inference from the failure to call the other perpetrators, who had been put to death. Did he acknowledge, if only to himself, that in the second trial he had placed the seven stockmen in double jeopardy? Did he perceive that he had ignored the presumption of innocence and reversed the onus of proof? Whatever his thoughts, Plunkett's balancing of the benefits and detriments of a third trial were heavily weighted against it.

***

As a result of the community backlash to the executions, the Governor lost much of his political will to continue any other prosecutions of a similar nature. By mid-1839, Gipps and the Executive Council had decided not to press any charges against Major Nunn for the Waterloo Creek massacre in January 1838. Governor Gipps did, however, establish a special force of 'Border Police', which had as its stated purpose putting an end to the atrocities being committed by both races in the squatting districts. The Border Police, in fact, focussed mainly on protecting white settlers and their stock, and were responsible for their own massacres of Aborigines in the years to come.[4] In May 1839, Gipps finally issued an edict enforcing his instructions from London of the previous year:

> *As human beings partaking of our common nature – as the Aboriginal possessors of the soil from which the wealth of this country has been principally derived – and as the subjects of the Queen, whose authority extends over every part of New Holland – the natives of this Colony have an equal right with the people of European origin to the protection and assurance of the Law of England.*[5]

The Australian Aborigines' Protection Society, which had been established in October 1838 following the arrests of the eleven stockmen, lost momentum and quickly disappeared.[6]

***

It should be noted that the Myall Creek massacre was one of a large number of mass murders of indigenous people committed in the early decades of the colony. The only reason so much is known about this particular incident is because it was one of the very few cases in which any of the perpetrators were brought to justice, and hence it was extensively documented. Numerous other mass murders were committed with complete impunity and were even sanctioned by the authorities.[7]

The struggle for scarce resources between the immigrant and the indigenous populations in colonial New South Wales resulted in so many indigenous deaths on so many occasions and at so many locations over more than a century[8] that one can only come to the depressing conclusion that racial conflict is endemic to the human species. The differences in force of arms between the two populations resulted in many more deaths on the indigenous side, so that whole tribes, like the Wirrayaraay, were decimated and some even exterminated throughout the Australian colonies. Similar outcomes for indigenous communities have occurred in many parts of the world and in many ages. The prosecution of the eleven men responsible for the Myall Creek massacre was not only a rare event in the Australian colonies, but indeed in the history of European colonialism.

Following the two trials of the perpetrators of the Myall Creek murders, despite the admonitions of Justice Burton, the murders of Indigenous people continued unabated, and extended well into the twentieth century. However, the preferred method of extermination changed and greater care was taken to prevent atrocities coming to the attention of the authorities. The two trials in 1838 pushed the murders of Aborigines underground, so that instead of roaming gangs killing Aborigines by acts of violence, malevolent landowners and their agents preferred to leave poisoned food for them or to contaminate their waterholes. Mass murders by violence did still occur, but greater care was taken to dispose of bodies and remove all evidence. Some of these atrocities were committed by the Border Police, which had been established to protect the Indigenous population. Those responsible for the murders of Aborigines no longer bragged openly about their exploits, and instead only whispered about them to co-offenders and trusted associates.

14

LEAVE, LONDON AND THE END OF TRANSPORTATION

Within two days of the execution of the Myall Creek defendants in December 1838, John Plunkett sought the Governor's permission to go on leave so as to return to Ireland. He was weary from the ordeal of the trials and worn down by the constant criticism in the press and the public arena. He was also tired from the relentless duties of office that he had performed since his arrival in the colony six years earlier. He had in mind that on arriving in London he would explore a number of options, which included: a government posting in his native Ireland or even in England; a posting to another colony; or a return to New South Wales. Maria Plunkett was adamant that her preferred option was to return home permanently.

It was more than two years before Governor Gipps was able to release John Plunkett to return home. The main difficulty was the impossibility of finding someone suitably qualified to take over Plunkett's dual role as Attorney General and Solicitor General on the salary of only one position. In fact, the Governor was unable even to find someone willing to do both jobs on a double salary. Governor Gipps' preferred candidate for acting Attorney General was Roger Therry, who was willing to take over the position if someone else was offered the post of acting Solicitor General. However, London was unwilling to pay both salaries. The deadlock prevented John and Maria from leaving Sydney for a lengthy time.

***

While waiting for the Governor to resolve these difficulties, John Plunkett was still smarting from the injustice of having been unable to call Davy, the only eyewitness to the murders at Myall Creek, and he resolved to provide a remedy for the inability of Aboriginal inhabitants to give evidence in the courts. Ideally, he would have preferred a Bill to allow Aborigines to give unsworn evidence in all cases, but, recognising the difficulty of winning acceptance in the Legislative Council for any such measure, Plunkett settled on a more modest proposal for Aboriginal men and women to be permitted to give evidence in court where their testimony could be corroborated by the sworn evidence of non-indigenous witnesses. The *Aboriginal Evidence Bill* was passed by a majority in the Legislative Council on 8 October 1839. However, Chief Justice Dowling advised the Governor that the measure was contrary to the rules of evidence in England, and therefore liable to be rejected by London under the doctrine of repugnancy. So, the Bill was remitted by the Governor to the English Attorney General, with this explanation:

> *The measure was introduced at the desire of the Attorney General, in consequence of the difficulty in obtaining convictions which he experienced in several cases, wherein native blacks have been concerned, either as the accused or the injured party, and the dissatisfaction which has been expressed in the colony when a criminal has escaped.*[1]

The English Attorney General obtained the opinion of two eminent English barristers, who advised that the proposed provision was 'contrary to the principles of British jurisprudence'. Their rationale was this:

> *To admit in a criminal case the evidence of a witness acknowledged to be ignorant of the existence of a God or a future state would be contrary to the principles of British jurisprudence; and the Act is loosely worded with respect to the admission of such evidence and the weight to be given to it that we do not think it could be attended with any advantage.*[2]

The disallowance of the *Aboriginal Evidence Bill* was conveyed in a dispatch dated 11 August 1840 from Lord John Russell in London to Governor Gipps in Sydney. The result was that Aborigines remained excluded as witnesses in the colonial courts of New South Wales. Governor Gipps received the disallowance of the legislation most unfavourably because it allowed whites to continue perpetrating crimes against Aborigines with impunity.[3] It also resulted in many Aboriginal defendants being unjustifiably acquitted because it was acknowledged that they were unable to provide a defence to a charge.

The ineligibility of Aborigines to give evidence was one of the reasons why white colonials were able to continue their murderous activities against the Indigenous population. In 1842, George Augustus Robinson, the Chief Protector of Aborigines, wrote to Governor Gipps:

> *At present the evidence of Aboriginal natives, by reason of their ignorance of the knowledge of God, is inadmissible in our courts of law; and hence, properly qualified religious instructors, to impart to them the truths of Christianity, and prepare them for the reception of their legal rights, as proposed by the Right honourable the Secretary of State, is, in consequence, absolutely needed. It were much to be regretted that the Colonial Act of Council on Aboriginal evidence was disallowed, for it frequently happens that for want of this evidence the highest and foulest crimes go unpunished.*[4]

The following year Robinson again pointed out that:

> *There is … reason to fear that the destruction of the Aboriginal natives has been accelerated from the known fact of their being incapacitated to give evidence in our courts of law. I have frequently had to deplore, when applied to by the Aborigines for justice in cases of aggression committed on them by white men, or by those of their own race, my inability to do so in consequence of their legal incapacity to give evidence.*[5]

***

Prior to his departure for England, Plunkett was once again involved in a case in which an Aboriginal inhabitant was denied justice because of his ineligibility to give evidence. The case involved an Aboriginal man known as 'Neville's Billy', who in November 1840 was charged with the murder of John Dillon at Ullabalong near Yass by spearing him.[6] There was a real question as to the identity of the murderer, as there had been a group of Aborigines in the vicinity at the time of the spearing. Plunkett opened the Crown case by explaining:

> *There were no cases of a more painful description than those against the Aborigines, who, from their ignorance of our language, manners and customs, as well as of our laws, could only take their trial at a disadvantage, as the state of the law prevented them from calling on others of their tribe to give evidence in their defence.*

The only real evidence against Billy was a verbal dying declaration made by the deceased, John Dillon, to William Jackson, an illiterate border policeman, a short time before Dillon died of his injuries. Being illiterate, Jackson had been unable to write down the dying declaration and was therefore forced to give evidence of it from memory at the trial eight months later:

> *'The prisoner speared him through the window of the hut under the arm-pit of the left arm, and then the person who speared him looked in through the window and said, "ah, ah!" I believe he said it was Neville's Billy who speared him.'*

Jackson also testified to a conversation in pidgin English with Neville's Billy when he arrested him several months after the murder:

> *'I said to prisoner, "what for you tumble down [kill] Waddy Monday?" (the black name given the deceased from his having a wooden leg) when he said that Billy, Paddy, Puckamulloi, Woagli, and Pialla [all other members of the accused's tribe] told him to kill the deceased.'*

On the defence side, Billy's Aboriginal companions, who presumably had witnessed the events in question, were unable to be called because of their inability to take the oath. The trial judge, Chief Justice Dowling, gave this grave warning to the jurors during a summing up which was clearly aimed at securing an acquittal:

> *'They were a jury of intelligent, British subjects, called on to administer justice to a savage, who was ignorant of the language, laws, and customs of civilized life; and [he] called on them to mark the situation in which the prisoner and the judges were placed in such trials. By a fiction of law he was amenable to British law. He was accused of the murder of a British subject, a white man, one of a race of men who had seized on his native land. He was by fiction of law, a British subject, and as such was entitled to be tried by his peers, his equals. Were the jury his equals? Did they know his language, his habits, or his customs? He took his trial under many disadvantages, so much so, that he was not in a situation to conduct his own defence – he could not even instruct his counsel. He might have witnesses, but they, by*

> *a legal technicality, not being Christians, would not be admitted to give evidence, and therefore it was that he said the prisoner took his trial under great disadvantages. It was in fact a one-sided trial, and therefore, he called upon the jurors, as Britons and Christians, to lay aside all prejudices, and give every attention to the evidence, which was not of that kind usually brought to support such cases.'*

Despite these severe admonitions, the jury convicted Billy of murder. The Chief Justice had no option under the law but to sentence him to death. John Plunkett, aghast at the injustice of the trial, pleaded for mercy, and Billy's death sentence was commuted by the Executive Council.[7]

The case reinforced the need to urgently reform the law to allow Aborigines to give unsworn evidence in the courts.

***

While Governor Gipps was waiting to find a temporary replacement for his Attorney General, the British government finally ended convict transportation to New South Wales. In both Britain and Australia during the 1830s, it had increasingly been acknowledged that transportation had an evil side that could only be avoided by abolition. The anti-slavery movement had achieved success by the passing of the *Slavery Abolition Act*, which progressively unwound slavery in the British Empire between 1833 and 1840. As slavery disappeared, those who had worked for its abolition focused their attentions on ending transportation. It had been mooted in the colony for more than a decade, with those who had benefitted the most from free labour predictably being the most vocal against abolition. With increasing numbers of free migrants, colonial society was anxious to be free of the hated 'convict stain'. Predictably, the major newspapers took opposing sides in a vigorous debate on the topic. Surprisingly, considering his liberal views on other issues, but also unsurprisingly, considering his extensive land holdings, one of the most vocal supporters of transportation was WC Wentworth. One of the greatest opponents of transportation was John Fairfax, who in 1841 became the proprietor of the *Sydney Herald*. John Plunkett was firmly in the camp of the abolitionists.

In New South Wales, it was predominantly the urban workers, both free men and emancipists, who opposed transportation, claiming that there was now a sufficiently large body of non-convict labour to service the needs of the colony. They feared, quite justifiably, that a continuing supply of free convict labour would undermine their employability and wages. As the British penal code was relaxed during the 1830s, those who were transported tended to be the more serious offenders, and increasingly there were fears expressed in all strata of Australian society that a continuation of transportation would increase the crime rate. The 1834 murder of prominent citizen Dr Robert Wardell by a serial convict offender in bush near the doctor's home at Petersham caused a massive outcry against further transportation. By 1840, the forces against transportation were overwhelming.

Meanwhile, in England in 1837, the *House of Commons Select Committee on Transportation* was established to advise the government on the future of transportation. Its head, Sir William Molesworth, was sympathetic to the causes of colonial self-government and the abolition of slavery, and this had a significant impact on how he conducted the Committee.[8] Evidence was received about the unpredictable nature of the convict assignment system. In its report in August 1838, the Committee concluded that transportation was not an effective deterrent to crime, that private assignments were iniquitous, and that the system of secondary punishment by flogging was retrograde. The report observed that a convict might be 'well fed, well clothed, and well treated by a kind and indulgent master, or he may be the wretched, praedial [relating to land] slave of some harsh master, compelled by the lash to work'. Molesworth relied heavily on the incidence of lashings to argue that the convict system was akin to slavery, which had been abolished in 1833. In a similar vein, his report quoted Governor Bourke's statement that the disciplinary laws of New South Wales, enabling single magistrates to order up to fifty lashes for insolence and other minor offences, amounted to a 'slave code'.[9] The committee recommended that transportation should cease as soon as possible.

On 22 May 1840, with a reformist Whig government in office, an Order-in-Council of the Privy Council removed New South Wales from the list of places to which convicts could be sent.[10] The order acknowledged: the dependence of the early colony on convict labour for its establishment, survival and expansion; the brutal convict origins of Australia; and the cessation of transportation arising from concerns that it was not a deterrent to crime and not a fair punishment for minor transgressions. Between 1788 and 1840, more than 80 000 convicts had been sent to New South Wales. About 85 per cent were men and 15 per cent women.

Almost two-thirds were English (along with a small number of Scottish and Welsh), with the Irish making up the remaining third. Many were first offenders who had been convicted of minor property offences. The assignment of convicts to private settlers formally ended the following year. New South Wales had officially ceased to be a penal settlement and could now more effectively move towards becoming a free, democratic and self-governing society.

***

John and Maria Plunkett waited patiently in Sydney for more than two years before the Governor finally found a temporary solution by appointing Roger Therry as acting Attorney General and William à Beckett as acting Solicitor General. Just prior to their departure, a public dinner was held in John Plunkett's honour, described as 'the grandest and most respectable event ever given in the colony'.[11] By then, much of the public opprobrium from the Myall Creek murder trials had died down. Plunkett was presented with a silver entrée dish inscribed: 'Presented to John Hubert Plunkett, Esq., M.L.C., Attorney General, By the People of New South Wales as a token of respect for his Public Character and esteem for his Private Worth, Sydney, March, AD 1841' together with the Plunkett coat of arms and crest.[12]

John and Maria finally set sail on the *Kelso* in March 1841.

***

John Plunkett's time in Great Britain was not all relaxation and pleasure. He used the opportunity to lobby the Colonial Office in London for legislation to make the New South Wales Legislative Council more democratic, so that it would consist of a majority of elected representatives. Previously, the Council had consisted only of unelected, 'ex officio' members who held high office in the colony and a few wealthy landowners chosen by the Governor. Plunkett advocated to the Colonial Secretary in favour of a wide franchise, however the influence of the Exclusives prevailed in their wish to restrict the right to vote to those of substantial property. What resulted from Plunkett's lobbying was the Imperial *New South Wales Act* of 1842, which enlarged the Legislative Council to thirty-six seats, of which twenty-four were elected and only twelve appointed by the Governor. Plunkett played a major role in assisting George William Hope,[13] the Under-Secretary of State for the Colonies, to draft the Bill, and Plunkett was given an opportunity to review the final version of the legislation before it was submitted to the Parliament at Westminster. In these ways he played a significant role in convincing the British Government to introduce the first steps towards responsible, democratic, self-government in the colony. Secretary of State Stanley later wrote to Governor Gipps:

> *I have also gladly availed myself of the presence in this country of the Attorney General of New South Wales, to obtain the benefit of his local knowledge and experience in the arrangement of many points of detail. Under these circumstances the Bill has passed without a dissenting voice through both Houses of Parliament.*[14]

It was later said:

> *Mr Plunkett was repeatedly consulted by the Secretary of State for the Colonies relative to the Bill for the Government of New South Wales, then being prepared for introduction into the House of Commons; and we have cause to know that much deference was paid to his opinions; and that it is to the suggestions made by him that many of the best features of the Act are attributable; particularly in the amendment of its qualification and disqualification clauses.*[15]

While in England in 1843 Plunkett was also instrumental in lobbying the British Parliament to pass the *Colonial Evidence Act* that empowered individual colonies to enact local Aboriginal evidence Bills, granting Aborigines the right to give unsworn evidence in courts. It was now permissible for New South Wales to enact such legislation, and Plunkett fully intended to introduce it if and when he returned to the colony. But, would the colonial legislators rise to the occasion?

While in the British Isles, Plunkett made subtle enquiries to see if he might be offered a suitable position in England or Ireland. However, he soon realised that the prospective positions in either location were far lower in standing than his existing position in New South Wales, and, in fact, no offers were forthcoming. At the time, Ireland was in a parlous economic state and there were few jobs. Having completed his private affairs and his lobbying activities, John, and a disillusioned, reluctant Maria, set sail for Sydney in April 1843.

***

John Plunkett arrived back in Sydney in August 1843 to find that William à Beckett had been confirmed as Solicitor General. The main reason that Governor Gipps chose à Beckett over Roger Therry was that he considered it undesirable from the point of view of public perception to have both senior law offices held by Catholics. John Plunkett resumed his post as Attorney General.

At the earliest opportunity, in 1844, Plunkett set about convincing the Legislative Council to pass an Act – now permitted by English law – allowing Aborigines to give unsworn evidence in court if their testimony was corroborated by a witness who had taken an oath. Plunkett addressed the Legislative Council in strong terms, pointing out that massacres had gone unpunished. His speech was reported in the *Sydney Morning Herald*:

> *The motive he [Plunkett] had in bringing in this measure was to put an end to bloodshed, and murder, and crimes which he feared were but too frequently perpetrated, but which escaped detection and punishment because the Aboriginal natives were excluded from the witness box. The crimes he feared were much more frequent than they would be, if the parties knew that they could not commit them with impunity. To this day, however great an outrage was committed upon the Aborigines or by them, the guilty parties could not be brought to justice unless there was one or more white men to give evidence as to the facts. Murder might be committed with impunity, and as he had said before, frequently was. Many cases had been brought forward which were sufficiently clear to him, but there was not legal evidence to go to a jury; in some cases indeed, the parties had been prosecuted, and convictions had been*

obtained, but it was not without the greatest difficulty, and this because the Aborigines who were witnesses of the crime were not permitted to make their statements in Court. The Imperial Parliament, when they passed the Act authorising the Council to pass such a measure as this, had all the circumstances of the case before them; they were well informed as to the nature and character of the Aborigines, and in the preamble of the Act they were characterised as uncivilised, barbarous, without any religious impressions, without any idea of a God, and without belief in a future state of rewards or punishment; and it was on this account that the Act of Parliament did not go the length of authorising the Council to place them on an equal footing with ordinary witnesses, but merely raised them to the level of approvers[informers]; their testimony was only to be regarded so far as it was corroborated by other evidence, and there were many cases in which the ends of justice were defeated, but in which it would not have been so if the statements of the Aborigines had been received, as those statements would have been fully borne out by competent witnesses.[16]

Plunkett went on to describe – somewhat inaccurately – the problems he had experienced nearly six years earlier in the prosecutions of those responsible for the Myall Creek murders. According to the report:

He [Plunkett] would mention one case only, which occurred in the neighbourhood of the Big River. Some eleven or twelve stockmen had been scouring the bush for some days in search of a tribe of blacks; about sunset one evening they came up with a tribe, although not the one which they were looking for;

the blacks were assembled around their fire, camped for the night; a rope was immediately put around the whole of them, twenty-four in number, and they were led away to a place about a mile and a half distant, where there were discovered signs which left no doubt that they had been most inhumanly massacred. But of this fearful slaughter there was no living witness except one, besides the perpetrators of the deed, and that one was inadmissible as a witness. That one was an Aborigine, distinguished from others as a tame black, having been for some time domesticated with some shepherds in the neighbourhood of the scene of slaughter. These shepherds, anticipating what was about to take place, but afraid to show themselves, sent this black to watch the murderers; and he contrived unseen, to get behind a tree on a slight eminence near the scene of slaughter, and witnessed the whole of the horrible affair. If this man's evidence could have been received, the shepherds would have been able to corroborate it; they would have deposed to the previous circumstances, to the leading away of the blacks, and to then sending the tame black to watch the proceedings, and they could have given evidence as to his conduct afterwards, so that the case would have been brought home to the guilty parties; but as the law was, the crime remained unpunished.

The newspaper concluded:

He [Plunkett] did not apprehend that much danger could arise to others from the admission of Aborigines as witnesses. The juries of this country would be well able to judge what weight should be attached to the evidence of the blacks. There were but too many whites in this colony who were utterly

> *unworthy of belief, even on their oaths and the juries of the country showed that they know well how to appreciate such evidence, by throwing it entirely out of their consideration. It was only just, he considered, that the Aborigines, however ignorant, however barbarous, should be protected from outrages on their persons and their lives, and this protection would in some measure be afforded by allowing their statements to be received in Courts of Justice, although those statements should not, on the other hand, be allowed to have any weight at all, unless fully corroborated. In the same way as Judges cautioned juries against receiving the evidence of approvers [informers], when that evidence was uncorroborated, so juries would be cautioned against receiving that of Aborigines; and the effect of the Bill, if passed, would be to restrain parties from committing outrages on the blacks, who now calculated on being able to commit them with impunity.*

In reply, Robert Lowe, barrister and member of the Legislative Council, said that the Bill would risk the lives of white people to the uncertain consciences of Aborigines. William Charles Wentworth attacked Plunkett personally by referring to his enduring criticism of the execution of those convicted of the Myall Creek killings by labelling them as 'legal murder' and a 'violation of every principle of law and justice'.[17] Despite the imprimatur of London, the Legislative Council rejected the Bill. For the second time, John Hubert Plunkett had sought to provide the Aboriginal population with access to the courts, and once again he had failed to convince his contemporaries of the desirability and fairness of this reform.

The failure of the 1844 Bill was, according to Professor Bruce Kercher, a reaction to the Myall Creek murder trials six years earlier:

> *The murders at Myall Creek had become a focus of the debate about law on the frontiers of New South Wales. Each side clung to its version of the second trial's outcome. The 1844 Bill failed largely because the majority believed an injustice had been done to the murderers and because of an irrational belief that the Bill would encourage further Aboriginal attacks. The formal legal position was that Aborigines were British subjects, but New South Wales was left without any means to begin to give them access to the British version of justice. They were subjects without enforceable rights.*[18]

In 1849, Plunkett tried for a third time to introduce a Bill for the admission of Aboriginal evidence, but again the Legislative Council rejected it. Plunkett could not understand the reluctance of his fellow legislators to allow this simple measure to be introduced, particularly because, in the meantime, South Australia and Western Australia had passed legislation permitting Aborigines to give evidence. It would not be until many decades later, in fact only in 1876, that New South Wales would finally allow Aboriginal persons to give evidence in courts, despite the fact that England had expressly permitted such legislation since 1843.

***

Within a year of Plunkett's return, the Chief Justice, Sir James Dowling, unexpectedly retired due to ill health, and shortly afterwards died. As the leader of the Bar, John Plunkett considered that he had first claim to fill the vacant position, due to what he claimed was a convention in England. However, he had a serious rival for the post in Justice Alfred Stephen, who in 1839 had come from Van Diemen's Land and taken an acting Supreme Court judgeship in Sydney, which had been made permanent while Plunkett was overseas.

John Plunkett and Alfred Stephen were both forty-two, they held similarly progressive views, and each had had an outstanding legal career to date. Plunkett had harboured a desire to one day be appointed Chief Justice since soon after his arrival in the colony. The idea of a Catholic taking office as Chief Justice anywhere in the British Empire appealed to his sense of vindicating history. He had faithfully served in public office for twelve years and had a good working relationship with Governor Gipps. Stephen, on the other hand, was an Anglican, whose father, John Stephen, had been one of the first Supreme Court Judges of the colony. Stephen also had the advantage that his cousin, James Stephen, was the Under-Secretary of the Colonial Office in London. John Plunkett and Alfred Stephen each thought that he had a superior claim to the position of Chief Justice, and the competition between them was intense for many months. Governor Gipps could not decide between them, so he left it to the Executive Council to make the final choice. Was this a convenient way of not alienating either of these two men, each of whom had contributed greatly to the colony? Did he know what way the Council would go, and wished to avoid the appearance of partisanship?

Apart from the Governor, there were four members of the Executive Council, all of whom were Protestant. The most influential was the Anglican Lord Bishop, William Broughton, who was implacably opposed to Plunkett and had openly declared that while he had a say in the matter a Catholic would never obtain a seat on the Bench in New South Wales. The next member was Campbell Riddell, who was the Colonial Treasurer. Riddell's appointment had been responsible for the departure of Governor Bourke, with whom Plunkett had worked so closely. The third was General Maurice O'Connell, the Commander of [Military] Forces, who, although he was a second cousin of Daniel O'Connell, was a Protestant with completely different political views to his famous Irish relative. The fourth member of the Council was Edward Deas Thompson, the Colonial Secretary. It came to a decision in the Executive Council on 7 October 1844. The Governor abstained and Stephen had three votes to Plunkett's one. When the decision was announced, it was met with general approval in the local newspapers, and it was finally confirmed by Lord Stanley in the Colonial Office in London in April 1845.

Plunkett was severely stung by the decision. Gipps offered him a position on the Bench as a puisne (standard) judge, but Plunkett would have none of it. If he could not be Chief Justice, he would not be a judge at all. He believed that New South Wales had lost an opportunity to show the Empire that real progress had been made in the equality of all citizens, regardless of their religion. Plunkett remained as Attorney General and the vacancy on the Supreme Court was filled by his co-religionist, Roger Therry, who, by his appointment, finally eclipsed his fellow countryman and erstwhile leader in professional rank.

William à Becket was appointed as resident judge in Port Phillip (Melbourne).[19] To his credit, Plunkett did not allow the decision to affect his long-term support of and respect for the new Chief Justice. Alfred Stephen went on to have a most illustrious and constructive career as Chief Justice for the next thirty years, winning universal respect and admiration. Nor did Plunkett's relationship with Therry suffer from the windfall appointment that the latter had received. In fact, after Therry went onto the Bench, their relationship improved.[20] Maybe, now that they were not frequent opponents at the Bar table, they were able to relate more readily as equals.

By passing over John Plunkett as Chief Justice, Governor Gipps and his Executive Council lost an opportunity to place the Colony of New South Wales at the forefront of religious tolerance and emancipation in the British Empire. New South Wales would not have a Catholic Chief Justice until 1988.[21]

***

Despite the abolition of transportation in 1840, during the ensuing years Britain gave ongoing consideration to its reintroduction as a way of avoiding the cost of building gaols in England. In New South Wales a huge majority of the population were against any reintroduction. Most of the community saw the future of the colony as a prosperous, vibrant, free, self-governing society rather than as a penal outpost of the mother country. However, there was continuing support in favour of resumption from a few of the larger landowners who were well represented on the Legislative Council, including WC Wentworth, who still exercised considerable political and economic power, and Henry Dangar, who had been elected to the Council in 1845. They were entirely motivated by self-interest and the prospect of further free labour. Henry Dangar's views were criticised by his local newspaper in the Hunter Valley:

> *Dangar has shown that he is one of those who are prepared to uphold the pecuniary interests of the woolgrower and the employer of labour at any sacrifice; he is for the resumption of transportation in any shape – either the old or the new, and has no objection to the importation of cannibals or coolies, providing that a profit can be extracted out of their labour.*[22]

In 1846, a Select Committee of the Legislative Council, chaired by WC Wentworth, was established to explore the issue. Plunkett, unfortunately, was absent, because he had been injured in a fall from his horse. The Committee ignored public opinion and voted in favour of resumption on certain conditions.[23] When the recommendations of the Committee were made public, they prompted a violent outcry in the community. Many well-attended public meetings were held in the latter part of 1846 and early 1847 to voice fierce opposition to the renewal of transportation in any form. Most of the newspapers, including the *Sydney Morning Herald* (renamed from the former *Sydney Herald* in 1842), were also firmly against the idea. John Plunkett's position was that a revival was unthinkable. At the first full debate on the topic in the Legislative Council in September 1847, he stated his unequivocal position:

> *If they could be so degraded as to ask again to have British crime poured in upon them, they would be forever unworthy of a place among nations of the earth.*

In September 1847, a majority of the Legislative Council voted against resumption of transportation. The resolution expressed the view that:

> *A return to the system of Transportation and assignment would be opposed to the wishes of this Community, and would also be most injurious to the moral, social and political advancement of the Colony.*[24]

However, in the meantime, because of the earlier Report of the Legislative Council Select Committee in favour of resumption, a letter came from Lord Grey, the Colonial Secretary in London, requesting a compromise: namely that convicts be sent to New South Wales as ticket-of-leave holders after serving a suitable reformatory period in Britain. The *Sydney Morning Herald* expressed the view that not one in a hundred of the citizens of New South Wales wanted transportation revived in any form. Despite this, the Legislative Council voted in April 1848 to accept Lord Grey's request, with two members opposing it – John Plunkett being one of them. Plunkett addressed the Council and explained that he was against the plan 'on the grounds that the social and moral interests of the Colony would be injured by the introduction of any class of criminals'. In late 1848, Lord Grey made preparations for the departure of the first ship – the *Hashemy* – containing 236 convicts. The stage was set for a violent public confrontation on its arrival.

When the *Hashemy* docked at Sydney in June 1849, there were mass demonstrations in both Sydney and Melbourne and there was even talk of sinking the ship in Sydney Harbour. Between 7000 and 8000 Sydneysiders turned up on a wet day to an anti-transportation rally in Barrack Square, at which it was suggested by some of the speakers that if England insisted on sending its convicts to New South Wales, a republic should be proclaimed. One of the speakers who addressed the crowd was a young Henry Parkes, who decades later was to play a major role in the Federation of the colonies into the Commonwealth of Australia.[25]

Reacting to overwhelming public pressure, in September 1850 the Legislative Councillors had a definitive debate on the topic, in which John Plunkett led the arguments against resumption. In a lengthy, eloquent and well-reported speech, he stated that 'it was impossible for the Crown Prosecutor of New South Wales to shut his eyes to the evils of convictism'.[26] He produced a vast array of facts and figures from the court system to prove that on the issue of crime alone transportation should never be reintroduced. He asserted that 'Transportation and free institutions cannot exist together'. In early 1850, the Council voted unanimously to abolish transportation for good. Plunkett's role in this decision was 'without parallel' and this period has been described as 'his finest hour'.[27]

15

PUBLIC EDUCATION, SISTERS OF CHARITY AND THE INCIDENT OF THE BIBLE

Over numerous years, the person who had shown the most obstinate resistance to many of the reforms that John Plunkett pursued was William Broughton, the Anglican Lord Bishop of Australia. Broughton was one of the most influential people in the colony and as a member of the Executive Council he had been able to thwart many of the progressive innovations that Plunkett had advocated. Broughton sided with the 'exclusives' on the issue of the civil rights of the emancipists; he stood against the introduction of a 'national' school system, preferring government sponsorship of parochial schools; he opposed the acceptance of unsworn evidence by indigenous witnesses in courts; and he was one of those who had voted against Plunkett's appointment as the first Catholic Chief Justice of New South

Wales. Bishop Broughton finally resigned his position on the Executive Council in early 1847. The person who replaced him on 30 March 1847 was John Hubert Plunkett. By then, Gipps had been replaced by Governor Sir Charles Augustus FitzRoy, who had arrived in the colony in August of the previous year.

By the mid-1840s, it had become apparent that the education system in New South Wales was seriously deficient. A Select Committee of the Legislative Council found in 1844 that more than half of the 25 600 children in the colony were receiving no education at all. Within two weeks of Broughton's departure and his replacement on the Executive Council by Plunkett, a significant grant of £2000 was made to establish the beginning of a national school system. As the religious authorities of the colony still jealously protected their right to their own denominational schools funded at public expense, the solution that Plunkett devised was a dual education system modelled on the Irish one that had been introduced so successfully many years earlier. In this new system, the denominational schools would continue to receive government support, but a public system, similar to the Irish National Schools, would be funded alongside them. Plunkett was convinced that such a scheme had inherent advantages that would allow families to make their own choices for the education of their children. The churches were firmly opposed to a dual system, perceiving (rightly in the long term) that a public system alongside their own would drain students, funding and resources from their sector.

It was John Plunkett who drafted the *National Education Board Act*, which became law in New South Wales in 1848. Governor FitzRoy asked Plunkett to become the Chairman of the new National Education Board, which Plunkett accepted with relish. He was joined on the Board by physician, politician, explorer, pastoralist, and philanthropist, Charles Nicholson[1] and by scholar and naturalist, William Sharp Macleay.[2] The Board faced a huge undertaking to set up a public education system. While the denominational schools had well-established administrative structures, buildings, teachers and curricula, the new Board had the job of establishing all these aspects from the bottom up. That makes it all the more remarkable that the members of the Board served without any financial reward. It is also noteworthy that Plunkett was able to serve as Chairman while maintaining his busy roles as Attorney General and member of the Executive Council.

At the time, there was no facility in the colony for the education and training of teachers, so Plunkett and his Board set up a new model school for the practical training of teachers in what had formerly been the military hospital at Fort Street in The Rocks area of Sydney.[3] The overwhelming success of the Board and the wide acceptance of its school system by the community at large can be gleaned from the fact that, by 1850, just three years after commencing, it had established forty-three schools and was in the process of creating another fifty-two.[4] Plunkett served as Chairman of the Board for ten years. On his retirement, his fellow Board members noted the 'untiring zeal and assiduity with which he sacrificed, year after year, the scanty leisure of a laborious public life to this self-imposed and gratuitous labour of love'.[5]

In the meantime, the religious hierarchies controlling the denominational schools felt under serious threat. One of the most vociferous critics was Plunkett's friend and co-religionist, Archdeacon John McEncroe, who by now was the

Director of Catholic Education in the colony. Plunkett was viewed by many of his fellow Catholics as having contributed little or nothing to advancing the interests of their church. Plunkett had always been careful to maintain the appearance and the reality of absolute impartiality in the performance of his public duties, and so the impression of his church leaders that he had not done anything special for them was quite accurate. What he had done, however, was to achieve a situation in which Catholics – and people of most other religions – were treated equally to the adherents of the dominant Anglican religion. The principal method of achieving this was to require public institutions to adopt non-discriminatory policies and practices. In a sense, what Plunkett introduced was an early version of the philosophy behind our present-day anti-discrimination laws.

***

Not content merely to establish a system of public primary and secondary schools, John Plunkett was one of those who were instrumental in establishing Australia's first tertiary educational institution – the University of Sydney. In 1849, William Charles Wentworth proposed in the Legislative Council the creation of the colony's first university; the motion was seconded by John Plunkett. Despite the fact that Wentworth was one of the wealthiest landowners in the colony and an anti-establishment figure who frequently attacked state officials, including John Plunkett, the two of them held many significant views in common, and *The Australian* newspaper, of which Wentworth was the founder and editor, had been supportive of many of Plunkett's reforms. Wentworth's mother had been a convict, and his rejection by the exclusives because of this had caused him to become a champion of the emancipists. Even nine years after the end of transportation in New South Wales, the social and political divisions between the exclusives and the emancipists endured. This division had been Wentworth's overriding concern during his many years of active politics in the colony. As one of the colony's leading political figures since the 1820s, and through his role as the editor of *The Australian*, Wentworth advocated for representative government, freedom of the press, trial by jury and the rights of emancipists. Despite his retrograde views on Aboriginal people giving evidence, he frequently spoke out against religious bigotry. On the question of a public university for the colony, Wentworth and Plunkett were united. Together, they drafted the Act of Incorporation of the new university. In accordance with the instructions they received from the Legislative Council, they created the legal framework for a university with no religious affiliation and one that did not require any religious test for entrance. They were both intent on avoiding the kind of discrimination that for centuries had kept universities in Great Britain and Ireland out of reach of non-Anglicans.

The joint motion for the establishment of the university hit a serious hurdle when one of the names on the list of proposed Senators of the new institution was the prominent surgeon, politician and philanthropist Dr William Bland. The opposition to Dr Bland derived from the fact that he was an ex-convict – even though he had contributed enormously to the colony since being pardoned thirty-five years earlier. This opposition was diametrically opposed to Plunkett's views on the rights of emancipists – that they should have equality with those who had never been convicts. However, there were sufficient numbers of exclusives on the Council to ensure that Dr Bland's name was removed from the list.

The *University of Sydney Act* was passed on 24 September 1850, and received the Governor's assent on 1 October, making it the first university in the British Empire outside the United Kingdom. John Plunkett was one of the fifteen people who became inaugural members of the University Senate. The University opened its doors in 1852 in the grounds of what is now Sydney Grammar School in College Street.

Within a year of the incorporation of the university, an issue arose that caused Wentworth and Plunkett great distress and illustrated only too clearly that there were still residual supporters of religious discrimination in the colony. In Plunkett's absence, due to his other arduous duties, the Senate voted in favour of a directive that appointments of academic staff should be restricted to distinguished candidates from either Oxford or Cambridge universities. At that time, those two pre-eminent English universities still did not allow attendance by Catholics, so the directive was in clear breach of the non-denominational status of Sydney University. In July 1851, Plunkett proposed in the Senate that candidates be considered from all the major universities in Great Britain or Ireland. His motion was rejected. Once again, John Plunkett had demonstrated his enlightened, anti-discriminatory views, and once again he had been thwarted.

In the first few years of the university, student enrolments were low. By the end of 1852, only thirty-eight students were actively attending classes. In 1853 there were sixty-five and in

1854 the number dropped to forty-seven. The Head of Classics, Professor John Woolley, expressed concern at the poor quality of many of the students, saying that he sometimes found it necessary to engage in rudimentary teaching before any genuine university work could be done. This underlined the need for a good grammar school to educate students – males only – to a level that would make them eligible to enter the university. As a result, another Select Committee was established by the Legislative Council in 1854,[6] and John Plunkett was one of its members. Later that year, the Committee recommended the establishment of a grammar school for boys with financial support from the government. The result was the passage in 1854 of the *Sydney Grammar School Act.* True to the philosophy of non-denominational, non-discriminatory education introduced by Plunkett years earlier, the Act stated that:

> *It is deemed expedient for the better advancement of religion and morality and the promotion of useful knowledge to establish in Sydney a public school for conferring on all classes and denominations of Her Majesty's subjects resident in the Colony of New South Wales without any distinction whatsoever the advantages of a regular and liberal course of education.*

The school opened its doors on 3 August 1857 in the College Street building that had previously been occupied by the University of Sydney. As Attorney General, John Plunkett was one of the first 'ex officio' trustees.[7] Under the leadership of the first headmaster, William Stephens, enrolments quickly grew and by 1859 they had reached 210. Unusually for the times, William Stephens had a kindly relationship with his students and rejected all forms of corporal punishment, banning the cane and outlawing the 'fagging' system so prevalent in the English great public schools (which were really private schools).[8] Fagging entailed younger boys acting as servants to more senior boys, who were given the right to discipline their charges, taking that duty away from the house-master who ran the dormitory. The system frequently resulted in physical and sexual abuse of the younger boys. William Stephens' values were too far ahead of his time, and a revolt by some of his staff led to an enquiry by the school's trustees and his unfortunate, abrupt departure.

On 27 February 1858, the University of Sydney received a Royal Charter from Queen Victoria, giving degrees conferred by the university rank and recognition equal to those of universities in the United Kingdom.[9] In 1859, the university moved to its current site at Camperdown. In 1865 John Plunkett was appointed as the fourth vice-chancellor of the university – a position he held until 1867.[10]

***

John Plunkett's efforts to remove all religious discrimination from major public institutions extended to one operated by members of his own faith – St Vincent's Hospital. Bishop Polding, the head of the Catholic Church in Australia, had requested the leader and founder of the Sisters of Charity, Mother Mary Aikenhead, who had established the Order in Dublin in 1815, to send a group of her Sisters to the colony to minister to the female convicts. As a result, five of the Sisters arrived in Sydney on the last day of 1838, to be met at the wharf by John Plunkett. They were the first nuns to enter the colony and attracted much attention on their arrival. They immediately set to work looking after the practical and spiritual needs of more than 800 female convicts at the Female Factory at Parramatta. The work of the Sisters brought instant improvement, for Bishop Polding wrote to Ireland in March 1839 that, 'within three weeks, an almost miraculous change had taken place in a gaol that had seemed full of hopeless misery, resentment and despair'. Plunkett was one of their constant supporters, both financially and practically. At one stage, the Sisters lived in his home. Maria Plunkett became very involved in their work and it became an important part of her life.

In 1855, John Plunkett helped the Sisters to acquire *Tarmons*, their first convent, situated in Victoria Street, Potts Point, and he later organised a public appeal to convert that property into their first hospital in Australia.[11] Those who responded to the appeal included residents from all sections of the community. In 1857, the Sisters opened St Vincent's Hospital as a free hospital with twenty-two beds. The Sisters did not confine their work to Catholics, but provided treatment to people of all faiths, without attempting to proselytise. A similar policy had applied for many years at the corresponding hospital in Dublin, set up by Mother Mary Aikenhead. Plunkett became St Vincent's Hospital's treasurer and one of its three trustees. As treasurer, he consistently used his position to insist on the non-denominational character of the hospital. St Vincent's epitomised Plunkett's view that public institutions – even those run by religious orders – should adhere strictly to non-discriminatory policies and practices, and offer services to all, irrespective of religion, status or wealth.

Plunkett's support for St Vincent's came into serious question in May 1859 when the 'Bibles incident' rocked the hospital. On 16 May 1859, a visiting Catholic curate from the Sacred Heart Presbytery on Darlinghurst Hill, Father Patrick Kenyon, took it upon himself to remove several Protestant Bibles[12] he had found in the female ward of St Vincent's Hospital. Father Kenyon informed one of the Sisters, Mary De Lacy, that 'it was not lawful for her and her sisters to supply these books and that if (he) should find they continued to do so (he) would feel obliged to bring the matter under the notice of the Archbishop'. Sister De Lacy brought the matter to the attention of Dr James Robertson, the hospital's Protestant medical doctor, who complained to Bishop Polding. The Bishop instructed the hospital that the Bibles were to be immediately placed back in the ward,[13] and Sister De Lacy was asked 'to inform Mr Kenyon, on his next visit to the Hospital, that he must not interfere in the management of the Hospital, that of course he could visit the Sick &c., but that he was in no ways to interfere in other matters, and that the books in question were not again to be removed from the ward'.

Further action ensued behind the scenes. Two days later, on 18 May, Dr Robertson submitted his resignation to Bishop Polding and on 26 May, Sister De Lacy also announced her resignation. Meanwhile, Father Kenyon was openly penitent for his actions. In a letter to the editor of the *Sydney Morning Herald* published on 7 June 1859, he stated:

> *All patients in the hospital, admitted into it irrespectively of their faith, and solely because they were sick and poor, might have, by all means their own books to use, might have their*

own ministers sent for at their request, to be their comforting friends ... If I erred in thinking those books were theirs [the Sister's], I am sorry for it, as men are sorry for an accident. I am more sorry for it, because of the great sorrow and misery that have grown up alongside of my act.

When John Plunkett heard about the removal of the Bibles, he was incensed at this breach of the hospital's non-discriminatory policy towards patients of other religions and horrified at the resignation of two stalwarts of the hospital who had contributed so much. He precipitously and publicly resigned his position as both treasurer and trustee, claiming that the incident had amounted to a breach of trust with the many donors to the hospital of other faiths. In what was an extraordinary overreaction, he even suggested that the hospital should be closed.[14] His resignation can only be categorised as rash and ill considered. Perhaps he had been affected by the departure earlier that year of one of his few friends, Roger Therry, to Ireland. Perhaps he was troubled by the spectre of an election for the Legislative Assembly that was looming two weeks later. The incident irrevocably affected the relationship between Plunkett and Archbishop Polding, who wrote that it was 'one of the most convincing instances of the folly of lay persons however good mixing in Church matters'.[15] Of Plunkett's role, he wrote:

He seems to consider that he may say and do whatever he deems right, but that the Church or Churchmen may not resent statements made publicly by him and which are injurious to religion or might be if not noticed. He has lost much of that he so much loves, popularity – by his interference about

St Vincent's and the very haughty position he has assumed in reference to all parties.[16]

In fact, the 'Bible incident' was but one of the triggers that led to the resignations of Dr Robertson and Sister De Lacy, as there had been earlier tensions between Archbishop Polding and these two senior personnel at the hospital. Religious politics had pitted the Benedictine nuns, who were answerable to Polding, against the Sisters of Charity, who were fiercely independent Ignatians. There had also been some antipathy from the Archbishop towards Dr Robertson, which may have had something to do with a certain Miss Gray, who was employed at the hospital and was a novitiate of the Vincentians – an order for women within the Catholic Church that allows them to make annual vows throughout their lives, rather than perpetual vows binding for life. Miss Gray's duties at the hospital were to assist Dr Robertson in the dispensary each day, and at his instruction to make up the prescriptions and generally attend to his needs. It became the view of her supervising Sister that Miss Gray began to 'neglect or omit her own spiritual duties under the pretext of duties in the hospital'. Ultimately, Miss Gray abandoned her calling and was 'taken by Dr Robertson to his own house, paraded through Sydney in his carriage and accompanied him to the Protestant Church'.[17] Such a defection was not easily forgiven or forgotten.

Plunkett's resignation deprived the Sisters of one of their staunchest supporters, and some of them, including Sister De Lacy, soon returned to Ireland. The incident was a classic demonstration of Plunkett's single-minded commitment to principle at the expense of pragmatism, even when directed at his own beloved church. It was a precipitous reaction to a relatively trivial event that was blown out of all proportion by many of the participants and observers. The newspapers had a field day. By going public and resigning his positions at the hospital, Plunkett needlessly distanced himself from an institution that he greatly treasured. It was not the only time in his life that John Hubert Plunkett wildly overreacted to what he perceived as a matter of principle, thereby denying himself a position of influence in a much-loved organisation that he had helped to develop over many decades.

16

DICHOTOMOUS AND DEATHLY DEBATES

It would be easy to think that John Plunkett's views were in every instance progressive and visionary, but that would be to ignore the reality. In retrospect, his approach to a few issues, particularly in his latter years, can now be viewed as regressive or narrow-minded. In fairness, one should view these failings as a product of his time. In a few cases, where he had held progressive views in his younger years, he changed his mind as he grew older. No prejudices were more ubiquitous in his day than those on Asian immigration to the colony.

With the discovery of gold in New South Wales in 1851, there was a massive increase in migration to the colony. It included Americans, Frenchmen, Italians, Germans, Poles and Hungarians. The influx also included a large contingent of Chinese. In fact, the Chinese were the third most numerous group after the British (including Irish) and the Germans. The Chinese miners were met with suspicion, resentment, racial intolerance and sometimes outward aggression from their Anglo and Irish counterparts.

Debate about Asian immigration had taken place in the colony on many occasions prior to the gold rush, but in November 1851, in the early stages of the frenetic wave of men from all over the world seeking their fortune in the Australian goldfields, the authorities feared that the Californian experience of unfettered immigration would be repeated in New South Wales. As a result, a debate about Chinese immigration occurred in the Legislative Council. Honorary physician at Sydney Hospital, Dr Henry Douglass,[1] suggested that 'free men' – meaning Anglo men and women – would be reluctant to emigrate to the colony if the Chinese were allowed to settle. In a speech brimming with xenophobia, he stated that the Chinese were:

> *A race of people addicted to vices which he could not mention, and which could not be mentioned in that house for fear the expressions necessary to name them should be reported in the public journals, and that their children might ask what those expressions meant.*

He added:

> *'We confess that we should not like to see the colony driven to such a choice as this. We are not partial to any admixture of races, particularly such an admixture as the Chinese and the Anglo-Saxon – the one so very different from and so vastly inferior to the other. We should like to see this colony preserve the English character which it has hitherto maintained ... We have no*

desire to see the dusky population of China mingle in our streets with the fair complexion of the Anglo-Saxon – or the temples of Buddha rise side by side with the Christians' house of prayer. We have no wish to see the habits and customs of paganism brought in immediate contact with those of Christianity. Our own countrymen – however fallen, however degraded – are dearer in our eyes than these benighted foreigners, and possess in themselves the germ of a great and extended civilisation. In a national point of view, the difference between a population of European Christians and Asiatic pagans is incalculable. The outpourings of all the hulks, and gaols, and penitentiaries of England, are better materials for the foundation of an empire than the best of the native inhabitants of Asia. However greatly they may be debased, they have a national character which vice and crime cannot divest from them – and which, in spite of themselves they must transmit to their posterity – a character which alone places them far before all the pagan communities in the universe. We would rather have these convicts, with all their anticipated pollution a thousand times over, than that the colony should be inundated with the benighted hordes of Asia, whether Tartar or Hindoo – Mussulman or Pagan.'[2]

WC Wentworth, also a member of the Legislative Council, advanced quite different views and suggested that it would be a breach of the comity between nations to restrict Chinese immigration because there was nothing stopping Englishmen going to China. He was sure that English workers would be prepared to work alongside Chinese workers.

The Colonial Secretary, Edward Deas Thomson, cautioned that, although he was against the immigration of Chinese, he doubted that the Council had the authority to prohibit it or to prevent private employers bringing them into the colony.

Attorney General John Plunkett stated his views on the topic in this way:

> *'He was strongly opposed to this species of immigration, and would be willing to concur in any legitimate means for discouraging it. For his own part, although as much opposed to a renewal of transportation as any member of that House, he did not hesitate to declare as the result both of his personal observation and of his official experience, that he would rather have 2000 convicts landed in Australia than 500 Chinamen. (Hear, hear.) They were objectionable in every respect. They would introduce a piebald breed. (Laughter.) They never could become acquainted with the English language or reconciled to English laws and English customs.'*[3]

By 1861, ten years after the discovery of gold, the Chinese made up 3.3 per cent of the population of New South Wales. Arising out of resentment and fear, a Protection and Anti-Immigration League was established to press for reduced Chinese immigration. In the same year, anti-Chinese sentiment reached new heights. On 30 June 1861, at Lambing Flat (Young) on the southwest slopes of New South Wales, about 3000 European miners banded together in a gang, called a 'roll up', and armed themselves with picks, whips, knives, sticks and anything that could be used as a weapon. They carried a flag on which was written 'Roll-up, Roll-up, No Chinese',[4] and overran the Chinese miners' camp. Chinese tents and equipment were destroyed, their gold plundered, and an unknown number of Chinese men were murdered. Although the official death toll was given as two, eye-witness accounts suggest between thirty and forty, and several hundred more were injured. Dozens of the Chinese men had their pigtails cut off – a matter of great dishonour.

As a result of the riots, anti-Chinese legislation was introduced later in 1861 when the New South Wales Parliament passed the *Chinese Immigration Restriction and Regulation Act.* The Act imposed numerous conditions regulating how long the Chinese could stay and whether or not they could bring their families, become naturalised, and work in the colony. The measure also raised a Chinese poll tax. Debate about the Act in the Legislative Assembly elicited varying approaches to the problem, including what we now view as sheer racism. Support for Chinese immigration came from pastoralists such as William Forster, who argued that the Chinese were an industrious and civilised people who could assist in developing the colony. Henry Parkes believed that further immigration of Chinese would lead to 'future discord, anarchy and civil war'. Others were more overt in their racism, such as Captain William Russell, a Hunter River pastoralist, who complained of Chinese 'vice, disease and dirtiness', and deplored the possibility of a 'mongrel population' resulting from the immigration of an 'inferior race'. Only in 1867, when the gold rush had almost run its course, was the Act repealed.

Plunkett's views on Chinese immigration, odious as they are today, must be seen in the context of his society. They would have been considered by most of his contemporaries as unremarkable and in line with mainstream attitudes. The surprising aspect of his approach to Chinese immigration was that it was at such variance with his unorthodox views on equality under the law for Aborigines, Dissenting Protestants, Jews and people of other non-Christian religions. His dichotomous views can best be understood as an expression of admiration for British civilisation and law, and a belief that a model society would embody the best that the British system could produce: equality under the law; freedom from discrimination; self-government; and abolition of corporal punishment, including the death penalty. The last thing that he wanted to see was a diminution of British culture, law or government. A multicultural Australia, unimaginable as it was at that time, would have entailed a denial of the superiority of everything British. Many thought that large-scale, non-British immigration would lead to a regrettable division of society into racial and cultural enclaves that would have little or nothing to do with each other. Such racial divisions had existed on the goldfields, and nobody thought it would be any different elsewhere. No wonder that most colonists were intent on maintaining the racial and cultural homogeneity of their society. These views were widely held in Australia until the slow winding down of the 'White Australia policy' during the period between 1945 and 1975, and they even prevailed in pockets afterwards.

***

Another area in which Plunkett's views could hardly be categorised as visionary was his opposition to the secret ballot. In 1858, New South Wales Premier Charles Cowper introduced the *Electoral Reform Act*, which abolished the last remaining property and income qualifications for voters and provided for universal, adult, male suffrage. In this respect, the Act had the support and encouragement of most legislators, including John

Plunkett. However, the Act also introduced the secret ballot, providing anonymity for voters at elections. This measure had already been introduced in Tasmania (renamed in 1856), Victoria and South Australia. It was such an innovative feature of voting that for a time it was known around the world as 'the Australian ballot'. Plunkett opposed the new way of voting on the basis that 'we should be willing to give our votes like men'.[5] While this approach illustrated the stridency with which he held his own views, it also demonstrated a lack of empathy for ordinary men who were less powerful and less firm in their convictions than himself.

***

By 1860, the now fifty-eight-year-old John Plunkett was enduring waning influence and failing health. It was under these circumstances that he came to some disturbing conclusions that seemed then, and still appear now, to be seriously at variance with his earlier progressive, liberal views, and suggest that his judgement had become clouded by age. In 1862, the *Church Act* was abolished, which removed state funding to the churches. Plunkett was troubled that the state was not providing any funds to any religion, and believed that this was a threat to the moral fibre of society. He also became increasingly concerned at secularism in public education. Finally, in a complete reversal of his stance over many decades, when Premier Parkes brought in the *Public Schools Act* in 1866, Plunkett opposed the measure and became a supporter of denominational schools. In anticipation of the disappearance of all state funding of religious schools, he set up an association to raise funds to support the Catholic system. The secular public education system had been his crowning achievement for decades, yet he was unable to see that Parkes's measures amounted to further progress – maybe because he had played no role in formulating them.

***

In other respects, however, John Hubert Plunkett remained a visionary in his time, in contrast to other leaders of the colony. The most notable example was in his opposition to the death penalty. Although Plunkett had been a most enthusiastic, forceful and successful prosecutor, leading to the execution of many defendants whose convictions he had secured, he was a strident opponent of the death penalty on moral and philosophical grounds. This contradiction had been sorely tested in 1835 when Plunkett was appointed for a short period as an acting judge to conduct the trial of two convict men confined on Norfolk Island who had been charged with murder. On their convictions, he had no choice but to don the black cap and impose sentences of death upon them.

The first curtailment of the death penalty in New South Wales came with some changes introduced during Plunkett's first full year as Solicitor General. In 1833, capital punishment was no longer available for relatively petty crimes such as cattle stealing, forgery and certain kinds of theft.[6] Then, in 1838, the colony adopted several major reforms that had been introduced in England the preceding year, when capital punishment was abolished for a wide range of more serious crimes, such as nonviolent burglary, attempted murder without bodily injury, riot, smuggling and slave trading. In

1845, Plunkett proposed the abolition of capital punishment for embezzlement, but it was rejected in the Legislative Council by twenty votes to two.

The next legislative reform of capital punishment in the colony was the abolition of public executions, and in this respect New South Wales moved ahead of developments in Britain. Plunkett spoke in favour of the change, stating that executions were 'extremely demoralising'. By this time, Plunkett was vociferously against the death penalty for any offence – a position he maintained for the rest of his life.[7] In 1853 the Legislative Council passed an Act to abolish public executions, but it required Royal assent before it could become law, which meant it only came into force on 11 January 1855.[8] Britain followed suit thirteen years later. When remission-of-death-penalty decisions came before the Legislative Council, Plunkett would excuse himself, because he was unwilling to be party to any decision to put someone to death.

In 1867, still in poor health and viewed as an elder statesman of waning influence, John Plunkett introduced a Bill in the Legislative Council for capital punishment in New South Wales to be restricted to offences that carried the same penalty in England. The newspapers that supported him, particularly the *People's Advocate* and the Henry Parkes – owned *Empire*, argued that the death penalty should be eliminated entirely. Plunkett asserted his preference for total abolition, but acknowledged that his Bill was more modest in seeking to align the law of New South Wales with England. He argued that:

> *The sooner the NSW parliament adopted his abolition bill, the better for the country, and the more honourable to us as Christian men.*

Quoting from a well-known English constitutional history book, he suggested that:

> *The deepest stain of English politics was the history of criminal law. The lives of men were sacrificed to a reckless barbarity, worthier of an Eastern despot, or African chief, than of a Christian state.*[9]

Plunkett referred to research in England that showed that wrongful convictions had occurred in which innocent men had been executed. He cited a poignant example of one of his own cases in 1841 in which a man had been wrongfully convicted of murder:

> *Mr Plunkett recollected one case which occurred in this colony, in 1841. Two men were in a public-house in Goulburn – one a settler, well to do – and the other an assigned servant in the neighbourhood. The case was heard before as able, as humane, as painstaking a judge as ever sat – Sir J Dowling. The men left the public-house at dusk, they were not intoxicated but elevated. They were heard talking loudly; the man to whom the house belonged was found murdered the next morning. The assigned servant went to his master's place and was described as he appeared the next morning. He was taken up as having been the last person with the murdered man. There was a doctor who gave extraordinary testimony – that it was not a gun-shot wound, that it was a stab. He made up his statement from the evidence. Altogether, the evidence seemed very conclusive, but the prisoner made a statement that he (Mr Plunkett)*

> *listened attentively to. He spoke so clearly, so naturally, so confidently, yet without bluster; he told such a story, in fact, that it made a deep impression on his (Mr Plunkett's) mind. The man was sentenced to death, and the case was coming before the Executive Council on a particular day. Now, he (Mr Plunkett) received depositions which showed him that a man – a bushranger, named Curran – was out bushranging, committing robberies, and fired at persons in this neighbourhood, and it occurred to him that Curran had committed the crime for which the other man was convicted. He was not a member of the Executive Council, but he took the papers there, and [Chief Justice] Sir James Dowling was staggered. The man's tale had been that as they were passing the bridge some man had fired, that the horse started, both fell, and he became alarmed, and ran home. And it appeared too, that it was from a gunshot wound that the murdered man died, and not from a stab; and subsequently, on the conviction of Curran, he at the scaffold, and in presence of the clergyman and others, said that he was the man who had committed the murder – had fired the shot – and that the man's tale was correct. The man had been sent to Norfolk Island, and on this he was brought back. He thought that such a case should make them pause before they inflicted the punishment of death, which was irrevocable.*[10]

The debate on Plunkett's Bill prompted a letter to the editor of *The Argus* in Melbourne from Frederick Lee, a member of the Society for the Abolition of Capital Punishment, on 9 December 1867:

Mr Plunkett, who for so many years ably and most honourably occupied the distinguished position of Attorney General of New South Wales, introduced a bill into the Legislative Council to abolish the punishment of death in certain cases, and to assimilate the law of New South Wales in that respect with the law of England. This bill was rejected by the Council without any attempt of philosophical reasoning save a miserable attack upon the bill by Mr E Deas Thompson, who had such a lame case as to be compelled to rake up some statistics twenty-three years old, gleaned from a work of no authority, to the entire suppression of Parliamentary statistics of 1866, or the authority of the home Government, and which statistics proved Mr Plunkett's position. Out of a House of eleven nominees, two only – the President and Mr Plunkett – were in favour of the bill; and it does appear rather presumptuous on the part of these nine nominees to assume to themselves a greater degree of wisdom than that possessed by both Houses of Parliament in the mother country, who enacted the repeal of these law after the strictest investigations by commissions at an expense of £100,000, and upon the unanimous recommendation of six ex-chancellors. I think, Sir, it proves to demonstrate that the Council represents nothing but their noble selves, and the rejection of the bill in toto (for there are sixteen crimes at present punishable with death in New South Wales), involves a gross and wicked libel on the people of New South Wales.[11]

The Bill was rejected by a large margin. New South Wales would only abolish the death penalty in 1955.

17

SELF-GOVERNMENT AND A SLOW DECLINE

In 1852, a Select Committee of the New South Wales Legislative Council was established with the concurrence of the Colonial Office in London to recommend a new Constitution for the colony that would make it self-governing. The committee consisted of ten members, of whom one was John Hubert Plunkett. WC Wentworth was its Chairman. The Committee sat for two years before agreeing on a model for final consideration by the Legislative Council and submission to London. There was substantial agreement between the Committee members on many issues, including the principle of a bicameral parliament along the lines of the British Houses. But on one issue there was considerable debate: whether the members of the Upper House should be elected or appointed. Always the

Anglophile, John Hubert Plunkett was firmly in support of the Upper House mirroring the British House of Lords, in which members were appointed by the Monarch. A group of the Select Committee members, including Plunkett, also advocated that those appointed to the Upper House should be granted hereditary titles, as in the House of Lords, so as to create an Australian aristocracy. Wentworth championed this suggestion, no doubt with an eye to his own prospects for recognition.

This was a very controversial topic throughout New South Wales. Should the colony attempt to emulate the mother country and establish its own aristocracy, or should it shun such affectations and create a more classless society, as the Americans had done more than seventy-five years earlier? People were divided on this issue largely based on the degree to which they saw the Westminster system as the quintessential model of good government, or whether they saw Royal appointments as creating undesirable social stratification. New South Welshmen had a choice to make: did they desire a local equivalent of the House of Lords, or did they want something distinctively Australian? When the issue of hereditary appointments was first ventilated in public in mid-July 1853, it was met with almost universal hostility in the newspapers and the general community.

The issue of hereditary titles was decided not at a meeting of the Legislative Council, or by vigorous debate in the newspapers, but in a place of entertainment at a public meeting called to oppose the proposals for an appointed Upper House. It took place at the Royal Victoria Theatre in Pitt Street, Sydney, on 15 August 1853. The meeting was attended by a huge crowd, where a motion was discussed that:

> *... the proposed Constitution Bill is radically defective and opposed to the wishes and interests of the inhabitants of this colony, who believe that a Representative legislature, consisting of two Elective Chambers, will alone possess that stability, energy, and usefulness which is maintained by public confidence, and without which no Government can permanently exist.*[1]

Twenty-five-year-old man of letters, poet and former 'boy orator' Daniel Deniehy gave a brilliant, witty speech in which he so thoroughly ridiculed the proposal for what he called a 'bunyip aristocracy' that it became a dead letter. Singling out by name WC Wentworth, James Macarthur, Terrence Murray and George Nichols – all members of the Legislative Council – he lambasted those who supported a local aristocracy:

> *Because it was the good pleasure of Mr Wentworth and the respectable tail of that puissant Legislative body, whose serpentine movements (loud laughter) were so ridiculous, we were not to form our own Constitution, but instead of this we were to have an Upper House and a Constitution cast upon us, upon a pattern which should suit the taste and propriety of political oligarchs who treated the people at large as if they were cattle to be bought and sold in the market (loud cheers); or as they indeed were in American slave States, and now in Australian markets (tremendous cheering), where we might find bamboozled coolies and kidnapped Chinamen. (Immense applause.)*
>
> *And being in a figurative humour, he might endeavour to make some of the proposed nobility to pass before the stage of our imagination, as the ghost of Banquo walked along in the vision of Macbeth, so that we might have a fair view of these*

Harlequin aristocrats (laughter), these Botany Bay magnificos (laughter), these Australian mandarins. (Roars of laughter.)

Let them walk across the stage in all the pomp and circumstances of hereditary titles.

At this point in his speech, Deniehy sarcastically described the aristocratic titles that might be taken by the four named legislators, and proceeded:

But, though their weakness was ridiculous, he could assure them that these pigmies [sic] might do a great deal of mischief. They would bring contempt on a country whose interest he was sure they all had at heart, until even the poor Irishman in the streets of Dublin would fling his jibe at the Botany Bay aristocrats. In fact, he was puzzled how to classify them. They could not aspire to the miserable and effete dignity of the grandees of Spain. (Laughter.)

They had antiquity of birth, but these he would defy any naturalist properly to classify them. But perhaps it was only a specimen of the remarkable contrariety that existed at the Antipodes. Here they all know the common water mole was transferred into the duck-billed platypus, and in some distant emulations of this degeneration, he supposed they were to be favoured with a bunyip aristocracy. (Great laughter).

It is remarkable to think that Australia rejected a local aristocracy and the class divisions that go with it largely because of a witty, sarcastic speech by a gifted young orator in a place of public amusement.[2] Although the issue of hereditary titles was resolved, the debate between those who supported an elected Upper House and those who preferred an appointed one still raged.

Plunkett took the position that if both Houses were elected it would lead to instability and the passage of hasty legislation, so he supported appointment to the Upper House by the Governor. Ever the Anglophile, he stated his reasons eloquently for favouring appointment by a system similar to the British House of Lords, even though that House had blocked Catholic emancipation for decades:

> *The result of a Constitution cannot be seen until after a long lapse of years or perhaps centuries. But if we desire the Constitution which we have devised should be of an enduring nature, what better model can we have than the Constitution of the land 'whose flag has braved 1000 years the battle and the breeze' ... All my readings, and my study, have inspired me with the greatest veneration for the noble Constitution of the United Kingdom. I believe it to be the most excellent of human institutions. It is no matter of theory or speculation, it is not a work of yesterday, that may be amended today and changed tomorrow; it is composed of many wheels, springs and balances, of counteracting and cooperating powers, all dovetailing in each other; and each of its parts seems to be fitted for the test; that to unsettle is to destroy ... I assert that the elective principle in an Upper House is not congenial to the British Constitution, and that it is now proposed for the first time ... I cannot conceive how monarchy can exist with an elective upper house.*[3]

In the result, those who favoured an appointed House won the day.[4] The *New South Wales Constitution Act* to establish self-government passed its second reading in the Legislative Council on 2 September 1853, and was then reserved by the

Governor and remitted to London. William Charles Wentworth and Edward Deas Thomson proceeded to London to advocate support for the Bill and combat any objections to it.[5] With some amendments, it was given the Royal assent by Queen Victoria on 16 July 1855 and proclaimed by the New South Wales Governor on 24 November 1855.

By virtue of the Act, New South Wales became a self-governing colony with a colonial Parliament, consisting for the first time of a fully elected Legislative Assembly and an Upper House – the Legislative Council – appointed by the Governor. The whole structure was modelled closely on the British Parliament. An Executive Council was established to advise the Governor in the exercise of his limited decision-making functions. Most importantly, the new Parliament had wide powers over domestic matters, including revenue raising and land, thereby side-stepping the overriding scrutiny of the Colonial Office in London and reducing the role of the Governor to a subsidiary one with the same limited functions as the Monarch in England.[6] The British Parliament, however, still retained an overriding power to disallow colonial legislation.[7]

The newly constituted Parliament met for the first time on 22 May, 1856.

***

With the introduction of responsible self-government and a fully elected Lower House, John Plunkett was firmly of the opinion that the old administration should make way for the new. Under the 1856 Constitution, the position of Attorney General was a political one, in that the holder was required to be a Member of Parliament. Plunkett decided that he would relinquish his post. Perhaps he realised that the influence of the new Attorney General would never be as strong as it had been during the twenty years he had held office, and so it was a good time to depart. Maybe he appreciated that he was a lone ranger who did not have the stomach for the lobbying and bargaining that membership of a Ministry of elected leaders would entail. In any event, he announced his retirement, which prompted an outpouring of accolades for the man now universally respected as an elder statesman who had guided the colony through more than two decades of progress – legally, politically and administratively. On 24 June 1856, the judges of the Supreme Court paid tribute to his twenty-four years as Solicitor General and Attorney General, when the Chief Justice said:

> *When the contests of party shall have passed away, and the voices of friendship and calumny have been like silenced by death, and the grave has closed over the generations which now know us, there will be no name recorded by the pen of history, in Australian annals, with juster or more enduring praise than that which belongs to Mr Attorney General Plunkett.*[8]

These lofty expectations would prove to be quite exaggerated. Plunkett was offered a public dinner in his honour by members of the Bar, but he declined, claiming that he was not yet finished in his public life, that he intended to maintain practice as a barrister, and that it would look too much like a 'valedictory manifestation' if the dinner were held.

Plunkett's last major achievements as Attorney General were to pass through the old Legislative Council two highly important Acts. The first was the *Marriage Act*, which for the first time legitimised civil marriages and gave equality of recognition to marriage celebrants of all the Christian religions. He had worked steadily on the Bill for four years, starting in 1851, until he was assured that it would pass, which only came about in 1855. He had 'hastened slowly' to achieve this monumental legislative step. In 1855, the Bill passed by twenty-seven votes to ten. Several months later, John Plunkett was responsible for the passage of the *Registration of Births, Deaths and Marriages Act*, which created the most detailed, centralised, public record keeping of these life events in the world, to such an extent that it became a model for other countries.[9] These life events had previously been recorded by religious authorities.

These two legislative provisions were Plunkett's final contributions to the laws of New South Wales under the old form of government. It can be seen that they both involved a further secularisation of public institutions and functions. The transition to responsible government in 1856 marked the apogee of John Plunkett's influence and power. Hereafter, at age fifty-four, he was increasingly viewed as an honourable elder statesman whose time had almost come to an end and whose influence had waned. The new guard, which would lead the colony forward under responsible self-government, did not include him.

***

In late 1855, John Plunkett decided he would stand for election in one of the four seats representing Sydney in the new

Legislative Assembly. However, because he was still working assiduously as Attorney General and due to remain in public office until the expiry of the old Council in early June 1856, he considered it inappropriate to publicly promote his own candidature. By early January 1856, the campaigning by others for the seats of Sydney had begun in earnest. Four prominent and seasoned politicians decided to form what was then called 'the bunch' but today we would call a ticket. They were Henry Parkes, Charles Cowper, James Wilshire and Robert Campbell. Two of them, Parkes and Cowper, were among the shrewdest politicians in the colony, and they had many supporters, one of whom – the clergyman John Dunmore Lang – was vehemently opposed to Plunkett's candidacy. It was Lang who raised the religion issue against Plunkett, suggesting that if Plunkett won a seat he would not be representing Sydney, but Rome.[10]

Although Plunkett was reluctant to campaign while still serving as Attorney General, he had substantial support in the community, and, most importantly, Reverend John West, the editor of the *Sydney Morning Herald*, was keenly promoting his cause. At this time, the *Sydney Morning Herald* had the largest circulation of any newspaper in Australia;[11] in fact, its daily circulation was higher than all but the biggest two papers in England. John West, a Congregationalist minister at the Pitt Street Church, had advocated strongly for the abolition of transportation and he was a keen champion of Aboriginal welfare, so he had much in common with Plunkett. At a critical stage of the election campaign, in an editorial on 22 February 1856, his paper summarised Plunkett's contribution to public life over nearly twenty-five years and noted:

The patriot of the highest character is the man who honestly and without reserve, abjures all pretensions unsuited to modern relations, and to colonial life; one who gives his days and nights to preserve the line which separates the civil rights and obligations of all from questions of religion.

The paper made this comment about John Plunkett's extensive career in the public sector:

... neither in his sympathy as an Irishman or in his profession as a Roman Catholic, will [he] ever sacrifice the general interests of the community, or suffer himself to be an instrument of any faction, whether polemical or national.

The paper went on to remind readers of some of his notable achievements, namely: ameliorating the worst aspects of the convict system, supporting public education, establishing the civil rights of minority groups, including the Jews, introducing new marriage laws, his support for the end of transportation, his general administrative talents, his determination to protect the Aborigines, and even his opposition to Asian immigration.

Finally, the paper commented on his personal integrity:

The personal character of Mr Plunkett is blameless. We do not think any human being – not himself infamous – would be found to question Mr Plunkett's honour, or cast the slightest stain upon his character as a man and a gentleman. In so long a career he must have awakened animosities, and come into collision with many; but it must be a rare degree of personal excellence, which through such various scenes, and in an office so calculated to create bitter recollections, has preserved to him the confidence of almost every respectable member of the community. All, whether his political antagonists or not, bear testimony to Mr Plunkett's worth, and acknowledge that whatever may be his opinions, he stands in the highest place as an honourable and upright man.

One aspect of that integrity was his failure to enrich himself while in public office:

While other members of his profession are found connected with banking establishments, have made large fortunes in speculative pursuits, and shared in all the advantages of a rising colony, the Attorney General has limited himself to his profession, and rejected all the means of gain which could in the remotest degree compromise the administration of justice.[12]

The *Empire*, on the other hand, couldn't hide its sarcastic contempt for John Plunkett:

Mr Plunkett has been a member of the Legislature the greatest length of years, but there is no man of prominence to whose account so little is set down in the records of the Legislative Council. Even his votes, if examined by any constitutional test, in nine cases out of ten would tell against him as a public man. Yet we have often seen occasion to admire Mr Plunkett; and when we have heard the bitter contempt for his intellect often expressed by the ablest of his contemporaries in turn, by Mr Wentworth, Mr Richard Windeyer, Mr Robert Lowe, and Dr Lang, we have thought he was unjustly treated.[13]

It was only several days before the elections for the four seats of Sydney on 17 March 1856 that John Plunkett felt comfortable to speak publicly in support of his candidacy. It was not enough. The people of Sydney looked to the new bunch to lead them and Plunkett came fifth. He was then nominated to stand for two country seats, Bathurst and Argyle, and he won them both.[14] John Plunkett was the only pre-1856 government official to be elected to the new Parliament. The election resulted in sixteen native-born representatives in the Legislative Assembly out of a total of fifty-four.

The new Assembly met for the first time on 22 May 1856. Plunkett had to choose between the two seats he had won, and so resigned as the member for Bathurst and took his place representing the electorate of Argyle. The first Premier of New South Wales – the position was then known as Colonial Secretary – was Stuart Donaldson. He offered the position of Attorney General to Plunkett, who declined it. However, another honour soon came in its place. On 6 June 1856, John Hubert Plunkett was appointed as the first Queen's Counsel in Australia.[15]

The first Parliament of New South Wales was a most unstable one, with the first two Premiers quickly losing the support of the Assembly. The first Ministry only lasted from late May until 22 August 1856, when Donaldson resigned as Premier. Charles Cowper took over as the new leader, and he also asked Plunkett to become Attorney General, which again Plunkett declined. A few weeks later, in September 1856, Cowper was also forced to resign, and Henry Watson Parker assumed the leadership. For a third time, Plunkett was asked to accept the position of Attorney General, and for a third time he refused.[16]

As a member of the Legislative Assembly, Plunkett assumed a principled stand. He was not part of any faction or interest group, preferring to remain independent and deciding each issue on its merits, and so he became the quintessential cross-bencher. By way of example, he argued for a rise in the salary of the judges, because in his view they were the worst paid public officers in the colony, and he voted against a motion to support the churches on a per capita basis because it was limited to the Christian churches and excluded the Jewish population.[17] At the same time, Plunkett took on a heavy caseload as a private barrister.

***

In January 1857, upon the resignation of Sir Alfred Stephen as President of the Legislative Council, John Plunkett was appointed to replace him. It was a great honour that recognised his massive contribution to the colony. However, his appointment was to last less than a year. In late 1857, a disagreement arose between Plunkett and Premier Cowper over the right of the National Schools Board, of which Plunkett was still Chairman, to make its own regulations or to appropriate public moneys. Cowper, who had been a supporter of the denominational school system, claimed that since New South Wales now had a responsible, elected Parliament, it was inappropriate for the Board to pass its own regulations and appropriate public moneys, as only Parliament should have those rights. Plunkett wrongly suspected that Cowper was trying to weaken the public school system. The dispute escalated and Plunkett unwisely sent an exchange of letters with Cowper to the newspapers. Cowper retaliated by requesting the Governor and his Executive Council to dismiss Plunkett as Chairman of the National Schools Board. As the Governor-in-Council was now a rubber stamp of the Parliament, the Governor had no choice but to accede.

This was a severe blow to Plunkett. For the second time in his life, Plunkett had acted rashly and publicly in a way that resulted in him losing a position of leadership in a major public institution that he dearly loved and that he had served with distinction for many years. To make matters worse, on 6 February 1858 Plunkett, in disgust, resigned as President of the Legislative Council, as a member of the Council, as a Justice of the Peace and from a number of other public offices. The newspapers and the public reacted with dismay at his resignations, but Cowper had won the day.

Plunkett's petulance and his failure to accept the realities of modern-day responsible government resulted in him losing what was probably his most treasured post. He had failed to ensure that he had the support of his Premier and demonstrated a lack of understanding of pragmatic politics in a new age. By resigning his post as President of the Legislative Council, he grossly overreacted and showed an unenviable surrender to wounded pride. By his own impetuous actions he needlessly deprived the colony of one of its most accomplished and highly respected elder statesmen.

Plunkett reacted to the public regret about his departure by standing again for a seat in the Legislative Assembly. He won the seat of Cumberland in September 1858; however, he failed to be re-elected in December 1860 in the first vote under universal male suffrage. Plunkett had lost his appeal to the electorate.

In May 1861, he returned to the Legislative Council, after being appointed for life by the new Governor, Sir John Young. In 1863 he was appointed as Vice-President of the Governor's Executive Council. Neither position entailed real power, but they both accorded him great recognition and respect.

***

During Maria and John Plunkett's many years in the colony, their relationship was sorely tested. John's professional obligations, and indeed his personality, kept Maria from enlarging their social connections to the extent she would have wished. During their time in Australia, her husband only wished to socialise with three people: Governor Richard Bourke, Father John McEncroe and Justice Roger Therry. John Plunkett was socially stiff, and few people were able or wished to befriend him. The only time he would let his hair down was at the annual St Patrick's Day celebration, which he organised, and at which he would play the fiddle. While Maria was interested in people and their affairs, when John was not attending to his official duties he was more attracted to music and books in the confines of their home. However, as Maria grew older, it was not so much their social isolation or that she had followed him to the far ends of the earth that affected her attitude to her husband. It was more her failure to bear children that most embittered her and caused her in later years to become caustic, contrarian and increasingly cantankerous towards her husband. Despite this, John continued to love Maria dearly, and patiently endured her moodiness and, later in life, her ill health from undiagnosed causes. Maria suffered from 'unspecified maladies born of ennui and frustration, and her restlessness was assuaged only by constant changes in climate', resulting in them spending months apart.[18] Maria would frequently go on her own to Melbourne and Hobart.

According to Hubert De Castella, who knew both Plunketts well, and whose wife was related to John:

> *It would be difficult to meet two characters less suited to each other, but despite which they passed a long life together. She, despite her amiability and her irreproachable conduct as a spouse, was egotistical, fantastic and jealous; he was kind, devoted to her and always patient. They had no children and this was without doubt their great tragedy. Madame Plunkett spent herself in regret and used it as a pretext to oppose all enterprise, all plans requiring stability. Demanding and changeable, if her husband proposed anything she didn't agree with, or was himself opposed to her wishes, there would be an explosion and the poor man, admirable in his sense of duty and in adherence to Christian virtue, when his love had been spent in these scenes, would submit. However, the tempests were for him alone; in the middle of one she could be calm and gracious to others, and as she was possessed of a truly brilliant intelligence and was for the rest an estimable woman, people blamed him, but her popularity did not suffer at all.*[19]

***

By early 1865, the health of both John and Maria was deteriorating. Although he was still a member of the Legislative Council, Maria wanted to move permanently to Melbourne, and John reluctantly agreed. His plan was that he would come to Sydney from time to time to fulfil his parliamentary obligations. In reality, it was his concern for Maria's mental health that convinced John they should relocate their home to Melbourne and he should put up with the inconvenience of frequent travel between the two colonies.[20] Once again, John and Maria were apart for long periods.

Later the same year, John Plunkett was appointed as the Vice-Chancellor of the University of Sydney. Despite poor health, he returned frequently to Sydney to attend sessions of the Legislative Council and to fulfil his role as Vice-Chancellor. It was said that:

> *Though he preferred New South Wales, and had here all his sympathies and friendship, yet the climate of the sister colony was better suited to the failing health of his lady. With that forgetfulness of self, which was one of the leading traits of his character, he gave up his own wishes and desires in view of the advantage to be derived by the loved partner of his life. Though residing in Melbourne, he was nearly as much in Sydney as in the rival city; and especially when the Parliament was sitting was accustomed to make prolonged stays in the town with which he had so long been identified.*[21]

In August 1865, Premier Charles Cowper was again in a precarious political situation. Desperate to shore up his government by using the reputation and recognition of John Plunkett to his advantage, he convinced Sir John Young to approach Plunkett and ask him to become Attorney General. It was a request that Plunkett could not refuse, so he reluctantly agreed to come out of retirement and assume the position 'until a younger and more suitable person [could] be found to take it'.[22] He and Maria both returned to Sydney. Within eight months – predictably – the Premier and his Attorney again quarrelled, and Plunkett once again resigned and returned with Maria to Melbourne. Shortly afterwards, in January 1866, Cowper's Ministry fell, and he was forced to resign as Premier.[23]

On 22 August 1868, Plunkett's good friend, Father John McEncroe, died. Roger Therry had departed Australia in 1859 and was now living in retirement in England, where he published his *Reminiscences of Thirty Years' Residence in New South Wales and Victoria*. Plunkett's only close friends were no longer with him, and he felt their absence deeply.

In April 1869, John Plunkett came to Sydney by steamer to attend to personal business. During the journey he felt feverish and sat on deck. By the time he arrived in Sydney he had a rash on his face, which he mistakenly attributed to sunstroke. It was in fact a condition called *erysipelas*, a serious streptococcal infection that attacks the lymph system, typically affecting the elderly when their immune system is compromised. In the absence of modern-day antibiotics, it was often fatal. He was laid up for several days at the Civil Service Club in Sydney, where he received medical attention that caused the rash to disappear. On returning to Melbourne and Maria, he managed to attend a meeting of the Melbourne Provincial Church Council, where he was the lay Secretary. It was his last official function. Within a matter of days, the rash reappeared and he quickly deteriorated, before passing away at his East Melbourne home on 9 May 1869. Bishop Polding was with him at the end to administer the last rites.

18

LEGACIES

John Hubert Plunkett's body was transferred to Sydney, where it lay in state at St Patrick's Church. His funeral service, including a full requiem Mass, was held there on Saturday 15 May 1869, conducted by Archbishop Polding and various other Catholic clergy. It was attended by the Chief Justice, the Premier, the Colonial Treasurer, the Postmaster General, the Attorney General, the Solicitor General, numerous members of Parliament, the French Consul, the Spanish Consul, a large number of barristers, officers and graduates of the University of Sydney, as well as many ordinary citizens. An eloquent and lengthy address on the life and character of the deceased was delivered by Father McCarthy, followed by the mournful music of the 'Dead March' from Handel's *Saul*.[1] The cortege – three-quarters of a mile long – proceeded down a crowd-lined George Street to the Devonshire

Street Cemetery.[2] John Plunkett had expressed a wish to be buried as close as possible to his long-time friend and confidant Father John McEncroe; however, this was not possible, and he was buried beside his first cousin, Captain Patrick Plunkett, about fifty yards from McEncroe's grave.[3]

On his death, John Plunkett was accorded accolades that acknowledged his contribution to the colony over thirty-seven years. The *Sydney Morning Herald*, which had both lavishly praised and savagely criticised him during his lifetime, frankly admitted their ambivalence over the years and laid out for readers to judge for themselves what had been his strengths and weaknesses:

> *Notwithstanding that we held opinions on points of controversy the very opposite of his own, these differences tended only to illustrate, in a stronger and purer form, the presence in his mind of those sacred principles of religious liberty which early suffering and later experience had made paramount in his thought and predominant in his conduct ... Mr Plunkett is decidedly liberal in his political opinions, but is somewhat diffident in the expression of them on ordinary occasions. It was to an act of indecision of this kind that the Corporation Bill of 1840 was lost. When the subject, however, appears of great importance, Mr Plunkett displays an energy and firmness which command universal respect. Mr Plunkett's eloquence is not of the first order, but he displays a highly cultivated mind, and an honesty of purpose which more than cover some slight defects of language and utterance.*

Finally, the paper ventured the opinion that:

> *He has left behind a noble reputation which will not diminish in the colony with the lapse of time.*

Despite this assuredness by Sydney's leading newspaper that he would not be forgotten, John Hubert Plunkett has largely been overlooked by posterity in the recognition of those leaders and heroes of the colonial period who were responsible for creating the institutions, structures, civil rights and values that underpin our nation.

***

Knowing that he was dying, John Plunkett made a will in his last few days, leaving everything to his wife Maria. However, his estate was worth a mere £2000. The paucity of this amount can be judged by the fact that his salary and pension had been £1200 per year ever since his original appointment as Attorney General in 1836. John Plunkett had left Maria in a parlous financial state in which she was unable to support herself. While most of his colleagues at the Bar had amassed great fortunes, Plunkett had dedicated himself to his office to an extent that was to his, and Maria's, financial detriment. He had been careful not to invest in anything that could cause a conflict of interest and had failed to make the kind of investments in land that had rendered many of his contemporaries wealthy.[4] His charitable contributions to a wide variety of causes covering a broad spectrum of society were frequent and generous. For example, in 1856 he contributed £200 – one-sixth of his annual salary – to the Sisters of Charity to assist them to buy *Tarmons*, the site of their first hospital at Potts Point. He had financially assisted a family member in great need.[5] The underlying reason for his impecuniosity, however, was that John Plunkett was totally uninterested in affluence and saw his real wealth in his accomplishments for the community and the progress that had been made to civil rights and the legal system since his arrival in the colony. His bank passbook at the time of his death showed a final balance of a paltry £87, and recorded recent donations to the Hebrew School, St Vincent's Hospital and the Good Shepherd Convent, which operated a home for destitute girls.

On Plunkett's death, his pension automatically ceased. A year after his death, Maria, now back in Sydney and in dire financial straits, petitioned the Legislative Assembly for an *ex gratia* pension, stating that her husband had left his 'pecuniary affairs in considerable embarrassment, his pension being almost the only property he possessed'.[6] Her application was refused,[7] and she was reduced to supporting herself by giving private lessons in music and French. Although the Catholic community rallied around her and attempted to support her, in the end she was forced to accept the charity of the eponymous Sisters for whom she had assiduously worked in a voluntary capacity for many decades, and who in turn housed her during her later years.

Maria died in August 1895 at the age of 82, having endured penury for twenty-six years after John's passing. One can only imagine that her umbrage during his lifetime at his focus on work and her frustration at their social isolation and lack of progeny were only exceeded by her resentment at how poorly he had provided for her after his death.

***

John Hubert Plunkett was a man of patent contradictions. Although it was widely known that he was a devout Catholic, it was equally broadly recognised that he abhorred religious partiality of any kind in public life. For this reason, the upper echelons of his church viewed him with suspicion and doubted his loyalty to their cause, although they took derivative pride in his standing and accomplishments. He was a man who saw his purpose in life as serving the public good, and yet he cared little for public opinion. He was in no way vain about his own abilities, and yet he would not hesitate to attempt to impose his strongly held views on others. He loved his wife Maria dearly, and yet paid scant attention to her frequent complaints of social isolation due to his actions as Solicitor General and Attorney General. One can only understand John Plunkett by knowing his past in Ireland and by appreciating the long history of persecution and discrimination that his forebears had borne during the dark centuries of domination and oppression by the English. It was no coincidence that his most treasured possession was the chalice that had been held during the celebration of the sacrament by his most illustrious and maltreated ancestor, Archbishop Oliver Plunkett. Maria Plunkett's obituary in the *Sydney Morning Herald* stated:

> *Sometime ago Mrs Plunkett presented the Cardinal Archbishop with precious relics of the martyred Irish Primate, Oliver Plunkett, consisting of a chalice, gold watch, and vestments. These relics came into the old lady's hands through her family, and are now preserved by his Eminence with the greatest reverence at Manly.*[8]

The chalice and vestments of Archbishop Oliver Plunkett are currently held at St Mary's Cathedral in Sydney.[9]

***

John Hubert Plunkett had a most illustrious career in New South Wales. Many of the reforms he introduced had a lasting effect on the colony, some of which have endured until today. During the Australian Constitutional Conventions prior to federation in 1901, there was no question but that the new nation would be secular, with no religion of state. In fact, the federal Constitution expressly precludes the Commonwealth from passing laws to establish any religion, to impose any religious observance, or to prohibit the free exercise of any religion. It also provides that no religious test shall be required as a qualification for any office under the Commonwealth.[10] It is in no small measure due to the actions of John Plunkett that this principle was accepted so early in the history of the colony. Similarly, the existence of a vigorous state school system side-by-side with religious schools – all funded by government – was due to a policy developed and pursued by John Plunkett. The University of Sydney and Sydney Grammar School, with their traditions of excellence in secular, liberal education, were, and still are, important community assets for which we should be grateful to those who were responsible for their establishment, including John Hubert Plunkett. Today, the University of Sydney is ranked among the best in the world,[11] while Sydney Grammar School is one of the foremost secondary schools in Australia. St Vincent's Hospital in Sydney is still one of the largest teaching hospitals in New South Wales, as it provides first-rate medical services to people of any religion without discrimination or proselytism.

As Solicitor General and Attorney General, John Hubert Plunkett brought great integrity and diligence to his high office during a time of enormous legal, social and administrative change in the colony. There can be few occupations more demanding and of more social value than to be the state's principal prosecutor of major crime, as Plunkett was for twenty-four years. In the author's view, there has been no Attorney General before or since who has had more influence on the passage of significant legal reforms than John Hubert Plunkett. Ironically, had he become a judge, it is likely that he would have had less influence on the development of the colony. His stand on a whole host of issues was progressive and farsighted. They included his views on: convict assignments, floggings, the abolition of military juries, qualifications for civilian jurors, the rights of emancipated convicts, the unrestricted power of magistrates, the obligation of the courts to punish those responsible for massacres of the Aboriginal population, the right of Aborigines to give evidence in the courts, the division between church and state, elected rather than appointed Legislative Councils, responsible self-government, secular public educational institutions at primary, secondary and tertiary level, teacher education, the provision of secular public health services, and the death penalty. Viewed in the context of his time, he showed great humanity, perspicacity, bravery and strength of purpose. In the author's view, he should be excused for those few idiosyncratic views that he espoused in later life that now appear retrograde and deeply flawed, such as his attitude to Chinese migration and his support for a hereditary

Australian aristocracy. His views on the merits of an appointed Upper House were quite unremarkable in the 1850s.

***

John Plunkett should be best remembered for his efforts to achieve equality before the law for all men. In order to assess his success at this broad and ambitious objective, it is necessary to look closely at the long-term effects of the Myall Creek murder trials. The two 1838 trials marked one of only a handful of times in the history of Aboriginal displacement that Europeans were punished – and punished appropriately – for the murder of Aboriginal Australians. Those trials stand as an early demonstration that Australian courts had the capacity to protect the weak and disenfranchised, to operate without fear or favour, and to treat all people equally, including those on the margins of society. That is not to say that the law always operated in this benevolent way, or even that it frequently did, but on the occasion of the Myall Creek murder trials it certainly did. Plunkett's advocacy and trial tactics succeeded in persuading a jury of twelve free men and freed men to convict seven white defendants for the brutal slaying of an Aboriginal child – representing twenty-eight members of that infant's tribe. In fact, if one takes into account the special jury that allowed the second trial to proceed, Plunkett succeeded in convincing twenty-four jurors of the need for justice arising from the deaths at *Myall Creek Station*. That he was able to do this in the face of almost universal hostility to the prosecution was nothing short of miraculous. It would never happen again during the colonial period, or even after the federation of the Australian states in 1901. Tribute must also be paid to the trial judge, William Westbrooke Burton, who set the tone for a fair second trial, and to the twelve jurors who were brave enough to convict the seven defendants in the face of hostile public opinion.

It has been argued that the Myall Creek murder trials were one of the early significant steps in differentiating Australia from the mother country.[12] The author disagrees. The process of delineating Australians from those back in the mother country began early in the history of the colony with the imaginings of the white population who saw themselves as pioneers in a remote and hostile, but enormously promising environment; where the bush was something that most people feared; where the Aborigine was viewed as a source of threat to be overcome; where convict labour was the backbone of the economy, but also offered hope and prosperity at the end of servitude; where struggle and strife stood side by side with the potential for undreamed-of prosperity; where opportunities for advancement – economically and socially – abounded in ways that never existed in the home country. All these self-imaginings made colonial Australia a very different society to the one most whites had left behind in England or Ireland. The trials coalesced much of the white population, including settlers, emancipists and convicts, and, in a perverse way, galvanised their self-image as pioneers in a fragile and vulnerable society. What the Myall Creek murder trials did was to demonstrate that even among all these imaginings of the white population, the colony still had in common with the motherland the fundamental tenet of British law: that justice was capable of being applied equally to all persons if those who applied it were sufficiently determined.

There is no doubt that John Plunkett suffered much residual resentment from diverse sections of the New South Wales community for his pursuit of the seven men who were hanged for murder. In 1849, eleven years after the trials, when Plunkett was pursuing one of his Aboriginal evidence Bills in the Legislative Council, a number of members spoke against it, claiming it was merely a device for Plunkett to be given more power, citing his role in the 1838 trials. Robert Lowe, John Foster, Charles Cowper, Edward Hamilton, Robert Fitzgerald and WC Wentworth all spoke against the Bill. The most vehement of them referred to 'the judicial murder of white men' in the Myall Creek case. Hamilton referred to 'the morbid philanthropy' demonstrated by Plunkett, who was solely responsible for the result of the Myall Creek case, which Hamilton categorised as 'the blackest stain on the criminal calendar of New South Wales'.[13]

Even some of those free settlers who held benevolent attitudes towards the Aborigines felt that the stockmen had been unfairly treated. Author, journalist and missionary Alexander Harris wrote in 1853:

> *From time immemorial it had been the custom for influential settlers to head parties like this, against the blacks. All former governors had sanctioned this method of proceeding, by immediate reprisals; and some of these men had thus been initiated into it. They were hanged for doing what they had been taught was perfectly lawful by their masters; and some of the masters [were] magistrates of the territory.*[14]

Tony Earls, one of the two principal biographers of John Hubert Plunkett, noted that:

> *Even to the end of his career, Plunkett suffered the open enmity of those who disagreed with his prosecution of the cases, to which his standard reply was that he would have been ashamed had he acted otherwise.*[15]

There is no doubt that the trials failed to stem the tidal wave of annihilations of the Aboriginal inhabitants of Australia. The hangings merely served to drive the murderous acts underground, so that more surreptitious means, such as poisoning, were used instead of brutal, bloody slayings by sword or bullet or herding over cliffs or into swamps.[16] However, one cannot assess the significance of the Myall Creek murder trials merely by that measure, just as one cannot assess the success of the Nuremburg trials in Europe after the Second World War by the number of genocides that have been perpetrated since in various parts of the world.

The trials in 1838 should be viewed as the earliest 'proto-war-crimes' trials in Australian history. There was undoubtedly an ongoing war, albeit rather one-sided, between the white settlers and the indigenous inhabitants whom they were attempting to displace. The war involved a systemic policy, approved or acquiesced in by the white authorities, of unlawfully exterminating those Aborigines who stood in the way of the expansion of white settlement or posed a threat to the pastoralists and their farming activities. In the author's view, the perpetrators of the mass murders at *Myall Creek Station* in 1838 were motivated by genocidal intentions and were an example of what we now call 'ethnic cleansing'. The fact that almost the whole tribe was decimated – including women and children – demonstrated only too clearly their genocidal intent. The subsequent sexual abuse of one female victim, which spared her life for what must have been a few excruciating days, illustrated the objectification of the victims. Recent history has shown that sexual violence in wartime often goes hand-in-hand with genocide, and that is why systemic sexual offences against enemy populations in war zones are now categorised as war crimes.

In addition, the actions of the perpetrators can be viewed as a classic example of what has become known as 'collective punishment' – a form of retaliation whereby a suspected offender's family members, friends, acquaintances, sect, neighbours or entire ethnic group is targeted for punishment, and where the punished group may have had no direct association with the act that is being punished. The victims in this case were living peacefully on the periphery of white pastoral society and had done nothing to justify their victimisation. Collective punishment has been categorised as a war crime since the 1949 Fourth Geneva Convention, and genocide has been categorised as an international crime by the Genocide Convention that was adopted by the United Nations General Assembly in 1948 and came into force in 1951.

By modern-day standards, the actions of the Myall Creek murderers were war crimes and part of a deliberate, state-sanctioned genocide of the Aboriginal people that today would be punishable by the rules of international criminal law. The fact that vast numbers of genocidal murders went unpunished would today provide evidence of state sanction. While such laws did not exist in 1838, the approach taken by John Plunkett towards the case was consistent with them, and demonstrated an enlightened and visionary attitude that was unparalleled in his time or for more than a hundred years afterwards. John Plunkett did not just prosecute eleven men for murder. He prosecuted his society for its connivance in the attempted annihilation of the Aboriginal people and their culture. His contemporaries subconsciously appreciated that fact, and as a result vehemently resented him at the time and for decades afterwards. It was a testament to his persistence and tactical skills that he convinced twelve jurors to convict seven of the perpetrators, because they were not only condemning those men to their deaths, but also stingingly rebuking their own society for the attempted genocide and ongoing displacement of the indigenous inhabitants.

The prosecutions conducted by John Plunkett against those responsible for the murders at Myall Creek should thus be seen as unique proto-war-crimes trials in an age when such measures were unknown. In the author's view, the 1838 trials had a subtle, long-term effect in promoting an underlying principle of justice and equality for all under Australian law. While they did not prevent future crimes of a similar nature, they stand as a beacon of humanity and interracial justice that illuminated the way for Australia to develop as a civilised nation. In the author's view, it is no coincidence that Australia today is at the forefront of developments in international criminal law. As a nation, Australia punches well above its weight in many international organisations and forums, but none more so than in the field of international criminal law. Australians were among the most enthusiastic and energetic participants at the 1998 Rome Conference, which led to the establishment in 2002 of the International Criminal Court at The Hague as the ultimate venue for the prosecution of war crimes, genocide, ethnic cleansing and crimes against humanity. Today, Australians are well represented at the Court and in its Prosecutor General's Office. John Hubert Plunkett was the first Australian prosecutor to point the way forward at a time when few other Europeans had the insight and courage to do so.

***

It is difficult to understand how a man who achieved so much for his society and was so revered in his lifetime has come to be so unknown in the general community today. Plunkett's contemporaries – Bourke, Gipps, FitzRoy, Wentworth, Macarthur, Cowper, Parkes, Forbes, Stephen, Dowling, Burton, à Beckett, Windeyer, West – are all better known than him today, so inevitably one must ask why.

In the author's view, there are a number of reasons John Hubert Plunkett has virtually disappeared from view in the history of colonial Australia. Plunkett left very few of his own papers. What he kept until his death were mainly letters sent to him, rather than the product of his own hand, so there was very little for later researchers to work with. The few papers he kept were left for many years after his death in the possession of a firm of solicitors, before being deposited in recent years in the State Library in Sydney. A further reason is that John Plunkett undoubtedly waned in his influence and judgement in his later years, and this may have caused a slight diminution in the esteem with which the community held him. A third explanation, and by far the most likely, is that John Plunkett did nothing to ensure that his name would be carried into posterity. He had an irascible personality and few friends, and, like his attitude to money, he cared little for how the public felt about him at the time, or how he would be viewed by history. His bank passbook at the time of his death illustrates how little regard he gave to the balance of his finances, and, in a similar manner, he cared little for the fickle fluctuations of public opinion.

It is also quite bizarre that there are so few memorials to this great Australian who did so much to initiate those freedoms and human rights we cherish so much today that we take them for granted. It begins with Plunkett's grave. As previously mentioned, in 1869 John Plunkett was buried in the Devonshire Street cemetery in central Sydney. When Maria Plunkett died in 1895, it was already known that the Devonshire Street cemetery was to be demolished to make way for the proposed Sydney Central Railway Station, so Maria was buried at the Waverley Cemetery in the eastern suburbs of Sydney, next to the grave of William Edmond Plunkett, the son of Captain Patrick Plunkett, John Hubert's first cousin.[17] The obituary for Maria Plunkett in the *Sydney Morning Herald* stated:

> *The old lady's grave is beside that of the late Mr WE Plunkett, and it is the intention of the latter's son (Mr William Patrick Plunkett) to have the remains of his relative, the Hon JH Plunkett, brought from the old Devonshire Street cemetery to Waverley, so that husband and wife who joined hands in marriage far away in Ireland when the nineteenth century was young, may towards its close peacefully rest here in Australia under the same mound of earth.*[18]

In 1901, when the Devonshire Street cemetery was demolished, Father McEncroe's body was reinterred in the crypt of St Mary's Cathedral, commensurate with his standing in Australian Catholic history. William Patrick Plunkett, a grandson of Captain Patrick Plunkett, arranged for his grandfather's body to be reinterred in a Plunkett family vault at the Waverley Cemetery.[19] At the same time, John Hubert Plunkett's body followed the captain's. However, only the captain and his immediate family were named on the memorial stone, so that John and Maria's gravesites made no mention of them.

There are few public buildings, streets or institutions that honour John Hubert Plunkett's name. It is painted above the door of the New South Wales Parliament and in the Legislative Council Chamber.[20] There is a plaque at the home of the Sisters of Charity in Potts Point, and his portrait hangs in the busy lobby of St Vincent's Public Hospital in Darlinghurst. His name is honoured by an annual lecture in legal history[21] and a centre for ethics jointly run by the Australian Catholic University and St Vincent's Hospital. The John Hubert Plunkett Society is a small group of Australian lawyers who desire to promote Irish cultural studies. There is a short street named after him in Woolloomooloo, which has been so truncated by the Eastern Suburbs Railway and Western Distributor that it scarcely still exists. Much better known is the eponymous primary school, which now lists its address as Forbes Street. There are several insignificant suburban streets that are presumably named after him in the Sydney suburbs of Kirribilli, St Leonards and Drummoyne, as well as in the country towns of Nowra in New South Wales and Dandenong in Victoria. The street in Drummoyne intersects with Gipps Street and is parallel to Broughton, Polding and Therry Streets.[22]

***

John Hubert Plunkett had a vision of Australia that was in some ways akin to the vision of America advocated a century later by Dr Martin Luther King Jr: 'equal opportunities in education, health, recreation, and similar public services; the right to vote; equality before the law'.[23] Like Dr King, John Hubert Plunkett fought tirelessly for much of his life to remove the many impediments to that equality. Like Dr King, he believed that advances in human rights had to be gained from within the system by lawful means. Like Dr King, he placed the achievement of his vision above his own personal interests and comfort. Both men eschewed personal wealth. Unlike Dr King, he was not a member of the most oppressed class – in Australia, undoubtedly the Aborigines – but in his place of birth he had been. Both men had been deeply affected by experiences of discrimination early in their lives. Both men were profoundly religious and used their faith as a source of inspiration and courage. Both men were moved by music. Both men had 'an inner urge to serve humanity' that could not be ignored or appeased. Both could look beyond the accepted conventions of their time to see eternal truths that today we view as self-evident.[24] While Plunkett achieved much through his courtroom advocacy, his skills as an orator and his ability to inspire others with words cannot be compared with those of Dr King. Unlike Plunkett, Martin Luther King Jr has been recognised by numerous memorials, buildings, neighbourhoods, streets, associations, libraries, a non-profit Center for Nonviolent Social Change, and even a national public holiday, which all attest to his greatness.

In Australia, we are short of heroes who have excelled in areas other than sport. We celebrate a most terrible military defeat at the hands of the Turks in 1915, even though it was planned and thoroughly mismanaged by the British. We hold up Ned Kelly as a national symbol – a bushranger who had a vile temper and a shocking record of violence, and who robbed from the rich to give to himself and his family. Our national heroes are often those who can hit, throw or kick a ball. Surely we can agree to fete a man who, in the early stages of our nation's existence, achieved so much in creating the freedoms, civil rights and public institutions that we enjoy today.

19

A DIFFERENT CHALICE

Not long after the disappearance of Davy and the release of the four remaining defendants who had been charged with the Myall Creek murders, the arrest warrant for the ringleader, John Henry Fleming, lapsed. Soon after, Fleming came out of hiding and resumed normal life. For the reasons that have already been mentioned, not the slightest attempt was made to bring him to justice. In October 1841, just over three years after the murders, he openly married Charlotte Dunstan at Wilberforce in the Hawkesbury River Valley. In 1842 he was appointed as a trustee for the erection of an Anglican church at St Albans. Like many of his brothers, he lived most of his life as a farmer in the Hawkesbury River district. In the early 1860s he moved to a farm at Wilberforce, where he became a highly respected member of the community. In 1882, he was appointed a Justice of the Peace, so it can legitimately, though loosely, be said of him that during his lifetime he went from mass murderer to magistrate.[1] The only person who expressed any concern about Fleming's appointment as a magistrate was Legislative Assembly member, Joseph Palmer Abbott, who noted in Parliament on 18 October 1882 that:

> *In the last Commission of the Peace he noticed the name of a man against whom a warrant for murder had at one time been issued.*

John Henry Fleming and his wife, Charlotte, had no children. In his later years, he was a popular member of his extended family and was renowned for regaling young nieces and nephews with blood-curdling tales of his exploits 'escaping from the blacks'. His account of the events of 10 June 1838 at the *Myall Creek Station* bore no resemblance to the facts, and was clearly an outright fabrication. According to a present-day family member, who was often told the story by her grandmother, who in turn was told by her mother, Maria Tuckerman (née Fleming), who was John Henry Fleming's niece, Uncle John would say this:

> *The cattlemen had been leading the captured group around the bush for a while hoping to attract the real culprits. They were very frustrated at not being able to get their hands on the ones they wanted – when finally deciding they had to do something. It erupted into an act of not being a straightforward act of taking aim and shooting, but a spur-of-the-moment atrocity.*
>
> *JH Fleming raised his gun and aimed at one particular man who he believed knew more than he was telling them, at first to scare him into talking, so he fired at him, not to hit him, but*

to scare him. To his shock and horror in a split second, every man with a gun had raised his gun and fired at the same time and kept firing until all the natives were down. John Henry admitted he probably killed one, but claimed he took no part in the mass killing of the others.

He was so distraught at what had been done that he left almost immediately and rode back to camp. In the morning he went with the men back to the massacre site to see what he could do. [He was] so traumatised and terrified by what he found that he just got on his horse and rode towards home on the Hawkesbury – not on a drunken horse as was written in places later, but at a measured speed to make sure his horse made the desperate ride to his home. However, by the time he reached the Hunter area his horse was tiring badly and he decided to call on a relative living in the area, specifically to borrow a fresh horse to continue on his way to Portland Head.[2] *Many Hawkesbury families had moved to the Hunter Valley and began farming there by 1820.*

He left his horse tied to a hitching rail in the village now known as Muswellbrook so no one would know who helped him in what he knew must soon come!

After he arrived back at Portland Head he was sheltered by a number of related families still farming at Wilberforce and Ebenezer. By then the Fleming daughters had intermarried with several Ebenezer and Wilberforce pioneer families and all were ready to help and protect him. The police never ever came looking for him, which even today is strange. He moved freely about the district, dressed as a woman. Many knew this and no one even considered giving him up to the police.

Eventually he got on a boat in Sydney, dressed as a woman and went to Moreton Bay to his brother Joseph.[3]

John Henry Fleming never expressed regret for his involvement in the Myall Creek murders. However, his later actions as a trustee and warden of St John's Church at Wilberforce possibly spoke of an underlying, even subconscious, appreciation of the evil he had done. In 1877, at the age of sixty-one, Fleming was responsible for the construction of one of the stained-glass windows in the south wall of the church, close to the chancel.[4] The subject of the window is Saint John the Evangelist and the poisoned chalice with an emerging dragon. The image is a reference to a legendary incident that, according to fragments of Greek and Latin texts, occurred to Saint John at Ephesus. The story goes that Aristodemus, the pagan high priest of the temple of Diana at Ephesus, challenged Saint John to drink from a poisoned cup to prove that his God was the true one. To prove the potency of the poison, two criminals were forced to drink from the cup, and promptly died. Saint John then blessed the cup and, according to various stories, a snake or a dragon emerged from it, thereby removing the poison. Saint John then drank safely from the cup, restored the two criminals to life, and Aristodemus was converted to Christianity.

At a simple level, the window is about the victory of Christianity over paganism, but at a deeper level it can be seen as the triumph of piety and faith over evil. Was the erection of the window at St John's an expression of hope by John Henry Fleming that through his faith and good work at his church and in his Hawkesbury River community he had expunged and neutralised the demon poison of his earlier life? Was the window a coded acknowledgement by Fleming of his role in the Myall Creek murders and a symbolic prayer that he had been restored to grace by his later good deeds? Whereas John Hubert Plunkett's chalice was a source of inspiration and a symbol of martyrdom in defence of faith, integrity and valour, was Fleming's chalice a valiant plea to atone for an evil deed that had gone unpunished in this world?

John Henry Fleming died in August 1894 at the age of seventy-eight. His funeral service at St John's Church at Wilberforce on 21 August was one of the largest in the area for years. Fleming had been a warden of that church for decades and he was well liked and highly regarded in his local community. There were few people still alive in his district who had a recollection of the 1838 murders that had occurred hundreds of miles to the north at Myall Creek, or of the subsequent trials in Sydney. Outside the church, the cortege was met by a group of children from the local public school, marshalled by their headmaster and his assistants, who formed a double-line guard-of-honour through which the mourners passed. Numerous wreaths were laid upon the coffin. During the service, Handel's 'Dead March' from *Saul* was played – the same piece that had been performed at the funeral of John Hubert Plunkett twenty-five years earlier. Fleming was buried in the Church of England Cemetery at Wilberforce. The local newspaper, the *Windsor and Richmond Gazette*, published an obituary that acknowledged the respect the deceased had been accorded by his community, stating:

> *As a resident he will be much missed for his kindness of heart and generosity to the poor; he was never known to refuse to anyone in want.*[5]

The article went on to record that he had been a member of the Hawkesbury Benevolent Society, which had provided much assistance to elderly residents in the area. It also informed readers that his health had been declining for several years, and that shortly before his death he had suffered a severe attack of influenza that had caused him much suffering, although 'through all his pain he was remarkable for his patience'. The only hint that John Henry Fleming had led anything but a conservative, honourable and law-abiding life was this seemingly innocuous reference in the obituary:

> *Deceased used to tell some stirring stories of the early days of settlement in the colony, and the trouble he had with the Blacks.*

***

Joseph Fleming, who was undoubtedly involved in helping his brother, John Henry, evade justice by hiding him in the outlying districts far to the west of the Moreton Bay settlement, had an interesting and varied working life in the years to come. In June 1839, he led the posse that captured Gentleman Dick's gang of bushrangers on the banks of the Big (Gwydir) River. Joseph was appointed chief constable of Wollombi in 1842 and inspector of distilleries in 1844 and held those positions until 1846. In 1847, he moved to Maitland, where he went into business as a butcher and established a boiling-down works. He moved to Ipswich in 1850 and established another boiling-down works there, and also became involved in political life. In 1886, he abandoned public life and became a storekeeper in Ipswich and Roma. He died in Ipswich on 23 September 1891.[6]

***

William Hobbs, the superintendent of *Myall Creek Station* who had been summarily dismissed by his employer, Henry Dangar, sued him in March 1839, for unpaid wages and was awarded £17. Hobbs never worked again as a station manager. Being unpopular in the Big River district for having reported the murders to the authorities, he left the area and joined the police, serving in Wollombi and McDonald River (ironically, the area in which some of John Henry Fleming's family lived). He married in 1842 and named his second son John Hubert Plunkett Hobbs. William then became a gaoler at Windsor and ended up as the governor of the gaol at Wollongong from 1865 until his death in 1871.[7] On modern-day maps of *Myall Creek Station*, the valley where the homestead is located is named Hobbs Gully.

***

George Anderson, who had been transported for life to New South Wales, and who played such a major role in the two trials of the Myall Creek murderers, was granted a conditional ticket-of-leave in September 1841. The condition was that he remain in Sydney in the employ of a Mr Townsend. In 1848 he was granted a pardon, and so became a completely free man, with the condition that the pardon would be void if he re-entered the United Kingdom. He remained in the colony for the rest of his life.

***

After the sacking of William Hobbs as Superintendent at *Myall Creek Station*, Henry Dangar appointed as his new manager William Wall, who had been a shepherd on the station, but based at Koloona, a few miles from the stockmen's huts, and thus not involved in the events of 10 June 1838. William Wall was employed at the station until he passed away in 1888. William Wall's son, John Wall (born 1852), and grandson, Cecil Wall, also worked for most of their lives on *Myall Creek Station*. Cecil ceased working on the station in 1937. In 1964 he provided Bingara resident Len Payne with a detailed, gruesome account of the murders that had been related to him by his grandfather – an account that differed in some respects from others.[8] In particular, Cecil described the massacre as having occurred inside a stockyard rather than against a fence. The author considers Cecil Wall's account as authentic and reliable. According to Cecil:

> *We were shown deep stains on the timber of the old stockyard and told that it was caused by the blood of the Aborigines.*

Cecil described how parts of the stockyard frame had still existed when he was a young man 'years before the last war'. Little by little it had collapsed, but sections of it stood for decades and the gate hung broken.

In July 1964, Cecil Wall and Len Payne went to *Myall Creek Station*. Cecil Wall identified the location of the stockyard where the massacre had taken place.[9] At the site they found the remains of the gate posts and two very large hinges about 18 inches long and weighing 18.5 pounds, which Cecil Wall identified as having come from the gate.

Years later, Len Payne was to play a role in attempts to erect a memorial to the slain Wirrayaraay at the site of the massacre.

***

John Blake, one of the four men acquitted at the first Myall Creek murders trial and not subsequently retried, was severely injured in a riding accident several years later and in 1852 committed suicide by cutting his throat. His great-great-grandson, Des Blake, who has effected a reconciliation with the descendants of the Wirrayaraay, said about his ancestor's suicide:

> *Did he have a guilty conscience? We like to think he did.*[10]

Beulah Adams, great-great-niece of Edward Foley, who was one of those hanged for the murders, has also been part of a process of reconciliation. She has said:

> *What Edward Foley did was a dreadful, dreadful thing. There's nothing that I can do to … to make it right. But I can say, 'Well, it shouldn't have happened. I'm sorry it happened.' And that's why I speak out today. So people will learn of the history, the dreadful history, in such a beautiful land. It should never have happened.*[11]

***

On the other side of the story is Sue Blacklock, a descendant of one of the two young boys who escaped from the approaching stockmen by jumping into the creek and swimming away. She said in 2001:

> *There were two brothers that were saved from the massacre. One of those little boys was my great-great-great-grandfather. My dad always told me about that. It was passed down from his great-grandparents right down to him, and he wanted to*

> *hand it down to his family. But I remember Dad when he'd speak about it. His voice cracked just like the memory just sort of hurt. I hear him now telling his grandchildren all about what happened out there, and how it was burnt … and were killed and then burned. We just kept it all hush-hush. We didn't want to talk about it because of how dreadful it was. And, um, I remember when we used to drive past that place. It … just had a feeling about it that I can't explain.*[12]

***

Neither Henry Dangar's reputation nor his financial fortune was seriously or permanently harmed by his ill-advised support for the accused stockmen in the Myall Creek murder trials. By 1850, he was one of the largest landowners in New South Wales, holding property covering an area of over 300 000 acres (121 407 hectares), as well as extensive commercial interests in the Hunter Valley and along the Great North Road between Sydney and Newcastle. He retired from public life in 1851. The following year he sailed to England and spent the next few years travelling on the continent, returning to New South Wales in 1856. He retired to a house at Potts Point in Sydney and died in 1861. Mount Dangar, Dangar Island, Dangarfield, Dangar Street in Armidale and Dangarsleigh commemorate his name, but his finest memorial was the proud boast of many of his employees that they were 'Dangar men'. Henry Dangar is viewed today by the Gamilaroi people as a sinister character who, behind the scenes, bore much responsibility for the murders.

Bill Dangar, great-great grandson of Henry, has said that his ancestor was essentially a good man, even though he was 'probably wrong' to appear to defend the perpetrators of the massacre.[13]

***

Robert Scott, co-founder of the Black Association and the man who convinced the eleven accused men not to break rank, was much less successful as a Hunter River landowner than his neighbour, Henry Dangar. However, he became quite famous for his social activities at his property, *Glendon*, as a host to artists, explorers, clergymen and scientists, creating a cultural centre unique in the colony for his time. He died unmarried in July 1844 aged forty-four.

***

After several years of complaining that the workload of Chief Justice was too heavy, and having several applications for leave refused until a suitable replacement could be found, Sir James Dowling finally collapsed on the Bench on 27 June 1844. His health in tatters, his application for leave was finally granted, but before his ship could depart for England, Dowling had a relapse and died on 27 September 1844. At the time of his death, he was preparing a volume of law reports containing the decisions of the Supreme Court of New South Wales during his time as Chief Justice. Upon his death, the venture lapsed, and the decisions of the court were not comprehensively published until they were made available to the public in digital form by Macquarie University in 1997–2005.[14]

***

After the second Myall Creek murder trial, Justice William Westbrooke Burton took leave to go to England between 1839 and 1841. Upon his return, he resumed his place on the Supreme Court. On 6 July 1844, he left New South Wales to become a judge in Madras, now Chennai, in India. This proved to be a costly move, because less than three months later the New South Wales Chief Justice Sir James Dowling died. Had Burton still been in the colony, he would undoubtedly have been appointed Chief Justice. While in India, he was knighted. In 1857 he returned to Sydney, where he was appointed to the Legislative Council, and he became President of the Council the following year. He left Sydney precipitously in 1858, after resigning his position on the Council due to a dispute with the government about the passage in the House of some land-reform legislation. He proceeded to London, where he died in 1888.

***

Within a short time of the Myall Creek murder trials in late 1838, procedures in New South Wales criminal cases changed markedly. In October 1840, with the passing of the *Prisoners' Counsel Act*, defendants' counsel were granted the right to address juries on the evidence. This prompted Mr Justice Willis of the Supreme Court to enter into conjecture about how the result in the second Myall Creek murder trial might have been different if defence counsel had had the right to address on the evidence:

> *Who can say what might have been the effect of an impassioned and eloquent defence by counsel on the minds of the Jury.*[15]

However, it was not until 1891, with the threat of eternal damnation for perjury having less of a grip on peoples' minds, that an accused was permitted to give sworn evidence at a trial.

***

Having acted as Attorney General during the two years that John Plunkett was absent from the colony, Roger Therry was elected to the Legislative Council in 1843. In 1844, he was appointed as resident judge at Port Phillip (Melbourne). In 1846 he returned to Sydney to take up a position as a judge of the Supreme Court. In 1850, together with John Plunkett, he was appointed as an inaugural Senator of the University of Sydney. He resigned his judgeship in 1859 and retired to England, where he wrote the book *Reminiscences of Thirty Years' Residence in New South Wales and Victoria.* He was knighted in 1869 and died in 1874.

***

In 1844, William à Beckett, lead counsel for all accused at both trials, was appointed an acting Supreme Court judge. In 1846 he moved to become the resident judge in Port Phillip (Melbourne). He remained there until his appointment in January 1852 as the first Chief Justice of the newly constituted Supreme Court of Victoria. In the same year, he was knighted by the Queen. As Chief Justice, he presided over the infamous Eureka stockade trials in Melbourne in February and March of 1855, in which miners were charged with high treason arising out of rioting at Ballarat. His summing up to the jury favoured a conviction, but popular sentiment held sway and the jury returned verdicts of *not guilty*. He retired in 1857 due to ill health, and in 1863 he moved to England, where he died in 1869 – the same year as John Hubert Plunkett.

***

Richard Windeyer, one of the junior counsel for the accused at both trials, later became an advocate for Aboriginal welfare and rights, and played a significant role in the establishment of the New South Wales Aboriginal Protection Society. He was influenced in this not only by his experiences during the two Myall Creek murder trials, but also by the trial in May 1836 of the two Aboriginal men, Jack Congo Murrell and Bummaree. By 1842, Windeyer was a large landowner in the Hunter River Valley. He was elected to the Legislative Council in 1843. In 1846, he spent Christmas day in Darlinghurst Gaol after being convicted of contempt of court by Chief Justice Sir Alfred Stephen, for calling John Darvall, his opposing counsel, a liar and shaping up to fight him during the hearing of a case. Richard Windeyer died near Launceston in 1847.

***

William Foster, the other junior counsel for the defence at both trials, had arrived in the colony in 1827, whereupon he was appointed as Solicitor General and Chairman of the Court of Quarter Sessions (now Chief Judge of the District Court). The following year he became Commissioner of the Court of Requests. From 1843 to 1845 he was an elected member of the New South Wales Legislative Council.

***

Mr Henry Keck, the gaolkeeper of the George Street Gaol where the seven Myall Creek murderers were hanged, became the first governor of Darlinghurst Gaol in 1841. He was later dismissed for having a variety of enterprising commercial schemes involving the misuse of prisoners to make money for himself.

***

After the execution of Archbishop Oliver Plunkett in 1681, his remains were buried in a London churchyard for two years and then removed to a Benedictine Monastery in Germany. Exactly 200 years later, in 1881, part of his body was transferred to the Benedictine Abbey at Downside, Somerset, in England. His head was brought to Rome, and from there to Armagh, and eventually to Drogheda in Ireland where, since 1921, it has rested in Saint Peter's Church. In 1920, Oliver Plunkett was beatified, and in 1975 he was made a Saint by Pope Paul VI – the first new Irish Saint for almost 700 years. In 1997, he was made the patron Saint for Peace and Reconciliation in Ireland. Today St Peter's Church in Drogheda is the site of a national shrine to Saint Oliver Plunkett.

***

Very few memorials mark the sites where Aborigines were killed by European settlers and their armed retainers during the 'war of extirpation' in colonial times. It took more than 160 years for a memorial to be erected at the location of the *Myall Creek Station* murders. It has come to represent a commemoration of the victims of all massacres of Indigenous people during the colonial era. The idea was first advocated by Len Payne, local cinema projectionist and Apex Club member in Bingara, the nearest township to the station. As previously mentioned, Len Payne had gone to the site of the murders with Cecil Wall, the grandson of William Wall who worked at *Myall Creek Station* in 1838 but was not involved in the murders. Payne recorded Cecil Wall's recollections of his grandfather's account of the murders. Payne first proposed a memorial to the victims of the massacre in January 1965 with the aim of 'reminding people of their lack of feeling for the Australian Aborigine'. Initially, the Apex club supported his proposal, however, there was resistance from other members of the local community who felt that a memorial would tarnish the reputation of the district and its residents – so his club abandoned the idea. The negative attitudes in the community were encapsulated in a strident letter to the *Bingara Advocate* from local resident, TJ Wearne, in which he expressed the view:

> *The whole idea is ill conceived, unconsidered and mischievous, and an insult to the Bingara people.*

Payne zealously, but unsuccessfully, maintained his advocacy for a memorial until his death in 1994.[16]

In October 1998, at the invitation of Sue Blacklock, a descendant of those who had survived the massacre, a conference on reconciliation was convened at the Myall Creek Community Centre, involving descendants of survivors, other members of the Gamilaroi nation, and supportive non-Indigenous people from the local community and Sydney, including members of the local Uniting Church.[17] A decision was taken to erect a permanent memorial and the Myall Creek Memorial

Committee was formed to put this into effect. Finally, in 2000, 162 years after the murders, a huge memorial stone was erected at the site of the murders. In an act of meaningful reconciliation, a moving dedication ceremony on Sunday 10 June 2000 brought together over 1500 people, including descendants of the survivors, the perpetrators, the Dangar family, and the Europeans who had done the right thing in 1838 by alerting the authorities. Eight years later, on 7 June 2008, at a memorial service marking the 170th anniversary, the site was placed on the National Heritage List.[18] Federal Heritage Minister, the Honourable Peter Garrett, said:

> *The fact that the descendants of some of the people massacred on that horrific day in 1838 and the descendants of those charged with the crime can come together in their own peaceful and personal reconciliation gives me great hope for our country and makes me very proud to be an Australian.*

The bronze plaque at the memorial site reads:

> *In memory of the Wirrayaraay people who were murdered on the slopes of this ridge in an unprovoked but premeditated act in the late afternoon of 10 June 1838. Erected on 10 June 2000 by a group of Aboriginal and non-Aboriginal Australians in an act of reconciliation, and in acknowledgment of the truth of our shared history. We remember them (Ngiyani winangay ganunga).*

The memorial at Myall Creek has come to represent the multitude of massacres that occurred all over Australia during a period of more than 120 years.[19] Although there are many known sites of other massacres, and a few memorials, we know more about the murders at Myall Creek than any other act of mass murder of Indigenous Australians – because of the two trials conducted in 1838. For that, there are a number of people to whom we as a nation owe gratitude: George Anderson, Davy, William Hobbs, Governor Sir George Gipps, Captain Edward Denny Day, the lone juror in the second trial who spoke out to correct the verdict, and especially John Hubert Plunkett. In the author's opinion, the story of what happened to the Aboriginal inhabitants in colonial times should be taught in our schools as readily as we teach the exploits of the great explorers. The two accounts are inextricably intertwined. A real acceptance of the horrors that were perpetrated against our Indigenous communities will bring with it an understanding of the long-term trauma that has been transferred down the generations until today. We readily recognise that the trauma of genocide during the Nazi period in Europe, in the former Yugoslavia during the 1990s, and in countries like Rwanda and Cambodia, can be deeply felt for many generations after the killings have ended. If we recognise that Aboriginal communities were subjected to massacres in a multitude of locations all over Australia for more than a century, there may be more sympathy for the current generations striving for equanimity, understanding and acceptance. Until we recognise that what occurred was a war of extirpation or annihilation – until we acknowledge that what was perpetrated amounted to an attempted genocide that today would be recognised as a war crime – we will not reach our full maturity as a nation.

ENDNOTES

Chapter 1

1 Now Court 3, King Street. At the time there were only two courtrooms. The Eastern Court was used as the Banco (appeals) Court. See http://designbase.com/heritagesites/KSsite/10heritage/history/kingsthist.html
2 In the New England district of northern New South Wales. The nearest large town is Inverell. The nearest small town is Bingara.
3 http://www.saintoliverplunkett.com/literature.html#book1
4 The English were anxious to avoid a repetition of the Irish rebellion that had occurred in 1641.
5 'The trial of Dr Oliver Plunkett', in Cobbett's *Complete Collection of State Trials*, London, 1810, volume 8, page 447.
6 For an excellent comparison between the convict system and slavery, see John Bradley Hirst, *Freedom on the Fatal Shore: Australia's First Colony*, Black Inc, 2008, chapter 2.
7 The thirteen female factories were situated at Parramatta (2), Bathurst, Newcastle, Port Macquarie (2), Moreton Bay (2), Hobart Town, Georgetown, Cascades, Launceston and Ross.

8 Tasmania.

9 See John Braithwaite, 'Crime in a Convict Republic', (2001), volume 64, *Modern Law Review*, page 11.

10 Lieutenant-General Sir Richard Bourke was the ninth Governor of New South Wales, between 1831 and 1837.

Chapter 2

1 Built in 1806 and home of the Plunkett family until the mid-nineteenth century. Described in 1851 as a 'superb mansion'; the entrance gates are still in use, but only low walls remain of the house and outbuildings. See http://landedestates.nuigalway.ie/LandedEstates/jsp/property-show.jsp?id=1154.

2 The Plunketts of Roscommon should not be confused with the family of Lord William Plunket, a Presbyterian from County Fermanagh, who was Ireland's Solicitor General and Attorney General (1802–07, 1822–27) and later Lord Chancellor of Ireland (1830–1841).

3 Tony Earls, *Plunkett's Legacy: An Irishman's contribution to the Rule of Law in New South Wales*, Australian Scholarly Publishing, 2009, page 24.

4 King's Counsel or Queen's Counsel.

5 Since the *Act of Union* of 1801, Westminster had been the Parliament of the United Kingdom of Great Britain and Ireland.

6 Earls, page 33.

7 It was not until 1858 that the political emancipation of British Jews was achieved with the passing of the *Jews Relief Act*. The Act removed the words from the Oath of Allegiance that stated 'and I make this Declaration upon the true faith of a Christian'.

8 Earls, page 50, footnote 85.

9 John Molony, *An Architect of Freedom: John Hubert Plunkett in New South Wales, 1832–1869*, ANU Press, 1973, page 10.

Chapter 3

1 Max Waugh, *Forgotten Hero: Richard Bourke, Irish Governor of New South Wales, 1831–1837*, Australian Scholarly Publishing, Melbourne, 2005, page 2.

2 Hazel King, *Richard Bourke*, Oxford University Press, Melbourne, 1971, pages 8–9, 12–14.

3 *Historical Records of Australia*, series 1, volume 17, pages 284–5.

4 Molony, page 13.

5 The equivalent of the current NSW District Court.

6 Dr Gregory D Woods '*A History of Criminal Law in New South Wales: The Colonial Period, 1788–1900*', Federation Press, 2002, pages 67–69.

7 Chief Justice Francis Forbes, Justice James Dowling and Justice William Burton.

8 '*Attainted Jurors Opinion*' [1833] NSWSupC 75. See: http://law.mq.edu.au/research/colonial_case_law/nsw/cases/case_index/1833/attainted_jurors_opinion/

9 For a discussion of the interaction between Aborigines and the courts, see Brent Salter, 'For Want of Evidence: Initial Impressions of Indigenous Exchanges with the First Colonial Superior Courts of Australia', *The University of Tasmania Law Review*, 2008, volume 27, page 145.

10 For example: *R. v. Jackey* [1834] NSWSupC 94; http://www.law.mq.edu.au/research/colonial_case_law/nsw/cases/case_index/1834/r_v_jackey/ See also: Russell Smandych, 'Contemplating the Testimony of "Others": James Stephen 'The Colonial Office, and the Fate of Australian Aboriginal Evidence Acts, Circa 1839–1849', 2004, *Australian Journal of Legal History*, volume 8, page 237.

11 *The Australian*, 17 May 1836. See also: http://www.law.mq.edu.au/research/colonial_case_law/nsw/cases/case_index/1836/r_v_murrell_and_bummaree/

Chapter 4

1 J Lowndes, 'The Australian Magistracy: From Justices of the Peace to Judges and Beyond', Part I, 2000, volume 74, *Australian Law Journal*, pages 509–532.

2 There was also another Plunkett in the colony: Edward Plunkett, the keeper of the Liverpool madhouse, who was unrelated. Molony, page 20, footnote 37.

3 David Plater & Sangeetha Royan, 'The Development & Application in 19th Century Australia of the Prosecutor's Role as a Minister of Justice: Rhetoric or Reality?', 2012, 31 *University of Tasmania Law Review* 78. For a report of the trial see *Sydney Herald*, 2 March 1837, page 2.

4 *Faunce v. Cavenagh* [1838] NSWSupC 24; http://www.law.mq.edu.au/research/colonial_case_law/nsw/cases/case_index/1838/faunce_v_cavenagh/

5 John Bradley Hirst, *Freedom on the Fatal Shore: Australia's First Colony*, Black Inc, 2008, pages 45–46.

6 It has been suggested that this was a cause of resentment between the convicts and the Aboriginal inhabitants. See Christine M Bramble, 'Relations between Aborigines and White Settlers in Newcastle & the Hunter District, 1804–1841', Dissertation, University of New England, January 1981, especially the conclusion at pages 79–80.

7 *R v Hitchcock and others* [1833] NSWSupC 114. See: http://www.law.mq.edu.au/research/colonial_case_law/nsw/cases/case_index/1833/r_v_hitchcock_and_others/. For Mudie and Larnach's version, see James Mudie, 'Vindication of James Mudie and John Larnach, Sydney, September 1834'; http://www.nla.gov.au/apps/doview/nla.aus-f1824-p.pdf.

8 Sir Roger Therry, *Reminiscences of Thirty Years' Residence in New South Wales and Victoria*, London, 1863, Sydney University Press, 1974, page 165.

9 Only five of them on the attempted-murder charge.

10 Roger Therry, page 169.

11 For a discussion on the allegations against Mudie and Larnach, see John Bradley Hirst, pages 171–2.

12 James Mudie, 'Vindication of James Mudie and John Larnach'.

13 London, 1837. See http://gutenberg.net.au/ebooks13/1300721h.html

14 Isobelle Barrett Meyering, 'Abolitionism, Settler Violence and the Case Against Flogging, A Reassessment of Sir William Molesworth's Contribution to the Transportation Debate', *History Australia*, volume 7, number 1, 2010, Monash University ePress, pages 6.4–6.5.

15 JM Bennett, *Sir William à Beckett: First Chief Justice of Victoria 1852–1857*, Federation Press, 2001.

16 See: http://www.law.mq.edu.au/research/colonial_case_law/nsw/cases/case_index/1834/r_v_jenkins_and_tattersdale/

17 See the extract from a speech by H Snelling QC, 'Some Remarks Upon the History of the Bar in New South Wales', The Bar Gazette, 1961, 2 NSW Bar Gazette, page 3.

18 Unrelated to the modern-day newspaper of the same name.

19 It should be recalled that in 1834 there were only about 70 000 non-indigenous people in the whole of New South Wales.

20 http://www.law.mq.edu.au/research/colonial_case_law/nsw/cases/case_index/1834/r_v_jenkins_and_tattersdale/

21 Ibid.

22 *Sydney Herald*, 13 November 1834.

Chapter 5

1 Alex Castles, 'The reception and status of English law in Australia', 1963, *Adelaide Law Review*.

2 Prue Vines, *Law and Justice in Australia*, Oxford University Press, Melbourne, 2nd edition, 2009, page 174. See also Enid Campbell, 'Colonial Legislation and The Laws of England', 1965, 2 *Tasmanian University Law Review* 148.

3 *Cable v. Sinclair* [1788] NSWKR 7; [1788] NSWSupC 7. See: http://www.law.mq.edu.au/research/colonial_case_law/nsw/cases/case_index/1788/cable_v_sinclair/

4 *Historical Records of Australia*, series 1, volume 17, pages 224–33. See Earls, pages 74–6.

5 *Historical Records of Australia*, series 1, volume 18, pages 201–07. See Earls, pages 77–8.

6 All mail had to come by sea – a journey of four months, or at least eight for return mail.

7 Earls, pages 69–78.

8 *Historical Records of Australia*, series 1, volume 18, page 472. See Alan Raphael Barcan, 'Opinion, Policy and Practice in N.S.W. Education, 1833–1880; The Development of an Educational Tradition'. Thesis submitted for the Degree of Doctor of Philosophy in the Australian National University, December 1962, page 17.

9 Barcan, pages 17–23. The issue of state aid to private schools continues to be a sensitive electoral issue.

10 A decade later, many of the same religious leaders recognised that they had lost out by opposing the schools proposal.

Chapter 6

1 The area is drained by the Namoi River and its tributaries, the Mooki River and the Peel River. https://en.wikipedia.org/wiki/Namoi_River. Current-day towns include Gunnedah, Narrabri, Quirindi and Tamworth.

2 Leonard L Payne, 'Then and Now – notes on the Myall Creek Massacre of 1838', pages 2–3, in *Papers on the Myall Creek Massacre, 1964–1979*, manuscript, National Library of Australia, BibID: 102008, MS 9619.

3 An attack involving plunder and pillage to buildings, property and/or animals.

4 John Ross (ed), *Chronicle of Australia*, 1993, page 240.

5 Annual Report of the Aboriginal Mission at Lake Macquarie, New South Wales – 1835, in *The Perth Gazette* and *Western Australian Journal*, 3 December 1836, page 810. See: http://trove.nla.gov.au/ndp/del/article/640187

6 Present-day Scone, more than 200 miles (350 kilometres) to the south.

7 To completely get rid of, kill off, or destroy somebody or something considered undesirable.

8 Acting Governor from 5 December 1837 till 23 February 1838.

9 Later Australia Day.

10 Situated near the present-day township of Bingara (pronounced with the emphasis on the 'i'), a small town in the New England region of New South Wales.

11 Pronounced '*bInga:ra:*' with the emphasis on the first 'a'.

12 Lyndall Ryan, 'A very bad business: Henry Dangar and the Myall Creek Massacre 1838', presented to a Conference of the Centre of the History of Violence, University of Newcastle, 27 November 2008, page 4.

13 Such breastplates were a clear marker of acceptance by white society. It was akin to the modern-day identification tags provided by military forces to the Press in war zones. A breastplate in the war zones between non-indigenous and indigenous combatants in the 1830s should similarly have protected the wearer and his tribe.

14 Located between present-day Manilla and Bendemeer.

15 http://www.the1788-1820pioneerassociation.org.au/Henry%20Flemming.html

16 The inn still survives at 104 Bathurst Street. Originally called the 'Blighton Arms', it was renamed the 'Macquarie Arms'. Next door is 'Mulgrave Place', a house built in 1823 where the Fleming family lived. Pitt Town was one of the five 'Macquarie Towns'

established by Governor Lachlan Macquarie in 1810. Although a site for the village was laid out near to the Hawkesbury River in 1811, due to frequent flooding it was relocated in 1815 to its present location further from the river.

17 Ebenezer.

18 See the article by Marie Turnbull in Clan Turnbull Ebenezer Newsletter, volume 4, number 2, July–August 2012, page 4. The article is available at: http://turnbullclan.com/tca/newsletters/ebenezer/2012_v03_n02_july-august.pdf.

19 Possibly a former slave from the Caribbean, who had escaped to England.

20 A light shotgun for shooting birds and small animals.

21 AJ Howard, *Bingera Run*, Australian Origins and Heritage Library, 2012. See http://www.bingara.com.au/files/uploaded/file/Bingera_Run_2012.pdf.

22 Later known as Jimmy Munro.

Chapter 7

1 See Len Payne, 'The Myall Creek Massacre' and 'An Interview with Len Payne, Bingara NSW, 27 June 1994' by Patrick Collins, referred to in Patrick Collins, *Goodbye Bussamarai: The Mandandanji Land War, Southern Queensland, 1842–1852*, self-published by the author. See also: http://www.goodbyebussamarai.com/page9.htm.

Chapter 8

1 Letter from William Hobbs to Police Magistrate Invermein concerning the Myall Creek Massacre, 9 July 1838, State Records New South Wales, series number 19437.

2 Now Denman.

3 Magistrate Day's greatest exploit in arresting bushrangers was yet to come. In December 1840 he was responsible for the capture

at Doughboy Hollow of the so-called 'Jewboy Gang', which had been active in the Maitland, Newcastle, Lake Macquarie, Wollombi, Dungog, Muswellbrook and Scone districts.

4 RHW Reece, *Aborigines and Colonists: Aborigines and Colonial Society in New South Wales in the 1830s and 1840s*, Sydney University Press, Sydney, 1974, page 146.

5 On 11 December 1838, John Henry Fleming's father, Henry Fleming, died aged forty-seven. It was said that he suffered greatly from the fear that his son would be apprehended and face a similar fate to the other perpetrators.

6 *New South Wales Government Gazette*, 12 September 1838, pages 81–84; see Reece, page 146.

7 See Patrick Collins, 'An Interview with Len Payne, Bingara NSW, 27 June 1994', referred to in Patrick Collins, *Goodbye Bussamarai: the Mandandanji Land War, Southern Queensland, 1842–1852*, self-published by the author. See also http://www.goodbyebussamarai.com/page9.htm.

Chapter 9

1 See Chapter 4.

2 See Chapter 4.

3 See: *Myall Creek Massacre*, NSW Parliament Hansard, 8 June 2000, page 6894.

4 14 September 1838.

5 *Sydney Herald*, 14 November 1838, page 2.

Chapter 10

1 This courthouse, since added to several times, is still standing. The author has conducted many trials in what was formerly the Western Court, but is now Court 3.

2 Questioning by the party calling the witness – in this case, the prosecutor.

3 Questioning by the opposing party – in this case, the defence.

4 Questioning by the party calling the witness to clarify or qualify any issue that has arisen during cross-examination.

5 He omitted to mention John Fleming. This may have been a technical requirement because Fleming was not on trial. In case Fleming was later apprehended, it was undesirable for there to be any publicity in the newspapers of his involvement, which could prejudice a subsequent trial.

6 This is explained later in Chapter 12.

7 Counsel's right to make an address to the jury after the prosecution case was only introduced in New South Wales in 1840 with the adoption of the 1836 English *Prisoners' Counsel Act*. See GD Woods, pages 145–148.

8 Letter to the editor, *The Australian*, 8 December 1838.

Chapter 11

1 *The Australian*, 27 November 1838.

2 *The Australian*, 27 November 1838.

Chapter 12

1 For a brief synopsis of his life, showing his wide education, life experience, interests and commitment to Aboriginal welfare, see the entry in the Australian Dictionary of Biography: http://adb.anu.edu.au/biography/burton-sir-william-westbrooke-1857

2 The association's involvement was admitted more than ten years later in the *Sydney Herald*, 29 June 1849.

3 This procedure is no longer applicable in New South Wales.

4 The *Sydney Gazette and New South Wales Advertiser* of 1 December 1838, page 2, also reported this part of the address.

5 See RH Helmholz & others, *The Privilege Against Self-Incrimination – its Origins and Development*, University of Chicago Press, 1997, pages 145–48.

6 See GD Woods, chapter 26.

7 This has become known as the rule in *Jones v Dunkel* – a High Court case. See (1959) 101 CLR 298.

8 For example, see *R. v. Burdett* (1820) 4 B & Ald 95 (106 ER 873). It was only in 2002 that this inference was declared by the High Court of Australia to infringe the accused's right to silence. See *Dyers v The Queen* (2002) 210 CLR 285.

9 For a more recent example, see *R v Williamson* [1972] 2 NSWLR 281.

10 See the decisions of the Privy Council in *DPP v Lynch* [1975] 1 All ER 913 and *Abbott v R* [1977] AC 755.

11 The questions from Plunkett have been inferred from the summary of the evidence recorded in the newspaper reports. In those days, there were no court reporters and the official record was the judge's notes. The newspapers reported a fairly full summary of the testimony from the witnesses, rather than the question-and-answer format of today's official court record.

12 A case in reply is limited to answering evidence in the defence case – in this instance, the character evidence.

13 *Prisoners' Counsel Act.* See *Sydney Monitor* and *Commercial Advertiser*, 26 October 1840, page 2; and GD Woods, pages 145–48.

14 The black cap was part of the official robes of a Supreme Court judge, worn when passing a sentence of death. It had its genesis in English Tudor court headgear. As styles of official dress changed, the cap was retained as an indicator of the formality of the occasion. It is still carried today by High Court Judges in England and Wales as part of their official dress.

15 10 December 1838, page 2. See Molony, page 144.

16 Reece, page 159.

17 *Sydney Gazette*, 20 December 1838, page 2.

18 Ibid.

19 Letter from JH Bannatyne to Windsor Berry Esq. relating to the Myall Creek Massacre, 17 December 1838 with postscript 18 December 1838, State Library of New South Wales. See: http://www.acms-search.sl.nsw.gov.au/search/itemDetailPaged.cgi?itemID=1336513

20 Governor Gipps' report to Lord Glenelg, 8 January 1839, *Historical Records of Australia*, series 1, volume 19.

21 Reece, pages 158–59. See also Roger Therry, *Reminiscences of Thirty Years' Residence in New South Wales and Victoria*, London, second edition, 1863 (reprinted by the British Library), page 283.

Chapter 13

1 See Molony, page 146.

2 *Sydney Herald*, 24 December 1838.

3 Neil Gunson ed., *Australian Reminiscences & Papers of LE Threlkeld, Missionary to the Aborigines, 1824–1859*, (Australian Aboriginal Studies number 40, Australian Institute of Aboriginal Studies, Canberra 1974), volume II, page 275.

4 See Colin Tatz, 'Genocide in Australia: By Accident or Design?', Indigenous Human Rights and History: Occasional papers, Monash Indigenous Centre and Castan Centre for Human Rights, Monash University, 2011, pages 23–24.

5 Reece, pages 176–77.

6 Reece, page 165.

7 From the 1840s and 1850s there were also Native Police forces (led by whites) in many parts of Australia that were involved in massacres. See Colin Tatz.

8 For a list of some that became known to the authorities, see Reece, pages 186–193. See also 'An unfinished and incomplete compilation of Frontier Conflicts, Wars and Massacres in Australia, 1770–1940s', compiled by Jane Morrison, Australian Frontier Conflicts, reproduced by the Friends of the Myall Creek Memorial and the Sydney Friends of Myall Creek, 2016.

Chapter 14

1 Sir George Gipps to Marquess of Normanby, 14 October 1839, in *Historical Records of Australia*, 1st series, volume 20, Governors' Despatches to and from England, February 1839–September 1840, page 368.

2 The Attorney General and Solicitor General to Lord John Russell, 27 July 1840, in *Historical Records of Australia*, 1st series, volume 20, Governors' Despatches to and from England, February 1839–September 1840, page 756. See generally Russell Smandych, 'Contemplating the Testimony of Others: James Stephen, the Colonial Office, and the fate of Australian Aboriginal Evidence Acts, circa 1839–1849', *Australian Journal of Legal History*, volume 8, 2004, pages 237–283.

3 See Russell Smandych, page 237, Parts I and II.

4 Public Records office (UK), CO 201/332, folio 238, Sir George Gipps to Lord Stanley, 3 April 1843, Despatch number 46.

5 Public Records office (UK), CO 201/344. folios 163-319. Sir George Gipps to Lord Stanley, 21 March 1844, Despatch number 68.

6 [1840] NSWSupC 78. See *Sydney Herald*, 5 November 1840; *Sydney Monitor*, 5 November 1840. See also David Plater & Sangeetha Royan, 'The Development & Application in 19th Century Australia of the Prosecutor's Role as a Minister of Justice: Rhetoric or Reality?', 2012, volume 31, *University of Tasmania Law Review* 78.

7 Molony, page 136.

8 Isobelle Barrett Meyering, 'Abolitionism, Settler Violence and the Case against Flogging: A Reassessment of Sir William Molesworth's Contribution to the Transportation Debate', *History Australia*, 2010, volume 7, number 1.

9 Isobelle Barrett Meyering, page 6.6.

10 *Order-in-Council ending transportation to New South Wales, 22 May 1840*, State Records New South Wales. See: http://www.migrationheritage.nsw.gov.au/exhibition/objectsthroughtime/order-ending-transportation-to-nsw/

11 *Australian Chronicle*, 4 March 1841.
12 Now in the Powerhouse Museum, Sydney.
13 Incorrectly described in Molony as DW Hope.
14 Molony, page 42.
15 Obituary in the *Sydney Morning Herald*, 19 May 1869.
16 *Sydney Morning Herald*, 21 June 1844. See http://trove.nla.gov.au/ndp/del/article/12421111
17 *Sydney Herald*, 21 June 1844.
18 Bruce Kercher, *An Unruly Child: A History of Law in Australia*, Allen & Unwin, 1995, pages 16–17. See also Russell Smandych.
19 William à Beckett went on to become the first Chief Justice of the Colony of Victoria.
20 Molony, page 262, note 57.
21 Chief Justice Murray Gleeson.
22 *Maitland Mercury*, 22 July 1848.
23 Molony, page 126; Woods, page 166.
24 *Sydney Morning Herald*, 16 September 1847: see Molony, page 129.
25 Henry (later Sir Henry) Parkes (1815–1896) was to become Premier of New South Wales on many occasions and was at the forefront of the movement promoting federation of the colonies into the Commonwealth of Australia.
26 See Earls, pages 144–49 for a good summary of his speech.
27 Molony, page 133.

Chapter 15

1 The Nicholson Museum at the University of Sydney is named after him.
2 Macleay's library and collection of specimens were transferred in 1890 to the Macleay Museum at the University of Sydney.
3 Now the SH Ervin Gallery on Observatory Hill.
4 Joseph Burke, 'The Contribution of John Hubert Plunkett to Education in the State of New South Wales, 1832–1869', BA (Hons) thesis, University of Sydney, 1961, page 76.

5 Burke, page 120.
6 Clifford Turney, *Grammar: A History of Sydney Grammar School – 1819–1988*, Allen & Unwin, 1989, pages 27–32.
7 The author is currently a trustee.
8 The fagging system remained a feature of most of the English boys' boarding schools until the 1970s and 80s.
9 Royal Charter of the University of Sydney. See: http://sydney.edu.au/policies/showdoc.aspx?recnum=PDOC2011/51&RendNum=0
10 At that time the position of Vice-Chancellor was not the same as today. It was a part-time position as deputy to the Chancellor.
11 Unfortunately, *Tarmons* was demolished in the 1960s.
12 Both the Catholic and Protestant Bibles incorporate twenty-seven books in the New Testament. The Protestant Bible, however, has only thirty-nine books in the Old Testament, while the Catholic Bible has forty-six. The seven additional books included in the Catholic Bible are: Tobit, Judith 1 and 2, Maccabees, Wisdom, Sirach and Baruch. The Catholic Bible also includes sections in the Books of Esther and Daniel that are not found in the Protestant Bible.
13 See Monsignor CJ Duffy, 'The Incident of the Moving of the Bible at Saint Vincent's Hospital, Sydney, 1859', *Journal of the Australian Catholic Historical Society*, volume 3, number 3, 1971, page 62.
14 *Freeman's Journal*, 1 June 1859. Also Molony pages 262–65.
15 20 June 1859.
16 9 July 1859. See Molony pages 264–65.
17 Dr Maxwell Coleman, 'Sr. M John Baptist De Lacy, Dr James Robertson and the Bible Incident Revisited', in St Vincent's Clinic Proceedings, volume 21, number 1, December 2013.

Chapter 16

1 Dr Henry Grattan Douglass (1790–1865) was an honorary physician at Sydney Hospital and one of the first teachers of clinical medicine in Australia. In 1854 he was appointed a director of the hospital, but resigned after two years to take a seat in the first Legislative Council under responsible government.

2 *Sydney Morning Herald*, 24 November 1851, page 2.

3 Ibid, page 3.

4 It is now on display at the Lambing Flat Folk Museum in Young.

5 *Sydney Morning Herald*, 31 March 1858.

6 Jo Lennan and George Williams, 'The Death Penalty in Australian Law', *Sydney Law Review*, 2012, volume 34, at page 666.

7 Molony, pages 168–69.

8 Lennan and Williams, page 665.

9 *Sydney Morning Herald*, 1 November 1867. See Amanda Kaladelfos, 'The Politics of Punishment: Rape and the death penalty in colonial Australia, 1841–1901', *History Australia*, 2012, volume 9, number 1, page 155 and page 162.

10 *Sydney Morning Herald*, 1 November 1867, page 2.

11 9 December 1867, page 6.

Chapter 17

1 *Sydney Morning Herald*, 16 July 1856, pages 4–5.

2 To this day Australians view official titles with some disdain. Witness the public reaction to the appointment of Prince Philip as an Australian knight by Prime Minister Tony Abbott in January 2015.

3 Earls, page 171.

4 The New South Wales Upper House members remained appointed until a referendum in 1977.

5 Anne Twomey, *The Constitution of New South Wales*, Federation Press (2004), pages 16-21.

6 See Woods, pages 167–68.
7 This was gradually surrendered through the enactment of the following legislation: *Colonial Laws Validity Act*, 1865 (UK), *Statute of Westminster*, 1931 (UK), *Statute of Westminster Adoption Act*, 1942 (Cwth), *Australia Act*, 1986 (Cwth), and *Australia Act*, 1986 (UK).
8 *Sydney Morning Herald*, 26 June 1856. See Molony, page 239.
9 Molony, page 215.
10 Earls, page 180.
11 Molony, footnote page 220.
12 *Sydney Morning Herald*, 22 February 1856.
13 *Empire*, 9 January 1856. The *Empire* was founded by Henry Parkes in 1850.
14 In those days it was possible for a candidate to stand for multiple seats. In the event of winning more than one, the candidate would have to make an election.
15 http://www.nswbar.asn.au/the-bar-asssociation/bar-history
16 Molony, page 244.
17 Molony, page 245.
18 Molony, page 278.
19 See Molony, pages xiii and 9–10.
20 During the 1850s and 1860s many shipping companies were established, providing a network of regular steamer services between the Australian colonies.
21 *Sydney Morning Herald*, 19 May 1869.
22 Molony page 276.
23 In all, Cowper was Premier five times.

Chapter 18

1 The 'Dead March' is a funeral anthem from George Frideric Handel's oratorio *Saul*, 1738. The libretto, taken from the first book of Samuel, tells of the downfall of King Saul and the destructive power of envy.

2 At the location of the current Central Station. The Mortuary railway platform is the only part of the cemetery still in existence.
3 *Sydney Morning Herald*, 19 May 1869.
4 In 1837, Plunkett purchased 1280 acres of land west of Wollongong near Mt Keira, which he named 'Keelogues'. By 1840 he had subdivided and sold it.
5 Earls, page 212.
6 Ibid.
7 However, Maria Plunkett's obituary in the *Sydney Morning Herald* of 17 August 1895 states that 'Mrs Plunkett had been in receipt of a pension from the Crown in consideration of her husband's long and splendid public services'. Presumably the Government relented at some time in the intervening years.
8 *Sydney Morning Herald*, 17 August 1895.
9 Because the chalice is in very poor condition, it is not on display. However, the vestments are in excellent condition and are on public display in a glass cabinet within the Cathedral. The whereabouts of the watch is unknown.
10 Section 116.
11 In 2015, it was ranked 45th in the QS World University rankings. Sydney University graduates have been ranked the most employable in Australia and 14th most employable in the world.
12 See for example Rebecca Wood, 'Frontier Violence and the Bush Legend: The *Sydney Herald*'s Response to the Myall Creek Massacre Trials and the Creation of Colonial Identity', *History Australia*, 2009, volume 6, number 3, Monash University Press.
13 Molony, page 155.
14 RHW Reece, *Aborigines and Colonists: Aborigines and Colonial Society in New South Wales in the 1830s and 1840s, Sydney University Press*, 1974, page 140.
15 Tony Earls, 'The Opportunity of Being Useful: Daniel O'Connell's influence on John Hubert Plunkett' in LM Geary and AJ McCarthy

(eds), *Ireland, Australia and New Zealand: History, Politics and Culture*, 2008 page 173.

16 For lengthy but still incomplete lists of massacres, see: https://en.wikipedia.org/wiki/List_of_massacres_of_Indigenous_Australians and http://treatyrepublic.net/content/history-australian-aboriginal-massacres

17 WE Plunkett had been the Under Secretary of the Department of Justice and Public Instruction. See his obituary in the *Sydney Morning Herald* on 19 May 1894, page 15.

18 17 August 1895, page 15.

19 Vault 42.

20 Earls, page 215.

21 The Francis Forbes Society for Australian Legal History.

22 There is a Lawry Plunkett Reserve and the adjoining Plunkett Street in Mosman, but the identity of this person remains unknown.

23 King's letter to the editor, *Atlanta Constitution*, 6 August 1946.

24 King spoke against the Vietnam war at a time when liberals had not yet come to criticise it. He fought against poverty of any kind.

Chapter 19

1 Christine Jones, *Murderer to Magistrate*, unpublished manuscript, 2009.

2 Ebenezer.

3 See the article by Marie Turnbull in *Clan Turnbull Ebenezer Newsletter*, volume 4 number 2, July–August 2012, page 4. The article is available at: http://turnbullclan.com/tca/newsletters/ebenezer/2012_v03_n02_july-august.pdf. The author is of the opinion that the story of Fleming's avoidance of arrest is likely to be as inaccurate as his account of the killings themselves.

4 Barry Corr, 'Window with a Dark Past', *Hawkesbury Gazette*, 10 June 2015, page 24. See Barry Corr, 'Pondering the Abyss: A study

of the language of settlement on the Hawkesbury Nepean Rivers', 2013. Available online at www.nangarra.com.au.

5 *Windsor and Richmond Gazette*, 25 August 1894, page 6.

6 See the Queensland Parliament website: https://www.parliament.qld.gov.au/members/former/bio?id=2042567882

7 Bert E Weston, 'William Hobbs', *Illawarra Historical Society Bulletin*, November 1985, page 68.

8 See Len Payne, 'The Myall Creek Massacre' and 'An Interview with Len Payne, Bingara NSW, 27 June 1994' referred to in Patrick Collins, *Goodbye Bussamarai: The Mandandanji Land War, Southern Queensland, 1842–1852*, self-published by the author. See also: http://www.goodbyebussamarai.com/page9.htm.

9 See Paync, pages 9–10.

10 'Bridge Over Myall Creek', *Australian Story*, ABC TV, 26 July 2001.

11 Ibid.

12 Ibid.

13 *Armidale Express*, 7 June 2013.

14 Bruce Kercher, '*Decisions of the Superior Courts of New South Wales, 1788–1899*', Macquarie University. For the homepage see: http://www.law.mq.edu.au/research/colonial_case_law/nsw/site/scnsw_home/

15 *Ex parte Nichols* (1830)1 Legge 123 at 133.

16 Matthew Da Silva, 'Aboriginal Massacre Site Commemorated', *Australian Geographic*, 15 November 2010.

17 http://www.myallcreek.info/index.php/massacre-story

18 http://www.environment.gov.au/heritage/places/national/myall-creek

19. A comprehensive list of massacres is contained in a 16 page brochure 'An unfinished and incomplete compilation of Frontier Conflicts, Wars and Massacres in Australia, 1770–1940s', compiled by Jane Morrison, published by Sydney Friends of Myall Creek, 2016.

BIBLIOGRAPHY

John Hubert Plunkett

Tony Earls, *Plunkett's Legacy: An Irishman's contribution to the Rule of Law in New South Wales*, Australian Scholarly Publishing, 2009.

John Molony, *An Architect of Freedom: John Hubert Plunkett in New South Wales, 1832–1869*, ANU Press, 1973.

Myall Creek massacre

Court transcripts concerning the Myall Creek massacre trials:

- *R v Kilmeister (No 1)* [1838] NSW SupC 105 http://www.law.mq.edu.au/research/colonial_case_law/nsw/cases/case_index/1838/r_v_kilmeister1/
- *R v Kilmeister (No 2)* [1838] NSW SupC 110 http://www.law.mq.edu.au/research/colonial_case_law/nsw/cases/case_index/1838/r_v_kilmeister2/
- *R v Lamb* [1839] NSWSupC 6 http://www.law.mq.edu.au/research/colonial_case_law/nsw/cases/case_index/1839/r_v_lamb/

'Australian Aborigines: Copies of extracts of despatches relative to the massacre of various Aborigines in Australia, in the year 1838, and respecting the trial of their murderers', House of Commons Parliamentary Papers (UK), 1839.

Patrick Collins, 'Goodbye Bussamarai: The Mandandanji Land War, Southern Queensland, 1842–1852', self-published by the author.

Brian Harrison, 'The Myall Creek Massacre', in Isabel McBryde, ed., *Records of Times Past: Ethnohistorical essays on the culture and ecology of the New England tribes*, Australian Institute of Aboriginal Studies, Canberra, 1978.

Geoff Lindsay SC, 'Aborigines, Colonists and the Law, 1838', background paper for the Australian Legal History School Essay Competition, The Francis Forbes Society for Australian Legal History, 16 March 2007.

Haydn Marsh, 'Native Tears: Conflict on the Colonial Frontier and *R v Kilmeister (No 2)*', *The ANU Undergraduate Research Journal*, 2011, volume 3, page 97.

Leonard L Payne, 'Papers on the Myall Creek Massacre, 1964–1979', including 'The Myall Creek Massacre – A Correlation of Known and Attested Facts from the Past and the Present Concerning the Infamous Myall Creek Massacre of 1838', private manuscript. National Library of Australia, BibID: 102008, MS 9619.

Lyndall Ryan, 'A Very Bad Business: Henry Dangar and the Myall Creek Massacre 1838', presented to a Conference of the Centre of the History of Violence, University of Newcastle, 27 November 2008.

Contemporary accounts

Sir Roger Therry, *Reminiscences of Thirty Years' Residence in New South Wales and Victoria*, (London, 1863), Sydney University Press, 1974.

William Westbrooke Burton, *The State Of Religion and Education in New South Wales*, London, J Cross, 1840.

'An Interview with Len Payne, Bingara NSW, 27 June 1994' by Patrick Collins, referred to in Patrick Collins, *Goodbye Bussamarai: The Mandandanji Land War, Southern Queensland, 1842–1852*, self-published by the author.

Collection of correspondence of Maria Plunkett and other miscellaneous documents, including the Plunkett family tree, Sisters of Charity, Sydney.

Colonial society

John Bradley Hirst, *Freedom on the Fatal Shore: Australia's First Colony*, Black Inc, 2008.

Race relations

RHW Reece, *Aborigines and Colonists: Aborigines and Colonial Society in New South Wales in the 1830s and 1840s*, Sydney University Press, Sydney, 1974.

Brent Salter, 'For Want of Evidence: Initial Impressions of Indigenous Exchanges with the First Colonial Superior Courts of Australia', *The University of Tasmania Law Review*, 2008, volume 27, page 145.

Other massacres

Roger Milliss, *Waterloo Creek: the Australia Day massacre of 1838, George Gipps and the British conquest of New South Wales*, McPhee Gribble, Ringwood, Victoria, 1992.

Colin Tatz, 'Genocide in Australia: By Accident or Design?', *Indigenous Human Rights and History: Occasional papers*, Monash Indigenous Centre and Castan Centre for Human Rights, Monash University, 2011.

Law, evidence, juries, prosecutors, lashings and the death penalty

John Braithwaite, 'Crime in a Convict Republic', 2001, volume 64 *Modern Law Review*, page 11.

Enid Campbell, 'Colonial Legislation and the Laws of England', 1965, 2 *Tasmanian University Law Review* 148.

Alex Castles, 'The Reception and Status of English law in Australia', *Adelaide Law Review*, 1963, 2 *Adelaide Law Review* 1.

See RH Helmholz & others, *The Privilege Against Self-Incrimination – its Origins and Development*, University of Chicago Press, 1997.

Rowena Johns, 'Trial by Jury: Recent Developments', NSW Parliamentary Library Research Service, Briefing Paper Number 4/05.

Amanda Kaladelfos, 'The Politics of Punishment: Rape and the death penalty in colonial Australia, 1841–1901', *History Australia*, 2012, volume 9, number 1, page 155.

Bruce Kercher, *An Unruly Child: A History of Law in Australia*, Allen & Unwin, 1995.

Jo Lennan and George Williams, 'The Death Penalty in Australian Law', *Sydney Law Review*, 2012, volume 34, page 659.

Isobelle Barrett Meyering, 'Abolitionism, Settler Violence and the Case Against Flogging, A Reassessment of Sir William Molesworth's Contribution to the Transportation Debate', *History Australia*, Volume 7, Number 1, 2010, Monash University ePress.

David Neal, *The Rule of Law in a Penal Colony: Law and Power in Early New South Wales*, Cambridge University Press, 1991.

David Plater & Sangeetha Royan, 'The Development & Application in 19th Century Australia of the Prosecutor's Role as a Minister of Justice: Rhetoric or Reality?', 2012, volume 31, *University of Tasmania Law Review* 78.

Russell Smandych, 'Contemplating the Testimony of "Others": James Stephen, The Colonial Office, and the Fate of Australian

Aboriginal Evidence Acts, Circa 1839–1849', 2004, *Australian Journal of Legal History*, volume 8, page 237.

Dr Gregory D Woods, *A History of Criminal Law in New South Wales: The Colonial Period, 1788–1900*, Federation Press, 2002.

Newspapers

Rebecca Wood, 'Frontier Violence and the Bush Legend: The *Sydney Herald*'s Response to the Myall Creek Massacre Trials and the Creation of Colonial Identity', *History Australia*, volume 6, number 3, 2009, Monash University ePress.

Education

Alan Raphael Barcan, 'Opinion, Policy and Practice in NSW Education, 1833–1880; The Development of an Educational Tradition', thesis submitted for the Degree of Doctor of Philosophy at the Australian National University, December 1962.

Joseph Burke, 'The Contribution of John Hubert Plunkett to Education in the State of New South Wales, 1832–1869', BA (Hons) thesis, University of Sydney, 1961.

Religion

Monsignor CJ Duffy, 'The Incident of the Moving of the Bible at Saint Vincent's Hospital, Sydney, 1859', *Journal of the Australian Catholic Historical Society*, volume 3, number 3, 1971, page 62.

Pastoral properties

AJ (Bert) Howard, 'Bingera Run', Australian Origins and Heritage Library, 2012. See http://www.bingara.com.au/files/uploaded/file/Bingera_Run_2012.pdf.

BIBLIOGRAPHY

Governors

Max Waugh, *Forgotten Hero: Richard Bourke, Irish Governor of New South Wales, 1831–1837*, Australian Scholarly Publishing, Melbourne, 2005.

Hazel King, *Richard Bourke*, Oxford University Press, Melbourne, 1971.

Pioneers

Russell Mackenzie Warner (ed), 'Over-Halling the Colony: George Hall Pioneer', Australian Documents Library, Southwood Press, Sydney, 1990.

General historical references

Historical Records of Australia, Series 1, 'Governors' Dispatches to and from England', Volume XVII, 1833–June 1835, the Library Committee of the Commonwealth Parliament, 1923.

Alan Atkinson and Marian Aveling (eds), *Australians 1838* Fairfax, Syme & Weldon Associates, Sydney 1987.

John Ross (ed), *Chronicle of Australia*, Chronicle Australasia Pty Ltd, 1993.

Numerous contemporary newspapers, especially the *Sydney Chronicle*, *The Sydney (Morning) Herald* and *The Australian*.

ABOUT THE AUTHOR

Mark Tedeschi AM QC is the Senior Crown Prosecutor for New South Wales. He has practised as a barrister in the criminal courts for almost 40 years, both for the prosecution and the defence. He is a Visiting Fellow at the University of Wollongong, a Member of the Board of Directors at the National Art School, and a Trustee of Sydney Grammar School. He is also a photographer whose works are held in many galleries and private collections. Mark lives and works in Sydney.

For more information, see his website:
www.MarkTedeschi.com.